AGNES
The Biography of Lady Macdonald

AGNES
The Biography of Lady Macdonald

LOUISE REYNOLDS

CARLETON UNIVERSITY PRESS
OTTAWA, CANADA
1990

© Carleton University Press Inc. 1990

ISBN 0-88629-131-3

Printed and bound in Canada

Carleton Women's Experience Series #2

Canadian Cataloguing in Publication Data
Reynolds, Louise, 1919-
  Agnes

(Carleton women's experience series ; 2)
Includes bibliographical references.
ISBN 0-88629-131-3

1. Macdonald, Agnes, Baroness Macdonald of
Earnscliffe, 1836-1920. 2. Prime ministers–
Canada–Spouses–Biography. I. Title. II. Series.

FC521.M28R48 1990   971.05'092   C90-090262-0
F1033.M125R48 1990

First printing 1979 Samuel Stevens Ltd., Toronto.

Distributed by: Oxford University Press Canada,
                70 Wynford Drive,
                Don Mills, Ontario.
                Canada. M3C 1J9
                (416) 441-2941

Cover design: Y Graphic Design

Acknowledgements

Carleton University Press gratefully acknowledges the support extended to its
publishing programme by the Canada Council and the Ontario Arts Council.

All photographs, with the exception of numbers 21 (Canadian Pacific Railway), 22
(in the author's possession) and 23 (courtesy of Mrs. David Partridge) are from the
Public Archives of Canada.

Dedicated
to the memory of
Jean Bull McMahon
whose daughter, Helen Small, by her
generous assistance, helped make possible
the publication of this book

Table of Contents

Introduction

Susan Agnes Bernard, Lady Macdonald, has entered Canadian history books as the second wife of John A. Macdonald, the eminent Conservative politician and first Prime Minister of Canada. Professional historians assessing the development of the Canadian nation have been interested in Agnes to the extent that John A.'s private life seemed to affect his public performance.[1] In particular, Donald Creighton, the principal biographer and acknowledged expert on John A. Macdonald, judged Agnes' character and actions in relation to John A.'s life and from John A.'s perspective. Indeed, Creighton has been accused of imposing his own patriarchal assumptions about the proper functioning of the family upon his analysis, and of viewing Agnes as domineering when her wishes did not conform to John A.'s preferences.[2] However, Agnes Macdonald also had interests separate from her husband. At the other extreme of approach, Jean Bannerman in *Leading Ladies, Canada*, an account of women's contributions to Canada, includes Lady Macdonald only in the section on "The Power of the Pen," as the author of "By Car and By Cow-catcher," "On a Canadian Salmon River," and "On a Toboggan."[3] Hence, historians interested in women's experience will welcome the reprinting of Louise Reynold's biography, *Agnes*, first published in 1979, which deals with all stages of Agnes' life and integrates the private, social and public spheres.

The biographical approach accords naturally with the recent interest among women's historians in life course history.[4] Louise Reynolds divides her book into three sections separated by the major events which structured Agnes' life – her marriage and the death of her husband. Ironically, the twenty-four years of marriage, the time which Agnes viewed as the most fulfilling of her life and for which there is the most information, is actually a shorter period than either the thirty years as a girl and "young spinster" or the twenty-nine years of widowhood. Sources for even elite women's lives frequently are difficult to obtain, so there are questions regarding the life of Lady Macdonald which cannot be answered fully. Nonetheless, from private family papers, correspondence in archives, and the diary which Agnes kept from 1867 to 1875, Louise Reynolds has pieced together the picture of a woman who, as she claims, merits attention in her own right.

Lady Macdonald emerges as a woman of intelligence, a quality ignored rather than contradicted in previous accounts of her relationship with John A. In addition, her lively adventurous nature and love of new modes of travel appear more clearly when shown as undiminished over the years. No one can dissuade Lady Macdonald from experiencing the thrill of riding the cow-catcher through the Rockies, in spite of the evident danger. She describes the crowded conditions aboard a scow on a New Brunswick salmon river as great fun and in her later years in England falls in love with the tricycle and the motor car. Certainly, as Reynolds emphasizes, "there was much more to Agnes than the Victorian ideal of devoted wife, mother and hostess." Yet Lady Macdonald was not a "New Woman" slightly ahead of her time either. While she evidently had a very good knowledge of political affairs and enjoyed listening to the House of Commons debates, she did not approve of votes for women. She had a talent for "scribbling" and published articles in *Murray's Magazine* and the *Ladies Home Journal*; indeed, it is possible that she undertook some of her travel escapades partly with publication in mind.[5] However, in contrast to her niece, Mary Agnes Fitz-Gibbon (May Bernard) who wrote for the Toronto *Globe* in order to support herself and her daughter, Lady Macdonald never had to earn her living by her journalism, and writing remained subordinate to her other duties and responsibilities.[6] The biography reveals how Victorian expectations regarding the character and behaviour of a lady affected Agnes at each stage of her life and how she accepted most of the conventions even if they did not always accord with her own personality.[7]

Susan Agnes Bernard, like other daughters of privileged families in the early nineteenth century, was educated to fulfill the social and familial responsibilities of a young lady, rather than to take paid employment. Born in 1836, she was the youngest child and only surviving daughter of Thomas Bernard, a Jamaican plantation owner, and his wife Theodora. Her upbringing was influenced by her gender as much as by her class. While her brothers were sent to England to finish their education and the two oldest entered the legal profession, Susan Agnes received instruction at home from her mother and then at school in Spanish Town. From age fifteen to seventeen, Agnes too continued her education in England, but only because she moved with her mother to the home of English relatives after the premature death of her father. In addition to her religious studies at the village vicarage, Agnes, as Reynolds notes, had lessons in the accomplishments expected of young ladies – singing, drawing, French. Another form of finishing education which a wealthy family might give its daughter was a European tour with a suitable chaperone. Because of family moves, Agnes had some of the advantages of exposure to different cultures and to the marvels of the nineteenth century, particularly enjoying the Crystal Palace in 1851, but otherwise financial concerns limited travel. Although Agnes' feelings about most of her education are not revealed, she clearly enjoyed travelling and in later years regretted that she and her mother had not seen more while in England. One other major trip essentially coincided with the end of Agnes' formal instruction; in 1854, Hewitt Bernard, who as eldest son was now considered the head of the family, was sufficiently well established to receive his mother and sister in Canada where he was practising law in Barrie, Ontario.

From the time Agnes Bernard came to Canada until she married John A. Macdonald thirteen years later, her life, like that of her mother, revolved around Hewitt. Theodora and Agnes accompanied Hewitt to Toronto when he became private secretary to John A. Macdonald and then to Quebec City when parliament moved there. With other young people of a similar background, Agnes participated actively in society, enjoying the popular outdoor activities of the mid-nineteenth century such as boating, sledding and tobogganing, as well as attending concerts and balls. Nor did she devote her time solely to pleasurable pursuits, even though these often masked the more serious purpose of establishing family social status, and for young women in their twenties like Agnes, of making contact with a suitable partner for the only career open to them – wife and mother. In the mid-nineteenth century, religion had a central function in defining life. Although women were excluded from positions of authority in the main churches, they provided much important support and piety was considered a fundamental feminine characteristic. Theodora Bernard took care to transmit religious values to Agnes so it is not surprising that Agnes attended the Anglican church regularly – twice on Sundays in Barrie – and also taught Sunday School in both Barrie and Toronto.[8]

On 16 February 1867, Susan Agnes Barnard married John A. Macdonald in the presence of an impressive list of guests at St. George's Church, Hanover Square, London. As Reynolds states, Agnes' wedding day was the most important of her life. With her marriage at age thirty, Agnes finally achieved a definite purpose for her life. In her diary she wrote that she had "found something worth living for – living in – my husband's heart and love." Although she obviously appreciated her social position as a "great Premier's wife," the prestige constituted the icing on the cake. Agnes Macdonald now was mistress of her own household. However, her new status did not lead to a rupture of family ties; Theodora lived in her daughter's house until her death eight years later, another example of the persistence of female relations in the nineteenth century. Unfortunately, there is little mention of Agnes' response to her mother's presence, but her shock and sadness at Theodora's death indicate continuing closeness.

As the wife of Canada's first Prime Minister, Agnes Macdonald occupied a place in Ottawa society second only to the wife of the Governor General. That social position entailed many duties and responsibilities as well as privileges and benefits; definitely Lady Macdonald was not a leisured wife. Only hints are obtained from her diaries and the comments of others about her tasks of household management. She always had servants but feared that when she neglected her supervision, "everything goes wrong downstairs among the servants." The duties evidently included overseeing domestic production, for at least at Earnscliffe, the Macdonalds, like many more modest Ottawa households, kept cows and hens. More attention is given to the entertaining expected of a Prime Minister's wife. During the session, Lady Macdonald gave dinners every Saturday night and also held receptions on special occasions such as New Year's. Many of her activities as hostess were undertaken, not in a supporting role to the host but in his absence, as John A. frequently was detained by business. Lady Macdonald also accepted her responsibility to give leadership in voluntary service to the community. Much of this activity still centred on the church, but the rise of women's organizations enabled women of various religious affiliations to cooperate in social work. Lady Macdonald used her influence to organize a bazaar which paid off the debt on St. Alban's Anglican Church in the absence of the rector who opposed such money-raising schemes. She also accepted the post of first Directress at the Ottawa Protestant Orphans' Home, an institution begun by the Protestant Women's Benevolent Society of Ottawa to care for children, and also elderly women, whose families could not provide for them, either temporarily or permanently. Not only did Lady Macdonald contribute her organizing talents and social position to a fund-raising concert for the Home, but she also spent time instructing the children, reading and teaching them catechism.

In spite of the importance of the social sphere, Agnes' first responsibility was in the private sphere to her husband, and, after her birth in 1869, to her only child, Mary. Both required much of her time and energy. John A.'s tiring work schedule, his drinking problems and his serious illness in 1870 caused Agnes continuing anxiety. Part of woman's mission in the nineteenth century was to exercise moral influence and combat corrupting influences which damaged the home. Through prayer, vigilance, and her own moral example, Agnes attempted to shield

John A. from the evils of alcohol. Caring for the sick in the family also was a traditional female role. During the six long weeks when he could not be moved from his office after his gall-stone attack in 1870, Agnes devoted all her time to nursing the husband who was twenty-two years her senior. In subsequent years, she not only tried to assure adequate rest and good medical attention but also at times assisted John A. by acting as his 'ears' in the House of Commons from her post in the Gallery. Intense sorrow over Mary's condition drained Agnes even more, for the baby whom she had anticipated with such joy was hydrocephalic and would never be able to walk or care for herself unaided. Both parents gave love and attention to Mary, and she always had nurses or companions to attend to her, but inevitably much of the supervision of Mary's daily needs, and especially of her mental development, devolved upon Agnes.

With the death of John A. Macdonald in 1891, Agnes lost the relationship which had been the basis of her social power as well as the centre of her personal life. A woman whose identity had always been defined by family relations, Agnes at age fifty-four faced a long widowhood with almost no family except a totally dependent daughter. Although she worried about managing money, having acquired control of a considerable sum for the first time, Lady Macdonald was spared the economic hardships often associated with surviving as a widow. She retained her zest for new experiences and new places, and, especially with the mixed blessing of her new title, Baroness Macdonald of Earnscliffe, continued to be invited to social functions. Yet the biography allows the reader to feel Baroness Macdonald's sense of restlessness and aimlessness as, lacking Canadian roots, she sold her Canadian property and wandered in Europe until her death in 1920 at Eastbourne, England.

Agnes, The Biography of Lady Macdonald is an appropriate book for the new Carleton University Press series on women's experience because, through the study of one individual, it reveals the complexity of the personal response to gender structures and ideals. In the view of John A. Macdonald, there may have been two separate and distinct Agneses, as defined by Creighton, one excitable and pleasure-loving and the other devout, repentant and serious.[9] The Agnes who emerges from the pages of the biography, seen from her own perspective and acting within a context of strong gender and class prescriptions, does not have a split personality.

Marilyn Barber

Department of History
Carleton University
July 1990

Notes

1. Donald Creighton, *John A. Macdonald; The Young Politician* (Toronto: Macmillan, 1952), and *John A. Macdonald: The Old Chieftain* (Toronto: Macmillan, 1955); P.B. Waite, *Macdonald His Life and World* (Toronto: McGraw-Hill Ryerson, 1975).
2. Barbara Roberts, "They Drove Him To Drink . . Donald Creighton's Macdonald and his Wives," *Canada: An Historical Magazine*, 3 (2), December 1975. 50-64.
3. Jean Bannerman, *Leading Ladies, Canada* (Belleville: Mika Publishing Co., 1977), 12, 355-56.
4. See Susan Mann Trofimenkoff, "Feminist Biography," *Atlantis*, 10 (2), Spring 1985, 1-9, for one analysis of the purpose, content and form of feminist biography.
5. See Barbara Freeman, *Kit's Kingdom: The Journalism of Kathleen Blake Coleman* (Ottawa: Carleton University Press, 1989), 81-6, for a description of Kit's travel and "stunt" journalism in the 1890s.
6. See Amy Ridley, "The Dual Struggle: Mary Agnes Fitz-Gibbon, Toronto Journalist 1899-1907," M.A. Research Essay, Institute of Canadian Studies, Carleton University, 1983, for further information on May Bernard who is mentioned a number of times in the biography.
7. Katherine McKenna, "Options for Elite Women in Early Upper Canadian Society: The Case of the Powell Family" in J.K. Johnson and Bruce G. Wilson, eds. *Historical Essays on Upper Canada: New Perspectives* (Ottawa: Carleton University Press, 1989), 401-24, provides a good comparison showing the impact of ideology on women's lives in the early nineteenth century. See also Barbara Welter, "The Cult of True Womanhood," *American Quarterly*, 18, 1966, 151-74.
8. Leonore Davidoff, *The Best Circles* (London: Croom Helm, 1973) and Leonore Davidoff and Catherine Hall, *Family Fortunes* (London: Hutchinson, 1987) show the connection between women's social role and family status.
9. Creighton, *John A. Macdonald: The Old Chieftain*, 6-7. Sandra Gwyn, *The Private Capital* (Toronto: McClelland and Stewart, 1984) in her chapter on Lady Macdonald, "The Lady or the Tiger", takes from Creighton the idea of opposed personalities but attributes the dual personality to Agnes' background and the circumstances of her marriage.

Acknowledgements

It seems to be the custom when writing acknowledgements, to include a final paragraph saying how much the author owes to the cooperation of his or her family. I wish to depart from this form and first acknowledge my grateful thanks to my husband, who supported me during the days when this book was just a vague idea, during the days when I was tied up in research and, finally, during those days when the work began to take form. He is the only person besides myself who has seen the book through every phase. He also typed its two drafts, fitting the time into his own demanding work as Canadian Ambassador to Ethiopia and Madagascar from 1971 to 1975 and later Ambassador to Costa Rica, Nicaragua, Honduras, San Salvador and Panama. That kind of cooperation deserves more than the closing paragraph.

To my publisher, Alan Samuel, and his wife, Valerie Stevens, who guided me through the early stages, I owe a special vote of thanks, and another to my editor, Lenore d'Anjou, for her patience and skill at juggling chapters around to bring out the best in them without losing the thread of the story.

This book ranges over a wide time span and moves from country to country — which means that there are a multitude of people to whom I am indebted. My research began in Canada when Dr. Donald Creighton, the expert on John A., put me in touch with the late Mrs. D.F. Pepler, who had inherited Agnes' diary. Both Mrs. Pepler and her daughters, Mrs. Peggy Sharpe, Mrs. Zan Critelli and Miss Totty Pepler, were more than kind in seeing that I had access to the diary as well as to family letters and scrapbooks. Information on Agnes' family also came from Mrs. S.B. Pepler and her daughter, Mrs. Susan West of Toronto, and from the late Mrs. Anastasia Van Eeghen of Florida.

My main source of material in Canada was, of course, the Public Archives, Ottawa. There I enjoyed the cooperation of the Dominion Archivist, Dr. W.I. Smith, and spent many hours in the Manuscript Division, where its Chief, R.S. Gordon, and his staff were ever kind and willing to help. From the day I began research there, when Walter Neutel was working in the Prime Ministers' Section in 1971, I was assured of complete cooperation. My special thanks to Carman Carroll, when head of this section, Jay Atherton, Roy Maddocks, Judith Cumming of the Auxiliary Service Section, Mary Psutka of the Historical Photographs Section and Juliette Bourque, Chief Librarian of the Historical Branch.

In Toronto, my work was made easier by the help given me by K.R. MacPherson, Supervisor, Private Manuscripts, Archives of Ontario; by the staff of the Canadian Department, Royal Ontario Museum; and by Ann R. Mack, General Information Centre, and Edith G. Firth, Head, Canadiana and Manuscripts Division, Metropolitan Toronto Central Library.

In England, my work was greatly facilitated by the always willing help of Mrs. J.M. White, Chief of the Public Archives of Canada Office in London. Through the courtesy of Mr. Robert Mackworth-Young, Royal Library, Windsor, and his assistant, E.H. Cuthbertson, I received copies of correspondence relating to Agnes' peerage. Peter Walme, County Hall, Hertford, supplied information which helped me imagine what The Hall, Bushey, was like in the early 1900s; George Baugh, County Historian, Shropshire, was working on a book which helped me with the history of the Mayne family. Further data came from Anthony J. Camp, Director of Research, Society of Genealogists, London; from Mrs. M.T. Halford, County Record Office, Shrewsbury; from Verena Smith, Honorary Secretary, Sussex Record Office, Lewes; from K.C. Harrison, City Librarian, Victoria Library, London; and from Constance-Anne Parker, Librarian, Royal Academy of Arts, London. Donald Smith's family was brought into the picture by his descendant, the present Lord Strathcona, over drinks in the House of Lords' Bar. Mrs. Katherine Broome, who is researching the Napier family, told me of Annie Broome's travails and travels and also gave me a copy of the MacKenzie family tree. John and Virginia Murray, of the family that published Agnes' articles in *Murray's Magazine*, discussed its Canadian contributor and sought old correspondence relating to her work. And the staffs of the Reading Room and the Colindale Newspaper Sections of the British Museum were unfailingly kind and provided me with much material.

Further afield, the setting of Agnes' holidays in Switzerland were investigated through the kind offices of M.R. de Courtin, Bibliotheque Nationale, Berne, and Laurette Wettstein, Archiviste, Archives Cantonales, Lausanne. For permission to read microfilm, I wish to thank librarians in as far-flung places as Addis Ababa, Ethiopia, when Rita Pankhurst was still Librarian at the University, and Geneva, where Julio Pommeranck of the United Nations Library was most helpful.

The Royal Trust Company, Ottawa, through P.H. Lewis, Manager, Personal Trust Department, assisted me in following Agnes' last few years of travel in Italy.

I wish to give special thanks to the late General Maurice Pope for allowing me to use freely the autobiography of his father, Sir Joseph Pope. In 1960, this book was edited by General Pope and published under the title: *Public Servant — The Memoirs of Sir Joseph Pope*.

I was most fortunate, throughout my work, to have the guidance of so well-known an historian as our friend Dr. R.A. Preston, Director of Canadian Studies, Duke University, Durham, N.C., and his wife, Marjorie, who often sent me material difficult to acquire when I was so far from the normal sources and who later, willingly, checked proof with me.

Although I said that family should not be relegated to the closing paragraph, I have to say that my children, each in his or her own way, have supported me throughout this work. As I look back over this extensive list, I recognize my gratitude to so many.

A major source of information regarding Barrie in the 1950s was Peter Moran, County Archivist, Simcoe County Archives, Sue Murdock, Assistant Archivist, also helped, as did Jean McNiece of the Simcoe County Historical Society. That my research coincided with some being done by Gary E. French benefitted me in shedding light on some Barrie families of the period.

There are many others in Ontario to be thanked. Mrs. Anne Mac-Diarmid, Archivist, Douglas Library, Queen's University, Kingston, had the Williamson Papers for me to read; Mrs. L. Simon, Windsor Public Library and Walter Evan Zimmerman, University of Western Ontario Library, were able to provide copies of some of Agnes' writings. Through the assistance of Janet Wright, Research Division, National Historic Parks Branch, Ministry of Indian and Northern Affairs, I learned more about the Macdonald homes in Toronto. Some surprising information on the religious life of the Macdonald family came to me through the Reverend Canon Bracken, Anglican Church Archives, Toronto, who put me in touch with the Venerable J.C. Clough, Coburg, and eventually with Canon H.M. Bedford-Jones, Maitland, Ontario, whose forebear wrote the most useful little paper quoted here several times.

Omer Lavallée, Supervisor of Special Projects and Corporate Archives, C.P.R., Montreal, gave me copies of relevant letters from the Van Horne correspondence. Life at Rivière du Loup was examined thanks to the kindness of our friend, Tony Price, who introduced me to his relative, Mrs. W.R. Eakin of Montreal, the present owner of the Macdonald cottage by the St. Lawrence. Her information was supported by a copy of a paper written about the inhabitants and history of Rivière du Loup by Irene Wolf, a descendant of one of the early settlers there.

Moving west, it was through the courtesy of a Winnipeg friend, Derek Bedson, that I made the acquaintance of Hugh Gainsford, the only living descendant of John A. More family information came from Father Athol Murray, Notre Dame College, Wilcox, Saskatchewan. In Alberta, the history of the cottage at Banff was made available through H.A. Dempsey, Alberta Historical Society, Calgary, and Maryalice Stewart, Director, Archives of the Canadian Rockies, Banff. In British Columbia, Tim Eastwood, Archivist, Archives of British Columbia, provided more family information for me.

Agnes was born in Jamaica, and it is with gratitude that I acknowledge an Ontario Arts Council grant which allowed me to visit that island. Once there, I was greatly aided by Clinton Black, Archivist, Jamaica Archives, Spanish Town, and by Bernard Lewis, former Curator, Institute of Jamaica, Kingston. At the Institute, I should also like to thank John A. Aarons, Head of Reference and Research, Avis Jones, Research Officer, and Mrs. Williams, Senior Librarian – only a few of the people who found material for me although the Institute was officially 'closed' for 'stock-taking'. Manley E. Lumsden, editor of the *Jamaica Sugar Digest*, drove me around one hot morning as we tried to locate just where Bernard Lodge had been.

* * *

This second printing of *Agnes: The Biography of Lady Macdonald* appears partly due to the interest shown in it by Pauline Adams, the editing and production coordinator at Carleton University Press. I am most grateful to her for her support and valuable suggestions. Dr. Naomi Griffiths from the Department of History of Carleton University read the book and recommended its re-publication to the Editorial Board. The fact that it was accepted as the second volume in the Women's Experience Series and was guided through this stage by Professor David B. Knight, the General Editor of the Press, is a matter of great satisfaction to me.

Author's Introduction to the reprint

This volume, appearing as it does some eleven years after the first, contains all the original material. Since then, various findings have added to our knowledge of this interesting woman, information gained by reading the diaries and letters of some Ottawans who were contemporaries of Agnes. More information about Agnes' daughter Mary, was unearthed through the resourceful research of Margaret Cohoe, a member of the Kingston Historical Society, while she was on a visit to England. Through her efforts some artifacts have been deposited in the Queen's University Archives and others may be seen on display at Bellevue House in Kingston. There is probably little more that can be added now to the story of Agnes and Mary, but life is full of surprises. Perhaps one day an old trunk will be opened and further letters of John A. and Agnes will come to light.

Helen Shaw
b. 1777
d. 1862

Hugh Macdonald
b. 1782
d. 1841

m.

Louisa Jean
b. 1818
d. 1888 unm.

James Shaw
b. 1816
d. 1822

William
d. inf.

Margaret
b. 1813
d. 1876
m.
James Gilchrist
b. 1806
d. 1895

John Alexander
b. 1815
d. 1891
m. (1)
Isabella Clark
b. 1809
d. 1857

Hugh John
b. 1850
d. 1929

John Alexander
b. 1847
d. 1848

m. (1) Mary Jane Agnes Murray
b. 1846
d. 1881

m (2) Gertrude Agnes Vankousnett

John Alexander
b. 1884
d. 1905 unm.

Mary Isabella "Daisy"
b. 1877
d. 1960

Thomas James Bernard
b. ?
d. 1850

Theodora Foulkes Hewitt
b. 1802
d. 1875

m

m.

Mary Margaret
Theodora
b. 1869
d. 1933

Hewitt
b. 1825
d. 1893

Rebecca Mary
b. 1828
d. 1834

Richard Barrett
b. 1829
d. 1861
*m.
Agnes Elizabeth Lally

Philip Hewitt
b. 1830
d. ?

Jane Elizabeth
b. 1832
d. 1834

Walter Stewart
b. 1834
d. 1869

Susan Agnes
b. 1836
d. 1920

† Annie Theodora (Dora)
b. 1859
d. ?
m. (1)
Francis Edward Philip Pepler
b. 1852
d. 1900

Mary Agnes (May)
b. 1862
d. 1933
m.
Clare Fitzgibbon

Agnes Florence
Frances Louise
(Babette)
b. 1886
d. 1944

Gerald
d. inf.

Philip
McCarthy
d. inf.

Bernard
Eykes

Roger
Crook
d. (W.W.2)

Edmund
Lally

Eric

Theodore
Francis
b. 1891
d. ?

Seth
Bernard

Ruth
Elizabeth

Theodora Agnes
Anastasia
b. 1899
d. 1974

Hewitt
William
Eyres
b. 1897
d. 1959

* m. (2)
(1873)

Dalton McCarthy
b. 1836
d. 1898

† m (2)
1907

E. Percival
Brown

1
An
Insignificant
Young
Spinster

On July 5, 1867, the wife of the Prime Minister of the new Dominion of Canada opened her new diary. 'My beautiful new Diary Book! I am ever so pleased with it and have been examining it and admiring it for full ten minutes! The lock too — ! My diaries as Miss Bernard did not need such precautions but then I was an insignificant young spinster.'[1]

When Susan Agnes Bernard made this first entry in her new diary, she had been the wife of John A. Macdonald for only a few months. Her life had taken an unexpected turn with her marriage, which was planned and carried out in a few weeks in London amid the flurry of final arrangements for the creation of the Dominion of Canada. Those were exciting, happy days, and, yet, a difficult time. Even the date of her wedding was dependent on the speed with which the British North America Bill could be prepared — and on the state of the British Colonial Secretary's health. Personal wishes had to await political demands. Throughout all Agnes' married life, she would find this to be true, and it is as well that she had her first lesson so early.

Finally, there was a lull in the talks, and on February 16, 1867, the Canadian delegates who were in London, as well as relatives and friends of both Agnes and John A., gathered at St. George's, Hanover Square, for one of the most important weddings in Canada's history. The new bride and groom even found a few free days to go up to Oxford for a honeymoon. Then it was back to the conference table for John A., and Agnes had a chance to learn more about her new husband's work, something in which she was to take a deep interest during the twenty-four years in which she was, in her own words, 'a great premier's wife'.[2] Even after John A.'s death, this interest was to continue, keeping her in close touch with Canadian affairs during her long widowhood when she lived abroad, 'an exile indeed',[3] as she said.

Those long years were far in the future. As Agnes admired her new diary, she was, however, very conscious of the change in her situation. Not only had she become Mrs. John A. Macdonald; before she had

had time to become accustomed to using that name, she had become Lady Macdonald. Now the title was only five days old and the challenge of bearing that honour was countered only by the challenge of opening the diary and making the initial entry. Understandably her thoughts turned to the days when she was in her own opinion, 'an insignificant young spinster'.

To do this meant going back thirty years in time, for Agnes was not a young girl when she married. It also meant transferring herself, mentally, to the distant island of Jamaica. There, she was born on August 24, 1836, to complete the family of Thomas and Theodora Bernard. They already had four boys, so the birth of Agnes was somewhat of an event, especially since two other infant daughters had been buried within two days of each other in early 1834, victims of one of the island's frequent epidemics. The family was spared any further tragedies for a number of years and Agnes grew up a healthy and happy child, along with her brothers, Hewitt, Richard Barrett, Philip Hewitt and Walter Stewart.

A few years before most of their children were born, Thomas and Theodora had decided to move from the capital of the time, Spanish Town, because of the poor condition of its drains, and had purchased a property some miles to the south of the city, a spot much more attractive than its name, Dirty Pit. It was on its 500 acres that the young Bernards spent part of their childhood. The land was partly cut up into pastures for sheep and cattle that their father raised, but there were other areas, such as Rock Hill and the land around The Pond, where a child's imagination could have free play and where youthful energy could burn itself off. There were lime and brick kilns to look in on, and Old Tom, Mary and other negroes working on the property always had time for a word with the children. When it was too hot to be outside, there were the wide verandahs of their home to provide a welcome refuge.

No trace remains today of the Bernard house itself.[4] Even the old landmarks have all but disappeared, but it is barely possible, with a little imagination, to see where the turn-in from Salt Pond Road might have been and to note that it leads to a piece of higher ground such as those on which the houses of landowners were traditionally built in order to take advantage of any cooling breezes.

None of the Bernards has left us a description of their home at Dirty Pit. But it is possible to get a picture of the countryside in which it was situated and its probable style by turning to the writings of Lady Nugent, wife of the Governor of Jamaica during the early part of the nineteenth century, who, like many upper-class ladies of that period, was an ardent diarist. The Nugents had, as their official residence, King's House, in Spanish Town; as well, they rented a country property called Government Pen, just across the road and to the south of the Bernard land. Of her first visit to the area, Lady Nugent wrote: 'The road to the Penn [sic] is most exceedingly pretty. Penguin hedges, which are like giant pineapples, with beautiful red, blue and white convulvuluses running all over them. There was also a variety of curious trees.'[5]

A few months later, on a visit into the Blue Mountains, west of Spanish Town, she had a view of the countryside that she found 'enchanting indeed. Imagine an immense amphitheatre of mountains, irregular in their shape and various in their verdure, some steep and rugged, others sloping gently and presenting the thickest foliage, and the most varied tints of green.'[6] As she looked across the Liguanea Plain towards the capital, she could see the harbours of Kingston and Port Royal as well as that of Port Henderson, which was only a few miles from Bernard Lodge. The plain was dotted with sugar estates, pens, negro settlements, and her overall impression was that it 'seemed like a paradise'.

As well as describing the scenic beauties of the area, Lady Nugent described the house and garden where she had been visiting:

[The house's] form is the usual one, of one story with a piazza, etc. The garden contains a great variety of flowering shrubs and fruit trees, and the hedge around it is of lime trees. . . . The limes were ripe and the yellow tint mixed with the bright green had a beautiful effect. Here and there the logwood is seen which is something like our hawthorn. In other places are seen rows of orange trees, the fruit just turning yellow; mangoes, red and purple; forbidden and grape fruit in clusters; and the acqui [sic], a tree that bears a large scarlet fruit. . . . Coffee too is a very pretty shrub, bearing a bright red berry. Besides these there are several trees from which perfumes are made but I forget their names. . . . But it is quite impossible to describe the great variety of plants, trees and shrubs that, at this moment, delight my eye and regale my nose.[7]

Growing up in a similar setting left its mark on Agnes who, as an adult, had a great love of outdoor pleasures. Wherever she lived after her marriage, one of the things of most importance to her would be her garden. As Lady Macdonald, she would take delight in her gardens in Ottawa and Toronto, and years later, as a widow, she would find feasts for her eyes on the Italian Riviera. From Alassio, in the spring of 1906, she was to describe the view down to the Mediterranean and then write of her garden there as

A sight to behold! Roses of size and fragrant . . . climb over the olive trees & hang in festoons loaded with blossom all over the place. Banksias are high hedges, a sheet of bloom. In one corner calla lilies glorify a wall draped with a mass of wisteria. In another salvia flames amid the branches of heliotrope which reaches to the high terrace & so on.[8]

It was her wish, she would say then, that her Canadian friends could see this garden, but, did she not, in her mind's eye, also see the long-ago gardens and the sweeping plains of her old homeland?

A more important influence on Agnes as a child and young girl was, naturally, that exerted by her family upbringing. To Agnes in 1867, looking from her new position as Lady Macdonald, that girl may have seemed insignificant. Yet she was not nor was her family. On her father's side, her ancestors were Huguenots who had sought safety in England after the Revocation of the Edict of Nantes in 1685.[9] There they had joined other members of the family who had fled France at an earlier date. Many of these had already settled in England, where they had intermarried and become settled, solid citizens of that country.[10] Others had moved, after a few years, to England's newly acquired colony, Jamaica, where the Crown offered land on good terms and the same rights and privileges as free-born British settlers would receive.

As early as the first part of the eighteenth century, the Bernards had owned plantations scattered across the island. Those who chose to make their living as planters had been, seemingly, good administrators and profited by their move across the sea. Other family members had sought an urban life, mostly as attorneys. Many had combined both fields of endeavour. The result was that the Bernards had soon become established members of a class of whom it was remarked: 'Resident planter-attorneys were the real rulers of island society. They filled the public bodies — not only the nominated Council but also the elected Assemblies. . . they supplied the officers for the local militia.'[11]

Some 150 years later, this description could be applied with equal justice to Agnes' father. In the family tradition, he both studied law and was an active landowner. In the same tradition, he assumed civic duties: as a young man he worked in Spanish Town, joined the volunteer militia, took on responsibilities in his church, St. James Anglican Cathedral, and became a firewarden. As time went on, he accepted directorships of various banks and other public institutions. In 1824, when he was still in his twenties, he took time out to marry Theodora Foulkes Hewitt, the twenty-two-year-old daughter of William Hewitt, a prosperous land-owner in the western parish of St. Elizabeth.

Through Theodora, Agnes' ancestry can be traced back to the Scottish Highlands of the thirteenth century. Stops along the way show many interesting forebearers, including Alexander Mackenzie, who joined the Darien Expedition[12] in 1698. After a year in what is now Panama, he was one of the handful of defeated men who managed to return to Scotland. Later, the sea called again, and he went across to Jamaica, where he married; his descendants formed the maternal branch of Agnes' family tree.

Before Agnes' birth, her father had entered politics, becoming a Member of the Assembly for St. Catherine's. His law practice led to other involvements: in 1826, he was a Justice of the Peace for the same parish; in 1831, Assistant Judge of the Supreme Court; in 1835, Justice of the Peace for St. Thomas in the Vale, as well as Custos Rotulorum for St. Catherine's. It was an impressive record of public service, one that was later reflected in the lives of several of his children, including Agnes. As wife of Canada's first Prime Minister, she showed, time after time, a dedication and a self-abnegation which came not from special training but from early example.

Industry and civic dedication, however, were not enough to ensure financial stability for the Bernards. Jamaica was, at this time, in the throes of economic turmoil. For over 150 years, its economy had been based on the production of sugar cane — a crop that had brought prosperity to hard-working planters but required an ever-increasing number of slave labourers. The bubble had burst when the swell of anti-slavery sentiment culminated in the British Parliament's passage of the Abolition Bill of 1808.

The planters could not have been expected to give in meekly to a change that meant the certain collapse of the island's economy. Indeed, for a number of years, the Assembly had refused to implement the bill. This, of course, had led to a revolt on the part of the slaves, who had attacked plantations on a large scale in 1832, burning houses and looting. The trouble had been put down, but the landowners had seen they would have to give in. They could count on no support from the British Government, which was faced with both public opinion and the economic reality that West Indian sugar was more expensive than the beet sugar now being produced in Europe. History had moved in support of the slaves, and in 1834 the Jamaican Assembly had acceded to the law.

All this had happened before Agnes' birth, but the results determined her life and that of her family. Even before abolition, the economic downfall of the Bernards — like most of the settlers — began. The revolt of 1832 had not touched Bernard Lodge, but Thomas Bernard, like the Hewitts, had land in the western part of the island where the violence reached its height. The list of properties burned shows:

List of properties burned

Prop.	Property	Buildings destroyed
Bernard, T.J.	Bellevue, St. James.	Residence 39 slaves
Bernard, T.J.	Colville, Westmoreland.[13]	31 "

6

After the freeing of the slaves, Thomas Bernard, like other plantation owners, was given money recompense for the loss of his work force but it was a pittance. In the same year he had to borrow money to keep going and, from then on, he went progressively into debt. His work as an attorney was also affected as the island's economy began its downhill slide. Soon he saw that he would have to give up Bernard Lodge, which he had hoped to leave to his sons in the same way that his father's property in Westmoreland had been handed down from generation to generation. The *Jamaica Almanack* tells a sad story:

Dirty Pit 507-3-23 acres	*Owned by*		
1824	Bramwell & Pike		
1828	Thomas J. Bernard		
1831	Thomas J. Bernard,	65 slaves,	
		125 stock	
Bernard Lodge (name changed)			
1832	Thomas J. Bernard,	60 slaves,	
		102 stock	
1838	Thomas J. Bernard,	64 apprentices.	
1845	Robert Page.[14]		

It was in 1840, when Agens was still a very little girl, that the family moved back to Spanish Town, where Thomas concentrated on the professional and public side of his life.

It was not a welcome change for the children, especially the younger ones. By this time, the older boys were in school in England in Bath, near many of the family. But for Phillip, Walter and Agnes, the move meant giving up a spacious world of childhood freedom for the confines of a hot, dirty city life. There was some relief during the searing summer months when the family would rent a house in the welcome cool of the Blue Mountains, not always in the same place, as Agnes' letter of 1845 shows:

My dear Hewitt,
    I hope your mouth is well. Philip has quite recovered. . . . It is very cool up here. We are much more comfortable than we were last year, there is more furniture. . . . I have a little garden by the steps. I dig with the small hoe you sent me. . . .

                       Your affectionate sister,
                       Susan Agnes Bernard[15]

Whether the family was in Spanish Town or the hills, lessons had to go on, and Agnes told Hewitt that while the boys did 'theirs with Papa in the

Piazza', she was learning hers with her mother in a little back room. Not only did Theodora supervise Agnes' studies but also those of the boys when Thomas was at his work. As well, she took on the responsibility of seeing that they had good religious instruction. It is hard to say how her sons reacted to this — likely with childish reluctance — but Agnes, definitely, seems to have been somewhat of a rebel, as is evident in a little poem she wrote to her mother in the spring of 1844:

> Religion's paths thou makest me tread.
> Each night thou teach'st me 'ere I go to bed
> And every morning when I rise to try
> To pray with fervour to our God on high.[16]

Agnes was nine years old at that time, old enough to know that Theodora was trying her best to be a good mother to her. Feeling that she, herself, was not fully appreciating this, she admitted that,

> . . . I do not strive to please
> You, dearest Mother, in the least.

> But, for the future, I'll be good.
> I'll not be naughty or be rude
> But let my better conduct prove
> My sure affection & how deep my love

[sgd] Susan Agnes[17]

The verses, while charmingly honest, do not show Agnes as having any promise as a poetess. What they do indicate is a healthy inclination on the part of a nine-year-old to resent being tied down by discipline in general. She said that she was sorry and she promised to be good: that was the best she could do at that time. As an elderly woman, Agnes was to come across what she referred to as 'my juvenile letter' and commented, 'A young mischief if ever one was!'[18] By then she could look back on the peccadillos of her childhood with some amusement. How much easier her early married life would have been if she had then been able to take a similar lighter view of the difficulties which faced her. Instead, she was to turn to the strict religious teachings that had been instilled in her so early, and, while she seemed to gain personal strength from them, they did not encourage her to let her own true character come through.

Eventually, Agnes outgrew lessons at home and went to school in Spanish Town. By then the younger boys had been sent to England to finish their education, and Hewitt had returned to Jamaica and entered a law office. In the late 1840s, he formed a partnership with some friends in the capital, a normal course for a young man of his class and background. A good look at the country, however, showed that things were in a bad way. The economy was not showing any signs of recovery. According to the London stock market reports for November, 1849, the sales of both sugar and coffee were down and both colonial and foreign products were selling at lower than usual prices. Landowners — and, consequently professional men — were hard pressed, and there seemed to be nothing the British government or the Jamaican House of Assembly could do about it. Neither could they do anything to improve the lot of the masses of former slaves, who were finding freedom was not all they had hoped for and were often driven to what a local paper labelled 'notorious. . . idleness, dissipation and vagabondism.'[19]

As if both classes were not suffering enough, in 1850 the island was visited by another disaster. Asiatic cholera struck. One of its first victims was Thomas Bernard. He died on March 3, 1850, and was buried in Claremount Chapel in the parish of St. Ann's, not too far from Friendship, where he had spent summers with Theodora and the children.

Agnes was by now thirteen years old, old enough to be marked not only by her father's premature death but also by the horror of those days when one out of every thirteen persons on the island died. There seemed no way of stopping the spread of the disease. The Board of Health could only advise people to limit their diets to arrowroot pap made with water and 'more or less brandy'. Walter Stewart, Theodora's brother-in-law, who was working in the Board of Health, wrote to her with his own personal suggestions for dealing with the epidemic:

> Tell Hewitt to advise something like this to all his friends. Let each street be divided between as many residents as possible. Let each have a portion of things such as Brandy, Vinegar, Turpentine, Arrowroot, Sugar and Mustard deposited with them for those who may require it at a moment. . . and many a life may be spared.[20]

Despite these precautions, some 32,000 people died before the epidemic burned itself out. Part of the blame lay, as usual, with the drainage system, so it is slight wonder that Agnes was to worry so much about the drains in her first home in Ottawa.

After Thomas' death, Hewitt became the man of the house, and it was to him that Theodora turned for guidance. In her opinion, he was 'an excellent and honourable young man. . . a kind and affectionate son, now my natural protector to whom I look with perfect confidence.'[21] Except for her sister's husband and Hewitt, Theodora had no men in the family whose guidance she might seek at this time. Most of the family had already moved back to England.[22] With the rioting and the plunging economy of the preceding two decades many people had left Jamaica,

9

and there still seemed little hope of a secure future on the island.

With these thoughts in mind, the Bernard family tried to work out what they should do now that Thomas was dead. The local papers of the time carried a surprising amount of foreign news, especially news of other British colonies. From a careful study of them, it seemed to Hewitt that Canada was a country which, unlike Jamaica, was going ahead. He decided to close his practice in Spanish Town, move to Canada and use his legal experience to establish himself there. He also offered to take Richard along, thinking that the twenty-one-year-old, who was now reading law, could finish his studies in Canada. This plan of beginning again in a new country appealed to Richard, but Philip, at twenty, and Walter, sixteen, did not wish to leave their native land. Understandably, too, Theodora was not anxious for all her sons to desert her at once. She planned to stay on in Jamaica, for the present, with Agnes, who was still at school. After Thomas' death, she had moved to Kingston, in the hope that being nearer her sister and the change in itself would help her become more content with her widowhood. In the back of her mind, of course, was the idea that after Hewitt was settled in Canada, she and possibly the rest of the family might join him there, if he suggested it.

As it turned out, however, Theodora and Agnes were the first to leave the island. The pull of England was strong and Theodora was having a difficult time adjusting to life without her husband. The move to Kingston had not been the answer, she found, and living on a reduced income was not easy. She never was confident in money matters, and, possibly for this reason alone, she decided to take the definite step of moving away from the land where she had always lived. With Hewitt's help, she made arrangements for herself and Agnes to sail for England in the summer of 1851. Before leaving, she was anxious to get a clear picture of her finances and, in this, she sought the advice of James Rennals, an old friend and one of her late husband's trustees. In a letter which is strangely like so many of those which Agnes was to send to Joseph Pope, one of John A.'s trustees, a half century and more later, Theodora wrote: 'I think it will be convenient for me to go by the packet of the 12 August as all my arrangements will be completed by that time and I should be very much obliged if you could give me a little of your time. . . that I may understand perfectly how I am in regard to money matters.'[23]

In late June, Agnes (or Susy as she was called at that time) stopped school and went with her mother on a round of farewells. Of the immediate family, there were left only Theodora's sister, Susan, her husband, Walter, and their children. It did not seem likely that they would meet soon again, if ever, and, as it turned out, Agnes never did see her aunt after that, although many years later she would see a great deal of her cousins, Louisa and Annie Stewart, in England.[24] The hardest good-byes of all were with Philip and Walter, the two brothers whom she would never see again. Although the plan was that they should all meet in Canada, it appears that Philip later went to Mexico, where he died, and Walter stayed in Jamaica to work on a sugar plantation until his death in 1861. As for Agnes' friends, she despaired of seeing them again with the despair only a fifteen-year-old can know. She was to be happily surprised when, from time to time, one or another of them would later turn up in Canada or in England. It all seemed so definite, so final during those days in the summer of 1851.

The packet was late and it was not until August 14 that they got away. At last and with very mixed feelings came the day when Theodora could note in her little pocket diary that on

Aug. 14	Susy and I left Jamaica in the Great Western.
Aug. 15	Very sea sick.
Aug. 16	Very sea sick.
Aug. 17	the same.
Aug. 18	Porto Rico — very severe gale.
Aug. 19	St. Thomas — changed at ten at night into the 'Dee'.
Sept. 8	The Lizard Point.
9	Arrived at Southampton.[25]

The three-week passage (an average for those early days of steam or steam and sail combined) had been undertaken during the hurrricane season, and it was, doubtless, a great relief to be on dry land again.

From Southampton, they went up to London by train, a type of transportation that was something of a novelty for them. People were literally pouring into London from all parts of the country eager to see that marvel of the summer of 1851, the Great Exhibition. To Agnes, who knew England only from her brothers' tales, it was all very strange and wonderful. The Exhibition, especially, was beyond belief, and the Crystal Palace, which has been called 'A Midsummer Night's Dream', was just that for the young girl from Jamaica. She was to see many exhibits in that building in the future, but even had she known this, her enjoyment would not have been dimmed by what she was seeing in 1851. What was disappointing, however, was that the colonies' sections had so little on display; nothing there could tell her much about the land where she hoped, one day, to live.

After two days of battling crowds, and still feeling tired from the voyage, Agnes and her mother left London to go down to the country where their relatives were waiting for them. There was the excitement of another train ride, with speeds up to and sometimes exceeding forty miles an hour, and then the joy of being reunited with Aunt Mary and

Uncle Dawson Mayne,[26] who met them at the station and took them to Woodfield, their home in a suburb of Shrewsbury. The Maynes were not the only relatives living in the area, and, after a few days rest, Agnes accompanied her mother on a round of introductory visits. Theodora's little diary reflects their travels:

Sept. 25 Capt. & Mrs. Mayne, Susy & I went to Hawkstone.
Sept. 26 At Hawkstone.[27]
Sept. 27 Left Hawkstone in the evening [to return to Woodfield].
Sept. 30 Walked. Saw the tree in which Owen Glendower saw the Battle of Shrewsbury.
   Oct.2 Susy, Mary and I went to Aston Reynolds, the seat of Sir Andew.[28]
           Went to Hawkstone with Mary & Susy, Mr. Charles Hill and Mr. and Mrs. Charles Taylor.[29]
           Children's Feast.
Oct. 30 Susy and I went to Tixhall Lodge.[30]
Nov. 10 Left Tixhall Lodge and arrived at Lacock.[31]

By November 10, Agnes and Theodora had been away from their home in Jamaica for nearly six months, and they were ready to settle down. They found a home with relatives who lived in the vicarage at Lacock, a little village near Bath, the heart of that part of the country where many Jamaicans sent their sons 'home' to study and settled if they returned from the island. In this picturesque setting, Theodora and Agnes lived for the next three years. It was a waiting period for them, and they seem to have tried to reconcile themselves to that situation, as well as to the inadvisability of too much travelling about in England. Possibly, the sheer cost of moving around was enough to convince them not to go on many visits, for Theodora's little notebook records, meticulously, the expenses of going to Lacock in the first place:

Expenses for Susy and myself from Shrewsbury to Lacock.

2 first class tickets to Stratford	10.4
to Birmingham	10.0
2 second class to Horsham	1.16.0
Fly at S.	1.6
Coffee for 2	2.0
Fly and toll gate to Corsham	6.0
	3.6.0[32]

Despite the excitement of England, there were many times when Jamaica was foremost in their minds. The bonds had been cut, but both Theodora and Agnes were still very much tied to Jamaica in sentiment and were dependent on the packet letters by which they kept in touch with their family and friends there. In the autumn of 1851, a letter arrived from Aunt Susan Stewart with the news that Hewitt, too, was about to leave Jamaica. Through one of her English cousins, Jane Nutt, whose husband had a small living at Mendup, near Bristol, Theodora had secured for Hewitt a letter of introduction to James Patton, a lawyer in Barrie, Canada West. Hewitt's other arrangements were now complete, reported Theodora's sister, and he would shortly be on his way.[33] For the moment, Richard would wait in Jamaica, but it was hoped that his wait would not be long. Theodora and Agnes, too, were looking forward to the day when they could join Hewitt, but it was acknowledged that Richard's turn should be first and that while they waited in England, mother and daughter would profit from getting to know their relatives there.

Their time was not, of course, spent completely in visiting or idleness. Agnes did some studies, and when she was at the Vicarage, it was natural that she should continue her religious education. Did she then remember her feelings of 1844 when her mother taught her to rise every morning and 'try to pray with fervour to our God on high'? Did she, like Elizabeth Fry, whom she read some years later, waken each day asking herself how she could best serve the Lord? Remembering the rebellious nine-year-old, one is inclined to doubt it, but, by now, a child's balkiness might have been replaced by a searching for answers. As a married woman going through a period of self-introspection, she would write in her diary that '[Fry] seems through life to have had an earnest, truth-seeking, intelligent mind. And furthermore to have been highly religious.'[34] Agnes, the young girl, not yet very far removed from the child, may, however, simply have been studying Church History or whatever else the Vicar or Theodora told her to study. She would not, in any case, have been as serious and soul-searching as the older Agnes would be.

Besides her religious studies, Agnes took singing lessons and, if the following account is typical, it is hardly exciting. Undoubtedly, it was the standard repertoire of a young lady of her time and station.

A quarter's instruction in singing given to Miss Bernard by . . . Berand.

£2.12.6

Peace of Mind	1.6
Mother's Lullaby	2.6
Exercises	4.0
Quarter ending 7th April, 1853[35]	

As her exercises required more time — or, at least, more money — it would seem that Agnes apparently had no more talent in this field than she had for poetry, and there is no record that she continued with her singing lessons. However, she was doing all the things that were expected of her as a young lady. She also took drawing lessons, according to Theodora's diary, the first being given at Lacock Vicarage in December, 1851. In this, she did show a certain ability, which is evident in some of her watercolours done in Canada many years later. A most important requirement for educated young ladies of the day was a knowledge of French, so Agnes also studied this in England. These lessons were, naturally, to be put to good use in Canada, and John A. would often remark how proud he was of her ability to speak to dinner guests from Lower Canada in their own language.

During this period of her life, Agnes had one regret — that she and her mother did not travel more in England. This feeling comes out strongly in a diary entry made twenty years later:

> Hawthorne's English notes [sic], which I am reading, annoy me a great deal. It is an amusing book to me, I suppose, in some way, or I should not read it, but he is sneering and prejudiced. In the bottom of his heart I can see he, in spite of himself, admires Oxford and our beloved Cathedrals, but in a grudging and reluctant manner. It makes my mouth water to think how much the beggar saw and my eyes water to see how little he appreciated![36]

It was early 1854 before Hewitt thought the time was right for his mother and sister to join him in Canada, as Richard had already done. Once more came the sadness of saying good-byes. Theodora, now in her fifties, must have found it no easy matter to part with her new-found relatives and friends; only the thought of being reunited with her two sons would have comforted her in this, as well as in the prospect of another long sea voyage. Agnes had also to leave new friends, but, for a girl still in her teens, the idea of a totally different life in Canada was probably intriguing. Hewitt's letters had told them much about Barrie and his friends there, and the move undoubtedly seemed a great adventure.

Their crossing was, wisely, set for late enough in the season to avoid the capricious spring winds and to allow their ship to travel up the St. Lawrence, which was, by then, no longer ice-bound. Their first contact with Canada was when they docked at Quebec City, little suspecting that they would later live in this city on the cliff. From there they travelled in a ship with less draft as far as Montreal, admiring the first glimpses of their new homeland. There was still Lake Ontario to traverse, and it was evident from the first that they were in a larger country than they had been able to imagine. It must have been with relief that they landed in Toronto, to be met by Hewitt, who assured them that they had only to travel a few hours north by the new Ontario, Huron and Simcoe Railway until they would be in Barrie, where they would be settled at last.

Hewitt had been in Barrie for more than two years before Agnes and her mother arrived and was becoming well established. His letter of introduction to James Patton had paid off in greatly facilitating his entry into his profession. And with his family background and likeable personality, he had soon become an accepted member of the small Barrie society, a circle into which Richard had been given an entrée on his arrival.

Shortly after his arrival in Barrie, Hewitt, following in the family tradition, had begun to devote some of his time to community responsibilities. One of his first interests was in the local Trinity Anglican Church. This small frame structure had been built in 1834, but the congregation had had its share of ups and downs. When the Reverend S.B. Ardagh became rector in 1842, he found it in a 'melancholy' condition, and his efforts to revitalize it took much time and effort. His parish extended as far as Owen Sound, and he had to live somewhere nearer its geographical centre than Barrie. From his home in Shanty Bay, he tried to visit all his churches as often as possible, but, given the condition of the roads at that time, his work was not easy. Little help came from the settlers who were primarily concerned with making a living. But in 1851, the Bishop of Toronto invited all the Anglican churches in his district to send lay members to the annual meeting of the Church Society in an attempt to get them more involved. To Hewitt, such involvement seemed natural, and, as soon as he was settled, he had taken on the post of church warden. Other influential members of the community had also begun to take more of an interest in their church, and, by the time Theodora and Agnes arrived in Barrie, Trinity Anglican Church looked after not only the spiritual needs of its members but also filled an important social need in helping people to know each other better.

So the church provided an easy introduction to life in Barrie for Theodora. She soon became a devoted attendant and worker, thus making friends and filling her life with new interests. Agnes, too, made friends through the church, which she attended twice every Sunday. She also taught in the Sunday School and, on Sunday afternoons, copied out the morning sermon. There would seem to have been little time for her to obey the advice given in one of the sermons she copied, to 'retire from the world, communing with your own heart in your chamber and be still to think over the sins of different natures which you have committed.'[37]

Just in case Agnes had time to commit any sins, Theodora continued to see that her daughter trod 'religion's paths' as firmly as she had in Jamaica and England. And now her efforts seemed more successful. Although Agnes had lived at Lacock Rectory for some time, she had not been confirmed in the Anglican Church. Now, in a little booklet in which she copied her notes on religion, she wrote: 'Began to prepare for Confirmation. March 16th, 1855. Confirmed by the Bishop of Toronto on the 27th of May — Whitsunday — 1855. Barrie, Canada West.'[38] By this time she had studied the differences between the Protestant and the Roman Catholic religions and had been enrolled in the Christian Knowledge Society by her 'affectionate Mother'. Her grounding in religious beliefs was as good as her mother could make it. Still there were traces of rebellion. On one of the pages of her notebook, perhaps in exasperation at all this study, she scribbled: '855 pages — 855 Sundays'.

The Bernards' lives in Barrie thus centered on the church and on the social contacts they made through the legal profession. There was little else for the middle class in Barrie then except, possibly, participation in the Temperance Society, the British American Friendly Society for the elderly and ill or the embryonic Barrie Philharmonic Society, which held weekly practices in the Barrie Common School House: 'Tickets, admitting the bearer to all performances and practicing, with the exception of special concerts, 5s. each, payable in advance. All persons desirous of purchasing tickets must send their names to the Secretary for the approval of the Committee.'[39] It seems there was no chance of any rowdy element ruining the concerts.

In the face of this relative paucity of offerings, what did a girl such as Agnes find to do in Barrie? She was already a well-educated young lady with the required accomplishments of her class. Higher education was not felt necessary for girls. The scope of her life must have seemed very limited in a town of some 1,500 persons, a town so new that its population had more than doubled in the eight years previous to 1854. Barrie did, however, offer compensations for being so much smaller and less lively than any place she had lived before. One was its closeness to the outdoors, which Agnes had learned to love as a child. A local paper considered the town

> beautifully situated on Kempenfeldt Bay . . . on a rising ground which slopes directly to the water's edge. . . . To the non-business man, the bay, sheltered from the sudden and violent gusts of wind which render its sister, Toronto, unsafe, . . . and abounding with inlets, bays and landings, affords ample opportunity of indulging in his *dolce far niente,* or should he prefer, somewhat more animated recreation in the piscatorial art. Here one may float along, dreaming lazily all the day through.[40]

Agnes may have done just that during some of these summer days. Hewitt had been Commandant of the Lake Simcoe Boat Club since 1855, and, with him and his friends, Agnes could have enjoyed the beautiful bay and sailing exploits which, when they were reported to friends back in Jamaica, caused envy as their friends only wished that they could 'get up' something similar.

It is unfortunate that Agnes did not leave us any record of her summer pleasures in Barrie, but many years later, she was to write of some of her winter activities. A description of a fishing trip published during the 1880s includes the memory:

Tommy cods! — meanest of edible fish.... Tommy cods! of which, in my very youthful days, I had one dark night caught eighty-nine specimens in three hours, through a hole in the ice, whither were they lured by torchlight, and whither their captors (for we were several on that occasion) were attracted by love of mischief and truant disobedience. [41]

In another of her writings for publication, there is a record of other winter activities.

In the more primitive days of Canada, when the fun was called 'coasting', and carried on in less exalted circles than is the case now, roughly made 'hand sleds' of common painted wood... were in constant use on natural slopes of hillsides, and formed the pet diversion of small boys and school-girls.... A pleasant flavour of mischief was added to the sliding attractions of that day, for Mamma often said 'No' and then came the excitement of being caught some bright moonlit night a mile or so from home, packed with one's bosom friend on a 'coaster', as the sled was called, tearing down a steep forest road-way, and then scudding away, breathless, dishevelled and nearly shaken to death, over the frozen surface of some lonely pine-fringed lake. [42]

The little girl who had promised 'for the future I'll be good' found opportunities, at times, to be refreshingly naughty some ten years later.

A definite advantage of Barrie was its proximity to the growing metropolis of Toronto. With the railway, one could go to Toronto on the morning train, have four hours for shopping and then return on the same day. Barrie, in 1854, boasted:

besides the usual proportion of all branches of trade... 3 Medical Men, 1 Druggist, 4 Lawyers, 3 Provincial Land Surveyors, 1 Draughtsman, 1 Gunsmith and Machinist, 2 Watchmakers, 13 General Stores, 2 Bank Agencies (Upper Canada and Commerce), 6 Hotels, 3 of them first class, 2 Printing Offices, 2 Weekly Papers (The Barrie Herald and Northern Advance), 1 Telegraph Office, also 4 places of worship. [43]

They had all this, and yet when Theodora wanted to buy a chest preserver and two pairs of mink mitts in preparation for the first long, cold winter ahead, she went to Toronto. No doubt the shops in Toronto offered much more variety than did those in Barrie. It also had cultural offerings of a somewhat higher level, and it was not uncommon for Barrie residents to go down for a few days simply to take advantage of its greater sophistication.

In all, life in Barrie could be made rich enough. Gradually, the Bernards began to feel so at home there that they, like many other residents of the town, began to invest in local property. Hewitt was the first Canadian landowner in the family, followed, in turn, by Richard and Theodora. The latter still had some money invested in England and used part of it to buy land in Canada, probably considering it a better investment. (It was not. None of their transactions made money for them and some they even lost by default.)

Even if the Bernards did not become rich through their Barrie land transactions, neither did they suffer. Barrie offered more than material wealth; it offered an agreeable way of life and was a good introduction to Canada for all the family. Both Hewitt and Richard became well established, Theodora found friends who had social and religious backgrounds comparable to her own, and Agnes used this time to move from girlhood into young womanhood. Shortly after they came to Barrie, she underwent an identity crisis not uncommon to young girls. For some time she could not decide so simple a thing as how to sign her name. A page from her notebook shows that she tried all different spellings and combinations. Was she to be 'Susan Agnes Bernard' or was she to be 'Susannah Agnes'? Rather, should she be 'Agnes Susannah' or, possibly, 'Agnes Susanna'?[44] It was as 'Susy' that she arrived in Barrie but when the time came to leave, early in 1858, she had decided. She was going to be Agnes. Somehow it seemed more dignified.

In February, 1836, a few months before Agnes had even been born, the Law Society of Upper Canada recognized 'Mr. John McDonald [sic] as candidate for a call to the Degree of Barrister at Law of this Society.'[1] He was then twenty-one years old. Before long, he became a politician as well as a lawyer, and by the time his path crossed that of the Bernards, in 1857, he had many years' experience in both areas. Looking at this experience and at his youth, it seems as if he had always been in training for the highest office in the land.

His mother, who had a strong influence on her son, had known that he was destined for greatness. Helen Macdonald, reputedly a strong personality and possessed of great intellectual powers, pinned her hopes on John A., her only son to survive infancy. (Those who knew her best remarked that, had she had a higher education, she would have become a noted woman in her own right.[2])

During the Macdonalds' early years in Canada, Helen's role was to hold the family together when her husband, Hugh, found that he was faced with the same lack of success that had led him, in 1820, to bring them over from Scotland to the Kingston area in the first place. Enterprise after enterprise failed, and, from the age of fifteen, John A. had to earn his own living. He had completed five years of grammar school, and that he had received even this much schooling was due, likely, to his mother's influence. Certainly education was not considered necessary for his sisters, Margaret and Louisa.

It was through Helen, too, that John A. secured an apprenticeship in the Kingston law office of George MacKenzie. The young man also boarded with his employer, and it was in that house that he got his first feeling for politics. During evening discussions, MacKenzie's interest in local issues made an indelible impression. At the same time, John A. learned something else that was later to stand him in good stead: he learned to debate. The precenter of Kingston's St. Andrew's Church, who was often referred to as a 'queer fellow' and a 'free-thinker of the worst kind', 'took a fancy to the clever lad and frequently engaged him in controversy regarding the Bible. I don't know that it did him much good but it taught him to argue.'[3]

In any spare time that he could find, John A. read to make up for what he lacked in formal education. He devoured books of all types and began to amass the store of knowledge that Agnes later remarked on in some wonderment: 'As for his knowledge, there seems to be no end of it. Where he found the leisure to collect so much general information — during twenty years of political life — surprises me.'[4]

Another pronounced and continuing characteristic of John A. was his sense of fun. According to his nephew-biographer, James Pennington Macpherson,[5] he was always full of mischief, quick with a come-back and unable to resist a joke.[6] This surely came to him from his mother, who was said to have had a pronounced sense of humour and to have especially enjoyed droll situations and droll expressions.[7] How many tense political moments John A. was able to smooth over with this happy inheritance. What a congenial friend and companion it made him in adult life. In this respect, he fared better than did Agnes, for her mother, although well-intentioned, lacked Helen Macdonald's sense of humour and was thus unable to temper her pious nature. As was to be expected, this rather bleak piety proved to have a strong influence on Agnes in later years when she faced problems that seemed too big for her to handle.

While Agnes was still scribbling childish poems, John A. was pursuing his career. Even before he was called to the bar in 1836, he opened his own law office, taking on George MacKenzie's clients on the latter's death. About this time, the Macdonalds moved back into town, and John A. was able to enjoy a rare period of home life. Even as he built up his practice, however, he had to assume more and more family financial responsibilities, for his father was a victim of drink. The Macdonald men always seem to have found it easy to drop into one of the many taverns that were part of contemporary life and share their frustrations with a glass or two. It was a tendency that John A. inherited.

In September, 1841, Hugh Macdonald died, and, soon after, under the strain of work and too much responsibility, John A. became ill. The family's great faith in the restorative powers of a visit to the land of his ancestors led him across the sea. It was one of many such trips he was to take in the search for health and one that was to have far-reaching effects. He went first to London, where he made many friendships that would long endure, and then went up to Scotland. This was what the family expected him to do. What they did not expect was that he would there fall in love with his cousin, Isabella Clark. It was a short courtship and, in the following year, Isabella came to Canada to become John A.'s wife.

The marriage was marked by tragedy, for Isabella was ill most of the time, so ill that she often had to be taken south to avoid the cold Canadian winters. The victim of an indeterminate disease, characterized by nervous tics, extreme fatigue and pain for which opium was the only available relief, Isabella attempted to carry on as John A.'s wife, but it was often beyond her powers. John A., who adored her, gave his life over to easing her misery in any possible way. He lavished time, attention and money on her, time and attention that, had she been in good health, he would have been spending on his law practice, which suffered from his absences. In 1847, she bore him a son who lived but a few months. A second son, Hugh John, was born in 1850; this time the baby lived, but Isabella's own health became steadily worse. Most of the time she was in Canada, she had to remain quietly in Kingston, under sedation, while John A., who by now had branched out into politics, tried to attend to his new, demanding duties.

It was a lonely, sad time for him, one that was to leave its mark. Just as his father before him, John A. turned to alcohol for solace. Isabella could do nothing to help her husband; she depended more and more on opium just to get her through the days. In a supreme effort, when the 1855 Parliamentary Session was about to open in Toronto, she did move down to the capital with John A. and little Hugh John, but household management was beyond her. The family had to live in a boarding house, depending on friends to care for the little boy much of the time. In early 1856, her condition became worse, and in December, 1857, she died.

It had been an agonizing time for all concerned, and the sequel was also difficult. Busy with two careers, John A. now moved into ten years of bachelorhood, during which he often had to be absent from Kingston. Hugh John was turned over to his grandmother and his aunts, Louisa and Margaret. He had also acquired a surrogate father since Margaret had been married to Professor James Williamson of Queen's University in 1852. 'The Professor', as he soon became known to all in the family, was to fill a need in the boy's life that his own father was not always able to provide.

Meanwhile, John A. tried to fill the emptiness of his life with work and boon companions who, more often than not, had a bottle on hand. When Isabella died, John A. had already been in politics for thirteen years and, in spite of his personal worries, had gone steadily up the ladder. From a start as a Kingston alderman, he had gone on to the larger political arena of the Parliament of Upper and Lower Canada in 1844. So tenuous was the union between the two Canadas that they compromised even on where their capital should be, moving back and forth between Toronto, Montreal and Quebec City. The 1844 Session was held in Montreal and, by then, the new Member for Kingston had already set the tone and substance of his later political philosophy. In his campaign speeches he had concentrated on the necessity of Canada maintaining a permanent connection with the mother country and avoided any references to the topic of the day, 'Responsible Government'. He had also been canny enough to discuss local issues, including the need for better roads into the interior. In emphasizing the need for transportation, he laid the groundwork for what was to become his major political battle in later years — his resolve to see the Canadian Pacific Railway constructed.

Step by step John A. advanced quickly up the political ladder, crossing swords at every rung with Reformer George Brown in an antagonism that was to last for decades. In 1854, John A. was named Attorney-General for Upper Canada, and by 1857 the forty-two-year-old lawyer from Kingston became head of the Liberal-Conservative Party.[8] In that year, the political team of Macdonald and Cartier,[9] which was to work together for so many years, came into being. In the same year, the Bernards entered John A.'s life.

With his heavy responsibilities as party head as well as Attorney-General, John A. needed the help of a good Private Secretary. As he read the pages of the *Upper Canada Law Journal and Local Courts Gazette,* a highly respected periodical to which he subscribed, he noticed more and more the work of its co-editor, Hewitt Bernard. Reading this and aware, too, of Hewitt's work for *The Herald,* a small Barrie paper which had been started to offset the influence of the local Reform paper, John A. detected thinking that often paralleled his own. Without hesitation, he contacted the Barrie lawyer and asked if he would consider moving down to Toronto to work as his Secretary.

It was an offer that seemed too good to pass up. Hewitt had accomplished the goals he had set in Jamaica over seven years earlier. Agnes and Theodora had been brought to Canada and seemed to be settled into their new home. Richard was well established and nearing the completion of his studies with the Upper Canada Law Society. All things considered, Hewitt thought that he might now be allowed to think of himself. Surely, in working with a man who held such a commanding political position, there must be an opportunity for advancement. With these thoughts in mind, Hewitt Bernard accepted the position of Private Secretary to John A. Macdonald.

His decision brought yet another change to the family. A life that had seemed more settled than any they had known since Thomas Bernard's death came to an end. Richard had to remain in Barrie to complete his studies, but Theodora and Agnes decided to go to Toronto with Hewitt. There was the tug of parting from their new and good friends in Barrie, but running counter to this was the attraction of returning to an urban way of life. Toronto was already a city and, as such, offered a more varied cultural and social life than Barrie, no matter how pleasant, could provide. As with leaving England, it must have been a hard decision for Theodora to make, but a look at Agnes' later life shows that she was always willing to travel, always ready for the next adventure.

It was not until late in February, 1858, that Hewitt's preparations for the departure were completed. During the interval, he, his mother and his sister said farewell to their new friends, beginning with the the first contacts Hewitt had made — the James Pattons. By now they could count many other prominent residents among their circle: the Lallys, to whom they were soon to be related by marriage; the Hopkins, with whom Richard worked for a time; the O'Briens, some of whom Agnes would keep in touch with even as an old lady; the Ardaghs, whose daughter, Martha, was a close friend of Agnes; Mrs. Boys, whose husband, Henry, was County Treasurer; and many others. The good-byes were sad but made with the thought that there would be frequent opportunities to meet again in Toronto or when the Bernards returned to visit Richard.

The move also meant many business details had to be looked after, and Hewitt delayed his departure to supervise the sale of some of the family's effects and to arrange for the shipping of the rest to Toronto. He did not feel he could leave these tasks to his mother, who was a hesitant businesswoman, nor would he entrust them to twenty-one-year-old Agnes. Finally he had to leave, while they remained in Barrie for a few days to carry out some last-minute tasks, which he carefully defined in a letter from Toronto. In a reassuring tone, he also told them: 'I have seen my Chief for a minute & he does not seem disgusted by my absence; so it was as well I remained, in fact there would have been a mess if I had not.'[10]

The same letter revealed he had a few misgivings about how his new situation would work out: 'My Chief intends applying for three Government nights in the Session which looks very much as if he intended to push matters through & get the Session ended as soon as possible. I shall be very glad when it is finished as it will make me more certain until the next.'[11] His uncertainty led him to suggest to Theodora that she make one or two farewells he had not been able to do personally. In particular, he wished his mother to write 'a little note to Mrs. Gowan,[12] saying that we begged the Judge (put his name in) would accept it. It may be advantageous hereafter.'[13] At the same time, he told her, 'Before leaving you should say to Miss H . . . you hoped to see her in passing thro' Toronto. Susan [Agnes] might offer her her bed, but it is problematical how we may get on so I would be guarded.'[14] Hewitt was taking no chances.

News of the appointment soon reached friends in England, who wrote to Theodora saying, 'It may lead to something else & Toronto I should think a pleasanter residence for you & Agnes than Barrie.'[15] In many ways it was. Although it meant making a new home for themselves, they were becoming used to this, and Toronto was not unfamiliar. On shopping trips and visits, the Bernards had come to know its commercial centre and to have some familiarity with its hotels and restaurants, as well as with the areas in which their friends lived. Now they had an opportunity to learn more of this developing city of over 40,000 inhabitants. A number of the red-brick buildings of its early days remained, but there were also some fine new limestone buildings and many of the streets even had gas lighting. Fine edifices and church spires marked the skyline, and the lake was never far from view.

It was the churches that first made them feel at home. Bishop Strachan, who had confirmed Agnes three years earlier, was at St. James Anglican Cathedral, and it was natural that the Bernards should follow up this connection. It was there they made their first friends in Toronto, some of whom turned out to be former Barrie residents. The move was made easier for Agnes in that she was soon in her accustomed role as a Sunday School teacher.

Toronto also offered welcome cultural attractions. Well-organized, amateur theatrical groups entertained the public. The Grand Opera House had not yet been built, but concerts were given in quite adequate halls. One of the finest of these was Shaftesbury Hall, and it was there that Agnes first saw John A. Hewitt pointed out his Chief, who was sitting in the front gallery with some ladies. Agnes recalled many years later: 'I remember distinctly how he looked; a forcible, yet changeful face, with such a mixture of strength and vivacity, and his bushy, dark, peculiar hair as he learned on his elbows and looked down.'[16]

Although John A. certainly seems to have made an impression on her, Agnes was too busy getting to know her new home to be overly interested in him. She also had to try to reconcile two vastly different pictures of the man — that reported by Hewitt and that painted by his constant enemy, the *Globe*. In any event, there was little opportunity for her to see him during the next few months. In February and during much of March he was ill with 'flu and away from the House a good part of the time. (Had she gone to the pub near his bachelor quarters on Bay Street, she might have found him there on occasion, but such places were out of bounds for young ladies.) Nevertheless, Agnes did begin to take an interest in Canadian politics about this time. This is scarcely surprising: Theodora was happy to be back in an atmosphere which had once been part of her life; politics seemed likely to become a way of life for Hewitt; and, in consequence, the subject must have been discussed frequently in their new home. Agnes even went to the House sometimes, perhaps hoping for a glimpse of that 'forcible yet changeful face', but it was not until July that she saw John A. again, and then it was in the midst of a fierce debate on selecting a permanent capital for Canada.

From her seat in the open galleries of the House, galleries that

were crammed with listeners, every foot of space [being] occupied in and around the chambers [she listened as] Mr. Macdonald was replying to the oft reiterated charges that, in defiance of distinct pledges, the Governor, Sir Edmund Head, had tendered advice to the Queen which led to her choice of Ottawa.[17]

The Members, tired of moving from one city to another, had tried to decide on the relative merits of Toronto, Montreal, Quebec City or, possibly, Kingston. When they failed to reach any agreement, the question had been left to Queen Victoria, who was in possession of the official report, as well as of a watercolour sketch of the remote lumber town from the easel of Lady Head. The Queen's decision had been in favour of Ottawa, and that decision had been made known to the Canadians early in January, 1858. It had seemed to be well accepted until July, when Brown, along with his political ally, Thomas D'Arcy McGee, saw in this a chance to make political mischief. In a motion that John A. thought was insulting to the Queen, Brown said he thought Ottawa was not suitable. Battle was joined. Years later, Agnes reminisced about it in a letter to Sir Joseph Pope:

I suppose you have often heard Sir John tell the story of how Sir E. Head promised not in any way to interfere about the selection of the capital & how he did not do so. On one of the first occasions I ever saw Sir John — and the first time I think I ever heard him speak he told McGee what he said was — as false as hell — in a parliamentary way of course but using those words. Sir John told me afterwards that what was so false was McGee's repeating the statement that Sir E. had interfered.[18]

During the few days after this contretemps, the floor of the House was a scene of great confusion as the well-known Double Shuffle developed. Brown succeeded in toppling John A., but the Reformer was 'king' for only two days, after which he suddenly found himself being referred to as one who *had* been Prime Minister. During all this confusion, Agnes could see that John A. maintained a very detached air. When the time came, he calmly cleared out his desk and moved to the Opposition side, seemingly unaffected by the upheaval around him. (He *was* detached, and, had Hewitt known him better, he might have guessed at the reason why and been alarmed. John A. was thinking of retiring. It was not the first time nor would it be the last, but he was never allowed, either by his own conscience or by pressure from friends, to take this step.)

Shortly after this excitement, the Bernards made a trip to Barrie to attend Richard's wedding to Agnes Lally. Agnes Bernard never did feel very close to her new sister-in-law, but with Richard, who often teased her, calling her 'vain' and nicknaming her 'Pug', she had a happy relationship. (One suspects that it was more relaxed than with Hewitt, perhaps because she and Richard were closer in age as well as in temperament, while Hewitt, the eldest and the one who had to bear the heaviest responsibilities, was much more serious.) About the time of his marriage, Richard opened his own law office in Barrie, but early in 1859, he and his wife moved to Windsor, where he struggled to get himself established before the birth of their first child later that year.

It was not long before the rest of the Bernards were moving again. In May, 1859, Toronto's turn at being the capital expired, and, although money had been voted for the construction of government buildings in Ottawa, it would be some years before they were ready. In the meantime, the Members and their staffs must pack up and move to Quebec City.

Agnes and Theodora went, too, but decided not to try to find a house of their own. Mrs. Patton, wife of Hewitt's former law associate, had often remarked on the excellence of Mrs. Steele's boarding house in Quebec City, and it was there that Agnes and her mother went to live. It proved very pleasant for them, especially when friends from Toronto, similarly affected by the change to another capital, decided to live in the same place. The opportunity to continue these friendships must have been especially happy for Theodora. After the Bernards had left Barrie, she had been the one who had held on most strongly to the old ties with her friends there and kept up correspondence with several of them, especially with Mrs. Patton. In these letters she heard how their little society was getting on; for example: 'Mrs. Gowan gave another small party; it was confined to young people. . . . Music — cards and games were the order of the evening — it passed off very pleasantly indeed. Mrs. G. and I regretted more than once that you and Miss Bernard were not present to share in the amusement.'[19]

Maintaining connections was especially important in Quebec City. When Theodora and Agnes had left Barrie for Toronto, the city had been more or less familiar to them. Not so Quebec City, which they had seen only briefly on their arrival in Canada in 1854. In aspect and in culture it was unlike any place in which they had ever lived. Agnes' Huguenot ancestors would have found it less strange, as its style was more that of seventeenth-century France than anything else. Like London, it was a city to explore, section by section. In both the narrow, crowded streets of the old town and the openness of the *haute ville,* there was something interesting to be seen at every turn. Reminders of the city's

French origin — street names, monuments, museums and churches — crowded against indications of the English presence — red-coated troops from the garrison and Holy Trinity Cathedral, near Place d'Armes.

As in other garrison towns in Canada, the British soldiers were a strong influence on local society.

> A regiment took its mess silver overseas. It also carried along its traditions and social mores. . . . They brought. . . the flavour of English 'society', fashions and manners that were little known in other parts of North America. . . . [They] formed racing, trotting, riding, sleighing clubs and packs of fox-hounds. . . organized 'cotillions' and balls; and they were joined in all these affairs by the upper stratum of the local people, especially by its young ladies.[20]

One young lady who quite enjoyed participating in some of these activities was Agnes. In Quebec City, she found an agreeable blend of what she had most enjoyed in Barrie and in Toronto — the pleasure of the outdoors and the society of young people of her own class. Years later she would recall:

> Tobogganing and coasting first became fashionable in Canada when adopted by those agreeable warriors who as officers of Guards, Rifles and Line, with their regiments were sent to Canada. . . . There were rinks crowded with struggling skaters, ballrooms red with uniforms, snow roads lined with tandems. . . and many a snowy hillside darted over by the hand sleigh or toboggan.[21]

A memory which she retained vividly was of a winter picnic to Montmorency Falls, a favourite gathering-place. 'About fifty strong, military and civilians, with a sprinkling of fair ladies. . . unpacked from a line of smoking tandems, piled with fur robes and foot muffs, we. . . stood waiting for orders what to do next.'[22] They spent the afternoon tobogganning, then:

> Before sunset we were called to dinner in a cave hollowed out at the base of the upper cone. . . . Once entered, we found ourselves in a wondrous fairy cavern. . . . There, on ice-carved sofas, were stretched dark rugs of fur; and on an icy buffet no end of good things were spread. . . . How we enjoyed that repast — what a capital drive we had home by tandem and starlight — what a merry dance in the Music Hall by way of a wind up.[23]

There was evidently no lack of entertainment in Quebec City for a young lady, and John A. contributed his share by offering a Valentine's Day Ball in 1860. Setting aside politics for a moment, he invited some 800 guests to a party which was said to have been more splendid than anything ever put on in Quebec City. The young officers of the garrison

27

were there in their bright dress uniforms, dancing attendance on Agnes
and the other ladies of society, young and old, who vied to out-do each
other in their dresses for this, the event of the season. The ball was held
in the Music Hall, which claimed to be the finest such room in North
America at the time, and John A. arranged special decorations for the
occasion:

> Its usual attractions were supplemented by tasteful decorations and
> designs.... Around the upper walls, above the gallery, had been hung
> graceful festoons of crimson drapery, looped at intervals by pendants of roses
> and evergreens. Below the galleries, facing each other, were two alcoves, in
> one of which dwelt a life-size Cupid.... In the opposite alcove was placed a
> copy of Canova's celebrated statue of the 'Dancing Girl'. Near the entrance
> were the Three Graces, bearing a chaplet of beautiful flowers.... In the front
> was a large bust of Her Majesty and near by, a fountain of Eau de Cologne.[24]

The evening was John A.'s. Thoroughly enjoying himself, he helped
stewards distribute valentines to all the ladies present. When it was time
for supper, 'There was another surprise in the form of a large pâté, from
which, when opened, there flew out four and twenty birds....'[25]

In the winter of that year Agnes first met John A. He apparently took
the initiative, reportedly paying Theodora a call during which he told
her he liked Hewitt very much and would like to get to know his mother
as well. Was this just a courtesy call? One suspects another motive — getting to know Hewitt's sister. He had first noticed Agnes several years
before, when he was dining with a colleague in a Toronto hotel. Agnes
and Richard had come into the room and caught John A.'s attention,
but his friend could only tell him that they were 'An English family settled on Lake Simcoe. I do not know their names.'[26] That had been in
1856; it was not until 1860 that he discovered the young lady whom he
had seen was his own Secretary's sister. Years later, Agnes tried to find
out what were his first impressions of her. The most serious answer she
could get was 'I thought you both very tall, very much alike, and that you
had fine eyes.'[27]

Agnes, then in her early twenties, was not a beautiful young lady. She
was, as John A. had observed, tall, and she had fine eyes. Otherwise she
has been described, rather unflatteringly, as being, 'Tawny...rather
"raw-boned" and angular. But she possessed a quick wit...and was
brilliant and piquant in conversation.'[28] John A. was probably first attracted by her personality, which may have reminded him of his mother
in her younger days. Whatever drew him to Agnes in the first place, his
admiration of her turned to love at some point.

Sources are conflicting as to when that point occurred; it is not clear, either, how well the two got to know each other during the years in Quebec City. On the one hand, it was asserted that 'their acquaintance grew to intimacy, [while the Government sat at Quebec], the somewhat limited circle of society and the professional relationship of Miss Bernard's brother bringing them into frequent contact.'[29] This is denied by others, who claim that John A. saw little of Agnes during this period and that rumours of his having proposed to her then were incorrect.[30] Whatever the truth, it seems likely that their acquaintanceship progressed to some degree of intimacy – otherwise their eventual marriage in 1867 was, indeed, preceded by a whirlwind courtship.

We may never know exactly what happened in Quebec City, but it is certain that during this period John A. was, as he had always been, a ladies' man, sometimes the pursuer, sometimes the pursued. His personal magnetism was great, and ever since Isabella's death he had been considered a fair catch. Several women are known to have set their caps for him, including Lizzie Hall, the widow of his good friend, Judge Hall of Peterborough. And there was more than one rumour about John A.'s supposed marriage plans during this period. Nothing ever came of them.

During these years in Quebec City, both Agnes and John A. suffered great personal sorrows. In October, 1861, Agnes' brother, Richard, died in Windsor at the age of thirty-two. His young widow and their baby, Dora, returned to Barrie where another daughter, May, was born a few months later.

In October of the following year, Helen Macdonald died. She had been an invalid for many years but had remained a dominant figure in John A.'s life. He felt her loss greatly, and, added to his political worries, it turned him more and more to his old solace — alcohol. There had already been days the previous spring when he had not appeared in the House, and the *Globe*, in glee, had reported that he was having another of his 'attacks'. Now, his drinking increased in frequency, and while it did not provide him the comfort he sought, neither did it allow him to escape attention. Not only the *Globe* but also *Grip*, the Canadian equivalent of *Punch*, made him an object of ridicule, as did his opponents in the House.

Agnes must have been well aware of what was going on. In addition to the jokes in the press, there were days when Hewitt did not even hear from his Chief. Although alcohol was consumed on a vast scale in contemporary Canada, she could see for herself that drinking had a far more disastrous effect on John A. than on most of the men she knew. It must have been impossible for her to come to terms with his problem, one that was little understood in those days. If John A. did, in fact, propose to her during their time in Quebec City, Agnes, with no informed opinion available to her as to how to cope with alcoholism, must have made up her mind that she could not risk the future as his wife. In 1862, she was twenty-six years old, seemingly not inclined to rush into marriage. At one time, during her days in England, family members had said they hoped Agnes 'has got a young Irishman',[31] but nothing more had been heard of such a possibility and Agnes had continued to live a satisfactory life as a single person. Why should she consider marriage to someone who could not control his drinking and who was, besides, considered a bit of a Romeo? The gamble was more than she was prepared to take, and she carried on with her own active social life, trying to forget the death of her brother Richard, while John A. sought forgetfulness for his particular worries in drink.

The political, as well as the personal, side of John A.'s life was having its ups and downs at this time. As he was painting a canvas of a Canada federally united with the Maritime provinces and Newfoundland, the tensions provoked by the United States' Civil War intruded. When the Trent Affair[1] made headlines in late 1861 and Anglo-American difficulties looked to endanger Canada's safety, it seemed obvious that the colony's defences should be improved. For this reason, John A. introduced a Militia Bill in 1862, only to see it go down like a lead balloon, taking the Government and himself with it. He then spent two years in Opposition.

Help for John A. and Canada's disruptive constitutional problems was forthcoming from a very unexpected source. In the spring of 1864, his old enemy, George Brown, let it be known that he would co-operate with the new Conservative Government if a lasting solution to Canada's problems could be found. The two antagonists formed a coalition, each seeing in it a hope of attaining his own desires. The country was on its way to Confederation talks, and Brown became a member of the Executive Council of the Province of Canada.

Agnes' life was only marginally touched by these events. There was the usual amount of social activity, and she also took up painting, which she had not done since her days in England. In the summer of 1864, she took her sketch book along on trips to the countryside near the capital, Quebec City. Back home, she worked these sketches in watercolours. It was 'the thing to do' and, although she was certainly not a great artist, she was probably as good as most of her friends. Several examples of her modest endeavours are still extant: scenes of Indians in canoes, Loretta Falls, Point Lévis, and 'Dear St. Feriol'.[2]

While Agnes was thus happily employed, John A. was working on his much more ambitious 'canvas', which involved a series of meetings to discuss Confederation with the Maritime provinces. With the other Canadian delegates, he went to Charlottetown, then moved on to Nova

Scotia and New Brunswick for more talks and the accompanying winings and dinings. Hewitt, who had gone as Secretary, reported back to Agnes that his Chief was very popular, especially with the ladies. There were even reports that a Miss Haviland of Charlottetown had fallen for his charms and that they were engaged to marry. Nothing more was heard of this rumour, however, and the talks went on in the conference rooms and around the dinner tables.

In the autumn, the Maritime delegates came to Quebec City, many of them accompanied by their wives and daughters. In the evenings following the talks, the Canadian hosts dispensed lavish hospitality, and during these parties Agnes got to know many of the ladies, forming friendships that, although she did not know it, would be renewed over many years.

After two weeks of hard discussions, John A. finally won out for union along strong constitutional lines. The conference was over, except for one final treat offered the Maritimers. This was a chance to see Ottawa and the new Parliament Buildings, which would be ready the following spring. When Brown had gone to have a look at them in the summer, he had reported they were 'magnificent. . . all surpassing fine. But they are just 500 years in advance of the time. It will cost half the revenue of the province to light them and heat them and keep them clean.'[3] What John A. and Hewitt found when they went up with the Maritime delegates was that the site now contained three partially finished buildings. The view, however, *was* superb and, from the point of view of defence, the Maritimers agreed that the choice had undoubtedly been wise.

Agnes and Theodora did not go to Ottawa, but what they had been hearing about the capital from others did not exactly make them eager to move there in a few months' time. Lord Monck, who had replaced Head as Governor-General, said the place could never amount to much, and his sister, Frances, went further in her condemnation of the capital. In her memoirs, she wrote: 'We were much disgusted by the squalid look of Ottawa. . . . The streets were so rough, like dirt roads. . . . I went on wondering how we could ever live there. . . . We all groaned over Ottawa.'[4] Even before she visited Ottawa, Frances Monck had heard about it from a Mrs. Adamson. 'She said, "What can you expect from a place where there is no water? You have to pay fifteenpence to a boy to bring you water; there are no waterworks". Mrs. M. asked if I had been there; I said no. "*Keep* out of it", said Mrs. A., "*as long* as *you* can!" '[5]

And that is precisely what Agnes and Theodora did. It sounded as if the place was 't'other end of nowhere' and when Hewitt corroborated all the tales, they made their decision. During their eleven years in Canada, they had adjusted to life in three quite different settings — Barrie, Toronto and Quebec City. The thought of another move, this time to a rough, unfinished town where they would need to make yet another set of friends, could not have seemed a very attractive proposition. On the other hand, England held family and friends, familiar institutions and a known way of life. Just as they had done fifteen years before, Agnes and her mother turned to them, leaving Ottawa for those who had no choice. Before the Parliament moved from Quebec City in the summer of 1865, they had their bags packed and their passage booked.

John A. was in England before them. He and Brown had crossed on the *China* in April to join Galt[6] and Cartier for further discussions on Confederation. Snags had developed over the past few months, one of the most persistent being where to find the money to extend the Intercolonial Railway to the Maritimes, a project which Nova Scotia and New Brunswick considered a prerequisite to union with Canada. (Prince Edward Island had already dropped out of the Confederation talks, and Newfoundland could not be considered a serious possibility.) Little was accomplished on this trip, but John A. had a good time and even Brown relaxed enough to join in a little horse-play on the way back to London from the Epsom Derby: 'Even George Brown, a convenanting old chap, caught its [the trip's] spirit. I bought him a pea-shooter, and a bag of peas, and the old fellow took aim at people on the tops of busses [sic] and shot lots of peas on his way home.'[7]

It was some years before Agnes heard this anecdote. She did not see the Canadian delegates on this visit, busy as she and Theodora were in getting to know London again. During their years in Canada, they must have sometimes thought longingly of the many things which only an old city could offer. They decided to live as close to the centre as possible and found accommodation in the Grosvenor Square area, near their friends and near so much that they had missed. It was good to be back, despite the disadvantages of grime and smoke, something Canadian cities were still spared. The Crystal Place was no longer within walking distance,[8] but there was so much to do and see. There were galleries and museums to visit, frequent concerts to attend, parks to wander through, and an abundance of *new* periodicals and magazines as well as books and no less than six daily newspapers.

On the whole, Agnes thought England 'a delicious country for the rich but I should hate it for the poor, and there is no denying, at least, I think not, that the middle class toady and fawn.'[9] This thought, though, was in retrospect. In 1865, it is unlikely she made any attempt to sum up conditions so precisely. Agnes and Theodora had chosen to return and, if they saw blemishes, they would not admit it, not even to themselves.

One of their greatest anticipations in going back had been the thought of renewing family ties. Unfortunately, the Maynes now spent most of their time in Ireland, as did Louisa Scott, Theodora's niece, who *had* 'got a young Irishman'. They were able, nevertheless, to see Louisa from time to time when she visited England, but they probably just missed seeing her sister, Annie.[10] When Agnes had first lived in England, she had not become well acquainted with this cousin, five years older than herself and recently married. It had been through the letters which Annie wrote to her Aunt Theodora that Agnes had first begun to have some idea of what her cousin's life was like.[11] They had included the usual chatter. about the children, but there had also been references to the 'fatigue and bustle of a London season', especially after Annie's husband, George Barker, had been knighted. Now that Agnes was back in London and accustomed to an active social life, she might have thought it would be enjoyable to be introduced to London society by Annie, but this was not possible. George Barker had died in 1861, and Annie had turned to writing to help support her two small children; through this interest she had met her second husband, Sir Frederick Napier Broome. They were married, suddenly, in June, 1865, and almost immediately sailed to New Zealand, where they were to become sheep-ranchers. If Agnes and Theodora saw them at all, it was very briefly.

While mother and daughter must have been disappointed not to see more of their closest relatives, there were still many cousins in the Bath region and many Jamaican friends in London itself. They spent some time, too, in taking trips, including one to the Channel Islands. A year later, back in Ottawa, Agnes reminisced about it:

Hot today — very hot — a blazing summer sun... shining full down on the unsheltered houses in the wide, dusty, ugly streets of this our capital. I lay on my sofa, *panting,* half asleep dreaming of the cool, flowery, shady lanes in the Channel Islands where I spent last summer, or of lazy moonlight strolls on the heather covered steep picturesque cliffs over the sweet, wide, calm, blue sea.[12]

Another trip was to Paris. Agnes did not visit it again until 1900, and her reactions then suggest what had impressed her in her youth. She found it immensely gay as to numbers and *go* but 'I miss the show and glitter of the days in 1866 when Napoleon and Eugenie in all their glory, made things lively. A republic is a dull arrangement socially in France.'[13]

The letters Theodora and Agnes received from Hewitt and from friends who had had no choice but to move to Ottawa must have convinced them that they had made the right decision in returning to England. Not until early September, 1865, did Hewitt and John A. manage to get away from Quebec City to the new capital. There they found that the Parliament Buildings were finished, lighted and heated, but surrounded by piles of construction debris.[14] The housing situation was even more disappointing. Ottawa was just a new, small town emerg-

ing from the wilderness. Less than forty years before, the Royal
Engineers had moved in to construct the Rideau Canal; their headquarters had been on the farm of Nicholas Sparks (near what is now
Sparks Street), surrounded by forest. When it acquired the name
Ottawa in 1855, it still could only boast a population of about
10,000. With the decision to make it the capital of Canada, progress was
speeded up, but the town was by no means ready to absorb all the new
arrivals in 1865 when the members of Parliament — and their families —
moved in.

One section of the town favoured by many because of its proximity to
the Parliament Buildings was Sandy Hill. It was there that John A. found
a house large enough to share not only with Alexander Galt, then
Minister of Finance, and J.C. Brydges of the Grand Trunk Railway, but
with Hewitt Bernard as well. These bachelor quarters became well
known as the 'Quadrilateral'.[15] Galt and Brydges came and went their
various ways, and John A. was often absent on business, leaving Hewitt as
its most permanent resident.

A frequent guest of Hewitt's at the Quadrilateral was the Reverend
Thomas Bedford-Jones, Rector of St. Alban's Anglican Church. The two
men had arrived in Ottawa about the same time and met while both were
still living in the Russell House, then the best hotel in town. As Reverend
Bedford-Jones remembered, 'On October 18, [1865]. . . at the dinner
table. . . a gentleman sat down beside me, and a conversation began,
naturally turning to Church matters. I soon found him to be a well-in-
formed and zealous churchman, and his manner exceedingly friendly
and sympathetic.'[16]

The two struck up a friendship and soon the Rector often dropped in
to spend an evening with Hewitt who was 'not a society man, and at the
end of his business day, was glad of what the Scotch would call a friendly
crack, or a little music, if he did not play Patience as he smoked a quiet
pipe.'[17]

The two men talked about the 'vexed ecclesiastical questions of the
day' and, on one occasion, Reverend Bedford-Jones remembered Hewitt
reading parts of a letter from Agnes, who had just made her trip to the
Channel Islands. He was much impressed by the graphic style in which
Agnes described her trip and thought her very talented, little knowing
that she would, before too long, become one of his most devoted
parishioners in the little church in Sandy Hill.

Hewitt needed those quiet evenings. His working days were far from
being calm, closely associated as he was with John A. and all of the latter's preoccupations during 1865-66. Many of the problems that had
been building up for years now had to be faced. Among them were: increasingly difficult trade relationships with the United States; the threat

of raids by the Fenian Brotherhood,[18] who had their homes bases close to the Canadian border; and John A.'s disintegrating dream of Confederation. Prince Edward Island had already pulled out of the talks, New Brunswick was becoming increasingly disenchanted with the idea, as it became clear the British Government's enthusiasm for the scheme did not extend to an open purse, and, in Nova Scotia, Joseph Howe was a strong anti-Confederation voice. In the end, it was external threats that worked to help resolve the internal issues. In June, 1866, New Brunswick looked across the border at the Fenians in Maine, who were rumoured ready to attack, and voted in a pro-Confederation Government. While that colony was spared any raids, the Fenians did soon cross the border into Canada by way of the Niagara River. This invasion from a point in the United States caused many Canadians to become more concerned with their geographic position and more determined to strengthen it by uniting their colonies federally. This boost to the cause of Confederation resulted in the scheduling of another round of meetings with the British Government. John A. hoped that at these even Joseph Howe might be won over.

The Maritime delegates crossed to London during the summer of 1866 but had to cool their heels waiting for the Canadian delegation to arrive. The confusion of a change of Government in Britain made it seem to John A. that there was no sense 'in my going home just now'.[19] It was November 14 before the delegation got away, and this time Brown was missing. He had resigned in November, 1865, disenchanted with the progress of trade talks in Washington, and was again back at the *Globe,* firing strong opposition editorials and lead articles. The coalition had been a short lull in the otherwise stormy relations between himself and John A. Brown's day as a pea-shooter was quite an exception; his style was more taking pot-shots at his opponents.

By late November, 1866, the delegates from all four provinces were reunited in the now familiar Westminster Palace Hotel, and the meetings began shortly afterwards with John A. in the chair and Hewitt again acting as Conference Secretary. Before the Canadians had left Ottawa, they had worked out a plan of action with Lord Monck in which they allowed three weeks or so to try to come to terms with the Maritime delegates. The schedule worked. By Christmas Day they had finished their preliminary work and sent a draft to the Colonial Office.

Those three weeks were not all work. Many of the delegates had brought their wives and daughters along to London, and they were not disappointed in the hospitality offered by their British hosts. John A., never one to sit aloof from fun, was often present at the parties. At times, however, he enjoyed a quiet game of Patience, which he, like Hewitt, always found relaxing. He also took long walks, especially when he felt it was better to proceed slowly with the particular issue under discussion. Possibly this was what he was doing one day in mid-December, 1866, when he took a stroll up Bond Street. As he made his way along this street, window-shopping here and there, he met two familiar ladies, Agnes and Theodora. It was a stroll that changed his life and Agnes'.

This may or may not have been the first time they had met each other since the London meetings had started. They both knew many of the delegates' families, so their paths could easily have crossed at some social function or other. And certainly Hewitt would have told John A. that Agnes and her mother were in London. So the magic of the Bond Street meeting is not known. What is known is that they met several times after that and, by the New Year, were making plans to marry.

Why did John A. wish to marry Agnes? It has been suggested that he married her for qualities such as 'a keen wit, a quick perception, a liberal mind and a certain unselfishness of heart which would well become the wife of a public man.'[20] All admirable attributes, no doubt, but it is surely doing John A. an injustice to suggest that he would marry anyone for reasons which simply add up to having a suitable chatelaine in Ottawa. He would not have had to make his choice in so analytical a manner. There had been other possibilities before, and ladies were still finding him charming. He must have seen more in Agnes.

And what made Agnes accept John A., particularly if the story of an earlier proposal is true? There had been repeated stories in the *Globe* referring to John A.'s 'weakness', so she could not have been reassured on that point. However, he did look better. Friends said that he had been trying to look after his health, *and* he was buoyant at the progress being made over the Confederation talks. He was a man of great personal charm, and one whom Hewitt continued to admire, after years of working with him intimately. Moreover, Agnes by now was thirty years old. Since her return to England she had travelled more and become more sophisticated, more tolerant of people. If she had refused one proposal, possibly, very possibly, she regretted it.

The truth of what sparked the romance or the details of either John A.'s or Agnes' feelings will probably never be known. All that can be certain is that he did propose around Christmas of 1866, and Agnes accepted. Her diary, which she began to keep in mid-1867, does not shed any light on why she said 'Yes', but it does give evidence of deep love and affection and the confession that 'I have found something worth living for — living in — my husband's heart and love.'[21]

Having won Agnes' acceptance, John A. said that he wished to be married as soon as possible so his new wife might share fully with him in all the social events planned for the end of the Conference. The only questions were when could they find time for a wedding and how quickly could Agnes prepare for this, the most important day of her life? When the crowded Conference agenda had been worked out with Lord Monck, no one had thought to allow any time for the wedding of the Chairman. After Christmas, the schedule looked more impossible than ever since discussions with the Colonial Office made it seem as if the final draft treaty could not be ready in time for presentation to the Imperial Parliament when it met late in January. Yet, somehow, it was, and somehow, too, Agnes managed to organize the details of the wedding. It finally appeared that they could find the necessary time in mid-February. (That date did not allow enough time for the banns to be read in the customary way, so it was only with the assistance of a special licence granted by the Archbishop of Canterbury that they were able to proceed with their plans.)

Whenever John A. had a free moment in early January, he went to his tailor's shop, in Hanover Square, to start getting his wardrobe in order. There he bought 'A Superfine Black Dress Coat with sleeve linings, corded silk breast facing [and] A Pair of Superfine Black Dress Trousers.'[22] Early in February he had his diplomatic uniform cleaned and pressed and bought a new sword case. He was ready for the wedding and for any diplomatic functions that might arise out of the Conference. It was more complicated for Agnes. She had to order her own dress of the traditional white satin and her veil of Brussels lace with its wreath of orange blossoms, and, as well, she had to think about the dresses to be worn by her four bridesmaids — Emma Tupper, Jessie McDougall, Joanna Archibald and Georgina Mayne.[23] These four ladies, it was later reported, wore 'dresses of white silk with white tulle tunics with folds of silk to match their bonnets, two of which were blue and two pink...four prettier bridesmaids can hardly be imagined.'[24]

Agnes had been a parishioner of St. George's Church, Hanover Square, for some time, so she decided to have the ceremony there. It was a suitably impressive church for a wedding that was one of the social events of the Conference, but, even so, when the morning of February 16, 1867, arrived and the bride, escorted by Hewitt, entered the church, there were 'so many present that...she had to pass through an avenue of friends, extending from the large entrance door to the very altar steps'[25] The wedding ceremony was performed by Bishop Fulford, the Metropolitan Bishop of Canada, who happened to be in London at that time, and the guest list was most impressive.[26]

So, too, was the wedding breakfast, which Hewitt offered as his contribution to the ninety or so guests. In the reception room at the Westminster Palace Hotel, so the *Daily Citizen* informed its interested readers in Ottawa, 'The tables were spread with every delicacy by a most

artistic *chef de cuisine* and with a profusion of the choicest plants in
endless variety in full blossom and perfume. On the plate of every guest
was a bunch of violets and snow- drops.'[27] During this 'brilliant' reception, only one toast was proposed, that being to the health of the bride. It
elicited a humourous reply from John A., to the effect that 'his public
mission in London was in favour of union and that, as a conscientious
man, he felt bound to carry out his own theory.'[28]

After the reception, John A. and Agnes left by the afternoon train for
a honeymoon in Oxford, albeit a very brief one because of the demanding schedule of the British North America Bill. A few days before the
wedding, the Bill had had its first reading in the House of Lords. The
second, crucial reading had to be got through quickly; in the Upper
House domestic politics were demanding the attention of all Members at
this time, and any delay of the Bill might spell its ruin. Howe was still
around, clamouring for Opposition support, which would mean defeat,
and John A. was worried. Luckily, he had found an ally in Lord Carnarvon, the Colonial Secretary, and thanks to his skill the Bill soon had
only the Commons to face.

On the same day that the Bill was to have its first reading in the Lower
House, Queen Victoria summoned John A. and four of the leading
delegates to what the Canadian chief described, in a letter to his sister
Louisa, as a 'special court', at which the Queen privately commended the
'very important measure' in which the Conference delegates had worked
so long.[29]

Agnes was not invited to this audience, but hearing about it from her
husband was almost as good as having been there. The details of it —
who was there, how the Queen looked, how she spoke, did she appear as
small as one thought, did she look very sad — were all fascinating to
Agnes. Indeed, all her days were fascinating now as she sat beside
John A. in the Gallery of the House during the latter part of February
and early March, watching the progress of the Bill. She was having a
preview of what was going to be a large part of her life — the role of a
very involved spectator in the game of politics, with all its disappointments and its successes. On March 8, 1867, she was overjoyed to see
John A. score a success when the Bill was finally in the clear. Three years
of hard work had resulted in triumph for her new husband.

When they had time to think about it, the delegates remarked on how
strange it was to see John A. married again. None of them — John A.
least of all — had expected any such thing when they left for London.
Friends back in Canada were also astonished. His old friend and colleague, Alex Campbell, wrote to John A. as soon as he heard news of the
wedding plans: 'And so you are going to subside into matrimony? I am
delighted to hear it and offer my best wishes to Miss Bernard. I confess to

old Weller's incredulity, "I didn't think you'd a done it." '[30]

It was quite a surprise, too, for John A.'s sisters, Louisa and Margaret, but a very pleasant one. He had been alone for too long and had been something of a worry to them. They were no longer young, yet, along with the Professor, they had the major responsibility for Hugh John, who had reached the age of seventeen. Now the boy would have a proper home to go to in Ottawa. They had never met Agnes, but they knew Hewitt and his family background; it was good to learn they now had a sister-in-law, young, but not *too* young, and from a good family. They sent their best wishes. 'I have been married some month & five days & feel as if it had been this day year',[31] wrote John A. in reply to their letter.

The days were truly flying by in a round of business and pleasure, both of which he shared with Agnes. She was no stranger to London by this time, but the society in which she moved as Mrs. John A. Macdonald was somewhat different from that of her unmarried days. Now she was being entertained in high official circles where politics, not simply sociability, were the order of the day. It was not long before she was even welcomed by Queen Victoria. John A. wrote of this great event to Louisa, but the Ottawa *Times* gave a fuller acount of Agnes' first presentation at court:

The Queen held a court at Buckingham Palace on the 27th ult., which the London papers say was brilliantly attended. Her Majesty was attended by several members of the Royal family and many of the great officers of State and most of the Diplomatic Corps were also present.... Among those who were presented to her [sic] Majesty on this occasion were Mrs. Macdonald by the Countess of Carnarvon.[32]

Agnes was enchanted by her new social life, John A. told Louisa. 'My wife likes it from its novelty to her, but it rather bores me as I have seen it all before.'[33] (He was not to be taken seriously in this blasé remark. He loved nothing better than the pomp and ceremony of his office and now that the new Dominion he had done so much to shape was finally coming into its own, one doubts he was fooling anyone, especially his sister.)

It was not until early May that John A. could get away from England and bring his bride back to Ottawa, the little city in which she had thought she would never live. The townspeople were waiting for them on their arrival and gave them a tremendous welcome.

Once in Ottawa, the Macdonalds moved into the Quadrilateral. Agnes had only a few days in which to organize her new responsibilities or even get acquainted with her new home before she and John A. went down to Kingston. The warmth of the reception there from both John A.'s constituents and his family was reassuring to the new bride and set the tone for many years of happy relationships. In no letter is there any hint that

Agnes and her in-laws — Louisa, Margaret, Professor Williamson and Hugh John — were ever on anything except the best of terms, and the Professor was to prove an especially good friend. The only misfortune was that Agnes entered the family too late to know what a friend she would have had in John A.'s mother, Helen.

The visit to Kingston had to be hurried one. The old custom of having two First Ministers was to be dropped under the new constitution, and John A. seemed the obvious choice as leader. In mid-May, a letter came from Lord Monck, who was still in England, telling John A. 'I write to authorize you to take the needful measures so as to have a ministry ready to be sworn into office and to commence the performance of their several functions on the 1st July.'[34]

The time seemed very short. Agnes must have felt that it was impossibly short for all that had to be done. She watched her husband tying up all the loose ends, deliberating for hours with representatives from each of the provinces in an effort not to offend anyone as he set about the formation of his first Cabinet. Somehow, by July 1, all was ready. John A. stepped out confidently as Premier of the Dominion of Canada. Beside him was Agnes, less sure of herself in her new role as 'a great Premier's wife'.

2
A
Great
Premier's
Wife

'This new Dominion of ours came noisily into existence on the 1st',[1] Agnes wrote in her diary. There was certainly cause for the complaint as well as for the pride in the remark. The importance of the day dictated that it should be properly celebrated as a holiday, and, in Ottawa, 'Never was a Magistrate's order more spiritedly carried out than the Mayor's proclamation requesting the citizens of Ottawa to observe the first day of the new regime as one of general rejoicing.'[2] On the eve of the great day, hundreds of persons gathered on the Ordnance Lands near the Cathedral. On the stroke of midnight, a huge bonfire was lit, followed by the pealing of bells, the lighting of Roman candles and rockets and a 100-gun salute. The festivities continued through the night until lacrosse and cricket games started at seven o'clock to usher in the day itself.

In the Quadrilateral all were up early. Their night had been broken by the noise of the celebrations, but the coming day was so exciting that sleep would hardly have been possible, in any case. John A. left early, as did Hewitt, the latter in his dress uniform as A.D.C. to Lord Monck. The players were taking their places but, on this day, there was no scheduled role for Agnes except that of onlooker.

Up on the Hill, the Judges and Members assembled, with as many of the public as could squeeze in, to hear Lord Monck invested as first Governor-General of the Dominion of Canada. It was said that 'not an inkling had the public ear of what was next to follow.'[3] It was even a surprise to the person most intimately concerned.[4] John A. listened as the new Governor-General told the gathering that, on instructions from Queen Victoria, their Premier was to be given the title of Knight Commander of the Most Honourable Order of the Bath in recognition of his services in connection with the Colonial Conference.

Ladies had not been admitted to the Chamber, so Agnes was not on hand to hear this announcement. She was not, however, kept long in ignorance of the news. If their Rector's memory is to be trusted, John A.

quickly had 'a messenger dispatched with [a]note to the great Premier's wife addressed for the first time as "Lady Macdonald." '[5]

It is hoped that Agnes was at home to receive this note, but she may have been out on the capital's streets, where there was much to see that day. The city was decorated by '. . . everyone who had a scrap of bunting.'[6] She and Theodora may also have been part of the large crowd that gathered on the Hill at noon to see Lord Monck take the salute of the new Dominion from the assembled military bands. Certainly it was after six o'clock before the new Sir John and Lady Macdonald were able to be together to share in the excitement of their imposing titles. They may have finished the day with a walk to see the splendid illuminations, public and private,[7] or watched the Ottawa City Council's great display of fireworks, which 'had a splendid effect all over the city. . . and so ended the first great Union day.'[8]

It was not until July 5 that Agnes found time to write a line in her new diary, the first one with a lock that she had ever owned. The precaution seemed necessary to her:

Now I am a great Premier's wife and Lady Macdonald and Cabinet secrets and mysteries might drop off. . . my pen. . . if I knew any Cabinet secrets which I certainly don't. . . but then a locked diary looks consequential and just now I am rather in that line myself — my husband's new title is just five days old — so — for a short time longer I may be excused for a little bumptiousness.[9]

There was little time to indulge in self-pride. Agnes was not only Lady Macdonald but also a wife and, for the very first time, mistress of a household. Theodora, from whom she had never been separated, would live with them, but would no longer run the household. The mother was now living in her daughter's house, and it was Agnes who had the responsibility of converting the former quarters of four bachelors into a family home. Galt and Brydges had moved out, but there remained the puzzling allotment of space. The 'resident bachelor', Hewitt, presented no problem to his sister; he could remain cosily settled with his books, his pipe, and his piano. It was the rest of the house that presented a challenge. Theodora needed a room, and larger quarters had to be found for Agnes and John A. than those he had used during his bachelor days. It would always be possible to make some temporary arrangements for Hugh John during his visits, which they hoped would be frequent, but there just was not any room for guests. When Louisa proposed making a visit early in 1868, John A. had to explain the situation to his sister. He told her that his study, where he had continued to do much work, as in his bachelor days, had had to be closed because of the foul odour from the drains, and, 'Dear old Mrs. Bernard insisted on giving up her bedroom for my use, & took possession of her son's, & he, Col Bernard, is now sleeping in the garret.'[10] Obviously, the house did not have enough room to meet the requirements of the Prime Minister's family, and yet, even with her self-confessed awkwardness in household management, Agnes was able, under normal conditions, to adapt the Quadrilateral to suit their varied needs.

She also made it into a home in the real sense of the word. It was the first one John A. had had for many years — and he evidently appreciated its relaxing atmosphere. Much to her satisfaction she noted that he would come home from work 'with a very moody brow, tired and oppressed, his voice weak, his step slow [and then]. . . ten minutes after he is making clever jokes and laughing like any schoolboy, with his hands in his pockets and his head thrown back. . . . He can throw off a weight of business in a wonderfully short space of time.'[11]

There were quiet, restful evenings, without visitors, when they had time to sit beside a cosy fire in Agnes' dressing room. She might read *Household Management,* seeking answers to some of her questions, while John A. played his favourite game of Patience. 'He says it rests his mind and changes the current of his thoughts more than anything else'.[12] Agnes has to be given credit for seeing to it that he was able to have a home where he had the peace to gaze into the fire, talk, read or play Patience.

He needed those moments of domestic peace. As Agnes lamented, 'Here — in this house — the atmosphere is so awfully political that sometimes I think the very flies hold Parliaments on the kitchen table.'[13] It was not possible, much as she wished to do so, to spare her husband from all the demands of his job; she could only see that his thoughts were diverted whenever possible. At times, it was hard for her to do this, for she was becoming more and more interested in what he was doing and could not resist discussing each day's events with him. She was attracted, at first, by the novelty of her situation and then began to be absorbed by it. One reason she gave was: 'I do so like to identify myself with all my husband's pursuits and occupations. He is so busy and so much older than I that I would soon fall out of his life if I went my own ways — as I might — disregarding his.'[14]

It was not easy, marrying as Agnes had, at thirty, to adjust to a life in which someone other than herself had to be considered first. Any marriage would have been enough to concentrate on, but marriage to the Prime Minister of Canada posed heavier demands. She made mistakes in coming to terms with her new position; at times, she was overly serious about it, and, for some weeks, did not even trust herself to write anything in her diary, being 'afraid of putting something in. . . which —

46

in time to come — I may find ought not to have been written. Living as I do — in the atmosphere of "headquarters". . . with the men who are now making part of the history of their country.'[15] At other times, she watched her husband and envied his ability to manage the House 'with infinite tact, grace and skill. It is charming to hear him adjust little differences by a few words.'[16] By comparison, there were days when she admitted that she could not even enter her kitchen and keep her temper. Had she had her husband's ability to laugh when things went wrong, it would have been easier for her, but she had to learn by trial and error to be both a wife and the partner of a politician of great importance. In the latter role, she knew she had to come to terms with his world and the only way to do this was to find out, at first hand, something of what was going on in the country.

The first chance presented itself early in July. A federal election had been called for August, but, in the meantime, John A. seemed to be concerned about a matter of provincial interest. Agnes wrote in her diary, 'A great "Coup" is being organized now-a-days. John has asked Sandfield Macdonald to be Premier of the local Parliament of Ontario. If he takes it, it will be what politicians here call a "bombshell in the enemy's camp."'[17] The 'bombshell' was that by taking up the challenge to run for the premiership, Sandfield would be prevented from supporting John A.'s old rival, George Brown, in August.

On July 9, Agnes and John A. went by train to Spencerville, where they met Sandfield. 'He said, "Well, I am going in for it, Lady Macdonald", & I answered, "I am heartily glad to hear it & trust & expect, too, it will be alright & for the best."'[18] When the discussion with Sandfield was satisfactorily completed, John A. and Agnes spent the day talking with people from the Prescott area, and, she admitted, 'I was right glad when we could go into the cool private car alone together. We locked both doors and John lay on the sofa and fell asleep in two minutes.'[19] It had been Agnes' first experience of politics in action.

Before the campaign was over in August, Agnes saw a great deal of electioneering at first hand. At times she loved it; 'Everybody pets us up and runs after us delightfully.'[20] But at other times she frankly confessed that 'I get tired of being flattered and coaxed and fêted and long to be alone with *him* somewhere — nobody knowing us or heeding us for awhile.'[21] Her mixed feelings were not unusual. At times, she felt some of the 'bumptiousness' of being Lady Macdonald — for it was still a very new honour — and, at others, like many political wives, she resented having to share her husband to such a degree. Living in the public eye, she found out, exacts its price, but if she wished to share in John A.'s political life, she had to accept its restrictions. 'July 13. Left Ottawa by an early train. Visitors in the private car all the way to Prescott. Talking!

Talking! forever smilingly receiving compliments and saying the same things — flattered and caressed ad lib. — all ready to fall down & worship the rising star.'[22]

From Prescott, they went on to Kingston by boat and spent some hours anchored in the harbour. 'It was a levée. . . all day people introduced — people to be talked to, ladies calling. . . and exciting political talk.'[23] In Toronto, their most important stop, it was more of the same.

> I was quite overwhelmed by visitors, engagements, parties, letters and all sorts of excitements. All through the intensely hot summer days & far into the close breathless nights my work went on, and seeing my husband so busy, being cognizant of the enormous machinery he was setting in motion, watching hour after hour the results of his skill in the diplomatic line — all this helped to weary & yet excite me — a novice in this kind of life. . . . [Yet] John is in great spirits & as long as I can help him by being cheery, and smiling, I am quite satisfied.[24]

Novice or not, it had not taken long for the bumptiousness to be replaced by reality.

On November 7, 1867, the first Parliament of the new Dominion was opened. The city was almost as excited as it had been on Dominion Day. Stores were closed and people lined the streets to see the new Senators and their wives and the new Members and *their* wives drive up to the Parliament Buildings. Agnes and other ladies present added their touches of colour to the ceremonies in the Senate Chambers. Then, as now, the wife of the Prime Minister and various distinguished ladies occupied seats on the floor of the Chamber, while other ladies graced the proceedings from the Gallery. Lord Monck's Speech from the Throne, a speech that Agnes had seen her husband amending up to the last minute, highlighted the enormous amount of work planned for the coming Session, including legislation related to currency, revenue, customs, excise, a new postal system, an enlarged Department of Public Works and, above all, the building of the railway to the Maritimes. The last issue was the most important politically. The summer elections had provided the Macdonald Government with a large majority from Ontario, Quebec and New Brunswick, but Nova Scotia was still against Confederation except on paper. Howe was still not won over and, as head of the Nova Scotian government, could prove a stumbling block unless some way were found to appease him and his constituents.

The following weeks were busy indeed, and John A. was immersed in work. This was very upsetting to Agnes, particularly since he continued to work on Sundays. Soon after their arrival in Ottawa, she had expressed the wish for a law forbidding Sunday politics. But seeing that her husband had so much to do and, possibly, hesitating to speak to him about her concern she put up with the situation, rebelling only in prayer. 'I made it for months a subject of very earnest prayer that my husband might prevent Sunday visitors and Sunday interruptions by refusing to see men on idle so called business or indeed — on any but very pressing matters.'[25]

Agnes soon had reason to believe in the power of prayer for, shortly after this, after the first pressure of facing the business of the new Parliament, John A. did give up Sunday business meetings and his relieved wife could write: 'This has been a very quiet, happy day. I am so thankful our Sundays are so regular and quiet now — that is, as a rule. . . . He — my own kind dear husband has been mercifully taught to see the right in this thing, and now we have so much happy rest after our morning service.'[26]

Going to church on Sundays had been a part of Agnes' life for as long as she could remember, and she did not give up the practice in Ottawa. John A.'s early attendance was intermittent and dependent on whether he was free of business, but Agnes always had the company of Theodora and sometimes of Hewitt, (although the latter was not consistently as faithful an attendant as his sister would have liked).

Their first place of worship in Ottawa was the old Court House, which had served as a church since 1865. It was 'a dirty, dingy chamber with windows on the western side and brightened only by a large portrait of the Queen over the Judge's bench. . . . On the right was the Jury box and on the left the Sheriff's. . . . During our services the elite and fashionable secured sitting in [these boxes].'[27]

The cornerstone of a new church for the Congregation of St. Alban the Martyr had been laid in May, 1867, before Agnes arrived in Ottawa, but the new building was not ready until year's end. So Agnes attended the services in the Court House for several months. It was not the awkwardness of this building as a place of worship but its surroundings that bothered her:

I could not help watching the prisoners, sitting close to the barred windows, eating their coarse dinners and looking into the yard. There was one boy — a brown-haired child almost — and I pondered over the strangeness of prison discipline that could allow that young criminal to associate with the villanous looking old blackguards who talked to him for half an hour.[28]

On those 'happy Sundays' when John A. went to services with Agnes, they usually went to St. Alban's, but sometimes appeared at the services of other denominations, since it was good politics to be seen in different churches. Also, according to Joseph Pope, John A.'s authorized biographer, while he was 'a firm believer in the truths of Christianity,

[he] cared little for external forms of worship, and was at times ready to accept the ministrations of the Presbyterian and Methodist churches.'[29] What Agnes thought about this indifference to form is not known, but she did accompany her husband wherever he chose to worship. Perhaps she was happy to accept any show of interest in things of the spirit.

Family prayers posed another problem. Agnes felt regret and guilt that neither her husband nor her brother seemed to have time enough for them. 'This is a grief to me and yet how to arrange it I know not. Sir John rises late — it is his only quiet time of rest — he could not, ought not to forego it. Then Hewitt says he has not time — he goes out so early — & the servants are Romanists.'[30]

Some years later Agnes would have her wish come true, when John A. began to conduct family worship personally, but during those early months in Ottawa, her only satisfaction about the religious life of her household seemed to be that 'Bridget, my new domestic, is a very devout Roman Catholic apparently. I am so glad she is for I think people who are religious are infinitely more trustworthy and altogether more pleasant to be with than people who are not.'[31]

There is evidence of no little pique in Agnes saying she found religious people more trustworthy and more pleasant to be with. These months were a frustrating time for her. She was far from satisfied, especially with herself. In trying to adjust to her new role, she sometimes attempted to change the habits of those around her, instead of making changes within herself. To some extent she realized this:

> How hard it is to know how to do right! I know I am very apt to be led astray by motives and know that analysing them too much is unhealthy for me, and I also know that my love of power is strong, so strong that I sometimes dread its influence on me when I imagine I am influenced by a sense of right.[32]

Agnes was not the first — nor will she be the last — wife of a prominent man to feel inadequate and dissatisfied. When the first excitement of being married, of being Lady Macdonald, of being the wife of such an important person, wore off, she began to take stock of herself. Her initial reaction was a mistake, for she compared her abilities and mastery of her new role to those of the person closest and dearest to her, John A. He was, she thought, 'the humblest, least assuming, most gently judging of mankind',[33] and she could not measure up to the standard she felt he set. What she overlooked, of course, was the fact that his greater experience of both life and politics, in addition to his much more carefree nature, made it much easier for him to deal with his own workload, full though it was. Then, too, Agnes soon found out that watching the Legislature from the Gallery or listening to others talk was no real preparation for living 'in the atmosphere of "headquarters" '. It was all rather intimidating, and, especially during the Session, when John A. had to spend so many hours in Cabinet meetings, she began to feel useless. She was also worried about her husband: 'It frets me very much to see him do so much, to know from his weary face that he is overburdened.'[34] She was afraid that he was working himself to death, and she did not know what to do to help. The only thing she could think of was trying to avoid having him recount to her all the details of his work, as tempting as it was to learn more about it.

In her anxiety, Agnes reached out for something to lean on, something to bolster her courage. John A., when he could no longer manage on his own, turned to alcohol as a release; Agnes, either of her own volition or with urging from Theodora, turned to her religion. It had always been part and parcel of her life, and now, unable, she thought, to know the best course of action, she began to rely more and more on the teachings of her youth and the practice of her adulthood. Prayer became her antidote in that troubled period, prayer for, as she put it, 'judgment, discretion, humility, forbearance . . . boldness, fearlessness and unworldly temper',[35] thus summing up all her faults, real or imagined.

Agnes also found much to criticize in her housekeeping, although she had to admit she had progressed beyond the awkward attempts of her first few months. By November she could write, 'We had a large dinner party last night — 12 — and everything was very nice indeed. John seemed in such good spirits & so satisfied that I was ever so happy'.[36] Yet even here she felt she needed to exert more self-discipline, to overcome what she believed to be a tendency to laziness. One day after she had breakfasted in her dressing room, she wrote, 'I must take myself to task for this. Everything goes wrong downstairs among the servants when I yield to temptation. . . [but] It is so dreadfully pleasant!'[37]

Entertaining was a necessary, if unwelcome, part of her obligations as wife of the Prime Minister, and it soon took on a pattern. During the Session, an especially busy time, she gave dinners each Saturday night, and these, along with her New Year's Day receptions and 'kettledrums'[38] became the times when Agnes put on her best dress and 'belonged to the public', as she remarked. Even in this area, she felt inadequate. The larger functions left her ill at ease unless John A. could be with her, (and, more often than not, his duties prevented him from making more than a brief appearance). She was especially critical of herself in the hostess' role of 'pouring' for 'I do this very untidily being like most women who dream of stars and love scribbling, anything but neat over my tea tray.'[39] How galling it must have been to see more adept friends obviously enjoying their own teas.

Being entertained she also found a mixed pleasure. It was still strange, when they dined at Rideau Hall to be taken in by the Governor, first Lady there. I try hard that these things should not tempt me. . . . My Heavenly Father in His wisdom has seen fit to place me in the position I occupy, unworthy, ignorant, idle me. He will give me — I trust & pray — grace & strength to fill it to His honour and glory. That is all my prayer![40]

Sometimes, it seemed to her, she enjoyed herself too much and let this new life go to her head; then she would pull herself up sharply by telling herself that 'The longer I live and the more I see the stronger is my conviction that a gay, unthinking life is not only wrong & perverted but most unsatisfactory.'[41]

Perhaps it was in search of the guidance Agnes felt she needed to fill her exalted position more adequately that she began taking Bible classes with the Reverend Bedford-Jones. Nor was this the only study through which she sought to improve herself. She decided the French she had learned in England as a child needed brushing up, too, so she spent hours puzzling over French verbs with the Sisters of the Grey Nuns' Convent. It was worth it, she felt, just to be able to see John A.'s pride when she used the language correctly. She was doing something right, after all.

For some months, too, she committed herself heavily to work at the Ottawa Orphans' Home. At first she went there to teach Catechism to the children, but it was not long before she found that she had to assume other duties:

I have accepted the post of 1st Directress. . . . [The Home] seems to be anything but a 'bed of roses' [with] the old committee quarrelling and a debt of nearly $3400 on the new building. . . smallpox in one part of the building and no water in the well. I went to see the 2nd directress, a prim woman on the defensive who soon thawed out when I spoke cordially.[42]

Before long, she felt that she should be devoting more time to the ill-managed home, but there was not enough time to go around. When she did manage to attend one of the monthly meetings, there was 'a full attendance, [but] too much talking and too little acting.'[43] Characteristically, Agnes decided she must try to do something about this state of affairs but then became discouraged. Yet she did not give up her connection with the Home, but continued to spend hours reading to the children and helping to plan a concert to relieve the debt on the new building, selling tickets to all her friends.

Bible classes, French lessons and Orphans' Home meetings were not the only demands on Agnes' precious time. She was also a member of a Tuesday Reading group. The ladies got started early in 1868 on a lofty tone with Parkman's *The Jesuits in North America*. Agnes had read part of it aloud with her mother a week or so previously and found it light and chatty — tho' interesting and graphic enough. Marvellous men indeed were those Jesuits in the wild forests of a then strange land.... Tame indeed is our religious faith in contrast with that which led them forth.... I have an idea there is much exaggeration — but granting that — there is still much left which ought to make us — idlers of the English church really ashamed.[44]

This book had not been John A.'s choice for the group. When Agnes had asked him for his suggestion, he mentioned something much lighter — Miss Berry's *Journal and Correspondence* — but some of the ladies thought differently and opted for Parkman. Agnes eventually wished they had taken John A.'s advice for she, at any rate, soon came to the conclusion that *The Jesuits* was an 'exaggerated account' and 'unnecessarily distressing'. As they read on, she was convinced that it was really a 'very melancholy sort of book . . . the whole failure of their gigantic plan for conversion is quite incomprehensible. It was begun and continued too much in their own strength. There seems to lack a looking into Jesus.'[45] *Travels in Abyssinia,* a book written by a British missionary, was more acceptable to her, and obviously to the other members as well, since they chose many travel books for their Tuesday reading.

By early 1868, Agnes had partially come to terms with herself. Her social and domestic duties began to lie on her shoulders a little easier and she was doing what she could to improve herself by reading and studying. Just then she and John A. were dealt a severe blow. His finances had been hovering on the brink of disaster since the days when he had neglected his law office to be with his first wife in her misery. Worse, when he had gone into politics, he had turned the running of his Kingston office over to his partner, who had died in 1864, leaving huge debts — his own and John A.'s. John A. had not worried much then; he had been too busy with the problems of Confederation to pay attention to his finances. Now he was forced to. In January, 1868, the Commercial Bank of Kingston failed and John A., who had long been a director, share-holder and solicitor, had to assume its debts. These plus those of his late partner meant that he was flat broke. To make good even some of his debts, he had to mortgage every piece of property he had acquired over the years.

John A.'s reaction to these financial worries was the same as to his political problems: he tried to drink them away. Agnes was at a loss as to what she should do. She was suffering from the neuralgia which was always to plague her during Ottawa's cold winters, and this illness made her feel even more unable to think her way through the situation.

It was difficult for her even to admit the problem. In mid-January, she wrote, 'Some things have happened to make this a rather trying week for me but thank God, all the clouds are passed away and all is brightness again.'[46] This was as close as she came to confiding even to her diary what her real 'clouds' were. Her actions were equally hesitant. 'I have given up wine — this for example's sake and because I think it is unnecessary'[47] she wrote in her diary. Indeed, many of her thoughts at this time seem to indicate a desire to deny herself pleasures that she had enjoyed in other days. 'May I see my duty about dancing parties and be taught to follow it,'[48] she begged. If more sacrifices were needed, 'I am giving up all novels, all those I mean which are so frivolous and numerous and are being written now. . . . I dislike all games of cards but "Patience". . . . I hope to be able to take a right stand against Balls and to set my face against theatricals.'[49]

It was as if she were paying a forfeit by surrendering those pleasures which might be seen as sinful. She probably felt that if she, herself, were less sinful, her prayers for her husband's health might be answered. It is also interesting that her worries were nearly always expressed in terms of John A.'s health (which *had* suffered greatly during this trying period) than of his excessive drinking. Undoubtedly it was easier for her to come to grips with problems of physical health than with alcoholism; so she, as well as Hewitt and Theodora, tried to coddle John A. during this time (which, sadly, coincided with the problem of the drains). All they could do, however, was to see that he changed his study. It was useless to fuss over him; he had never been accustomed to this and had to work his own way out of his alcoholic bouts, something he had always had to face alone.

Not until late March was there consistent optimism in Agnes' diary. 'I only hope and pray life's sunshine may never dazzle me. The shadow that has for so long dimmed its brightness has passed away. I trust its memory may never fade — but keep as ever, watchful and humble.'[50]

Agnes had come through this experience a much wiser person (or so she thought) and felt that in future crises, which might recur, she could best help her husband by being more loving and patient, by just waiting for him to free himself of his friend, the bottle. At the time, it was a great comfort to her to feel that, because of her self-denials or not, her prayers had been answered: 'My darling so cheerful and in good health. What a changed man in so many respects. Who am I to have been made the instrument of so much improvement. God in his great mercy had so ordered it.'[51]

Just when they were recovering from this trying experience, John A. and Agnes found themselves shaken by one of Canada's most tragic moments. On April 7, 1868, Thomas D'Arcy McGee was assassinated. McGee, a well-known opponent of Fenianism, had been warned by John A. to be on his guard against attacks by subversive elements within Canada and he had promised to be watchful. He was, however, one of the Government's chief spokesmen in the House and, at that time, efforts were being made for the pacification of Nova Scotia. On the night he was killed, the debate had gone on late. Likely thinking more about how it was going to be possible to keep the eloquent Howe from taking his province out of the Confederation than about his own safety, McGee set out to walk the short distance from the Commons to his rooming house. He was struck down just as he was about to enter.

Agnes, one of those closest to this sad incident, described it fully in her diary:

This is how it was, that dreadful night at half-past two o'clock on the Tuesday morning. Tuesday the 7th my husband came home from a late sitting. It had made me a little uneasy his being away so long, to begin with I knew he would feel tired and then a sort of dread came upon me. . .something might happen to him, at that hour coming home alone. About a ¼ past 2 I felt so restless. . .and I went into Mama's room. . .she was scolding me for sitting up when I heard the carriage wheels and flew down to open the door for my husband. We were so cosy after that — he coming in so cheery — with news of the debate — and sitting by my dressing room fire with his supper. . . . I was almost half asleep when I was roused by a low, rapid knocking on the front door — in an instant a great fear came upon me — springing up I threw on a wrapper — just in time to see John throw up the window, and to hear him call out 'Is anything the matter?'. The answer came up fearfully clear and hard. . .'McGee is murdered — lying in the street — shot thro' the head'. The words fell like the blow of an iron bar across my heart. . . . My husband and brother went down to the spot immediately and did not return until 5. I sat trembling with fear and horror. . .for one could not tell how many more assassins might be lurking in the grey lit streets. . . . We felt at once that the shot was fired by a Fenian. When John came home he was much agitated — for him whose self command is so wonderful. . . . All Tuesday was so wretched — news coming and going — hurried steps and visits. . .all were on the alert for the finding of the base coward who had done the foul deed. . . . John's face was white with fatigue, sleeplessness and regret and yet he never gave in or complained or was other than cheerful to me and kind. I lay on the sofa till the afternoon half paralysed! My reading party came and went, I had forgotten them.[52]

During the next few days, the House operated in an air of gloom. Agnes, from her Gallery seat, thought '. . .everyone seemed depressed. Perhaps it was poor Mr. McGee's vacant chair.'[53] To Agnes, personally, it was a shock that 'the man who had only three days before been in our house sitting at our table, should be lying lifeless and made lifeless in so frightful a manner.'[54] To John A., it was a matter of deep concern, as well as regret. Agnes could see that 'The investigations about the murder seem to evidence a painfully excited and rebellious feeling among the

Irish in our country. I expect that disturbs John more than he expresses.'[55]

As the facts were investigated, it became clear that the assassination had been the work of Fenians and that several individuals were involved. To Agnes' horror, there was a rumour that 'Buckley, the livery stable keeper, who has been almost a coachman of ours, is supposed to be deeply implicated. I shudder when I think how entirely my husband — chief crown law officer — has been exposed by driving with him.'[56]

Yet the Session had to keep going and there was so much work to be done that the Members often sat late into the night. On May 1, Agnes wrote, 'This promises to be a very busy month. As the Session draws near its end, the bustling becomes tenfold. Last night my husband went to the House as usual at 7.30 and did not return till 4.30 this morning. They were on "The Tariff." '[57] These late hours went on during much of the month. Agnes found them very trying. Sometimes she drove down with John A. and often stayed for the debate; at others, she dozed on the sofa in her dressing-room until he returned. Many of these long hours in the House were spent discussing the route of the railway to the Maritimes, now that money had been obtained for its construction, but, by the end of the Session, all that was clear was that the line would somehow connect Rivière du Loup with Truro, Nova Scotia.[58]

If Agnes thought that she was entitled to a peaceful summer after such a difficult winter, she was disappointed. The next lesson she had to learn was that a politician has to use the summer to visit his 'parishes'. She packed and went along, going first to Kingston and then on to Toronto with many stops enroute. At the end of July, she, John A. and Hewitt went by ship from Montreal to Halifax. This was an 'olive branch' trip that John A. felt necessary in order to win Howe over to the fact that the Constitution was not going to be changed to let Nova Scotia out of Confederation. Their initial reception in Halifax was very cool on the part of the provincial officials, but that was compensated for by the Governor, General Sir Charles Doyle, their host while in Halifax. '. . . such a pleasant, kindly host and we were féted everywhere — such constant dissipation as it was, flattering too, but so unsatisfactory and fatiguing, yet I know I liked it all. The prominent part I had to play, the pretty dresses to wear, the compliments to listen to!!!!'[59]

It was still very hard for Agnes to admit that worldly things pleased her. What she could and did take satisfaction in without feeling the least sinful was that, by the end of the visit, Howe had been convinced, at least in private that Nova Scotia's future lay in remaining in Confederation. A month or so after the trip, the news was such as to make Agnes write, 'Nova Scotia seems to be sobbing herself to sleep, at least let us hope so — fair green Nova Scotia.'[60] And by January 1869, she could muse that

Howe, 'the prime mover in the repeal cause, the most influential of all the public men [in Nova Scotia] is in Ottawa "negotiating" — strange phase of affairs indeed.'[61] John A.'s long wooing of the Maritime leader had finally been brought to a successful conclusion.

Meanwhile, despite the success and relative peace of the summer, Agnes was glad to settle into her own home again for she was now three months pregnant. In her self-censored diary, the first veiled hint of her condition appears in an entry made in late June: 'My strength feels failing somehow and I am not feeling well. It must be the great heat.'[62] By the end of September she was too ecstatic about the baby to restrain her naturally exuberant nature, which she had been denying for some months. Tossing aside any tendency towards the then-prevalent prudery which made many women loath to comment, even to their own mothers or sisters, on the fact that they were pregnant, Agnes wrote, glowingly, 'My "New Hope" so bright while so strange! Can it be that some day I shall have the sweet happiness of being a Mother? It seems so wonderful and yet so beautiful — I can hardly express what a new life it has given me. What a new life.'[63]

Looking back to one of her first diary entries, in which she said that, at last, she had 'found something worth living for — living in — my husband's heart and love', it is clear that Agnes was making a very personal statement when she wrote: 'I often think what an unsatisfactory experience women must lead, who, passing girlhood and having no particular vocation never realize the joys of wife and mother and spend their lives in trying to fill the void which nature has decreed they should experience.'[64]

Despite her joy, Agnes' pregnancy was not easy. She was often headachy and languid and, sometimes, she admitted, just out of sorts, so she gave up most of her outside interests, spending her days mostly in the Quadrilateral with Theodora. Housekeeping chores still took up much of her time, but there were still many hours in which to read, by turns, with Theodora, to embroider, to write letters and to keep up with the newspapers. After lunch she practised on the new piano which the Kingston voters had given her that summer, and she often walked over to the Department of Justice 'for my darling'.

During these late afternoon strolls, Agnes found that John A. liked to talk out his problems of each particular day. This was a welcome stimulant to her daily routine, restricted as it had necessarily become. During the previous year there had been frustrating times when she had deliberately tried to divert John A.'s thoughts away from his work, but now he seemed to want to talk things out.

One activity that Agnes never neglected during her pregnancy was her entertaining. During the Session, there were, as always, the dinner parties and she gave her usual New Year's At Home.

Visiting began soon after noon and I had such a busy, pleasant day. Luncheon going on from then till 5.30 and about 90 callers. I like so much this old-fashioned custom — it is so truly kind and cordial and friendly — my husband helped me and so did my dear old mother and we all enjoyed ourselves.[65]

Agnes' pleasure was enhanced by her memories, and she felt that it was 'the happiest New Year's Day I can remember since I was a child, and used to have a holiday and little presents and play and romp in the sunshine of my far-away native land.'[66] How natural, now that she was soon to be a mother, that her thoughts should go back to her own childhood.

During the last weeks of her pregnancy, Agnes often felt 'poorly', and depended very much on John A., who was 'necessary for me, for he is such a tender loving care-taker and nurse.'[67] She did not move far from the Quadrilateral, except to take an occasional walk or drive when the weather was good. It was not until early February that she felt able to make one call that protocol demanded — a courtesy call on the wife of the new Governor-General, Lady Young.

Mama and I drove to Rideau Hall and found her ladyship reclining on a chintz sofa, in a room heavy with the scent of hyacinths[,] arrayed in a rich robe of violet satin, thickly quilted and trimmed with Swansdown. She was close to a blazing wood fire and the double windowed room was very hot.[68]

Agnes found it difficult to breathe in such an atmosphere, and she wrote that the scene was one of 'too much luxury [and this] tho' wonderfully pretty to look at is not healthy or wise.'[69] Lady Young was definitely never one of Agnes' favourite chatelaines of Rideau Hall, but her reaction on this first visit was quite possibly intensified by the jealousy that one who was feeling 'poorly' and whose clothes were becoming more and more uncomfortable every day might well feel.

On February 7, Agnes noted in her diary that she ought to write not only on eventful days, but 'This is likely to be one for me however for I am . . . suffering.'[70] It was April before she was able to return to her diary-keeping, and then she could write, 'She is lying asleep in her blankets — my very own darling baby — my little daughter, the sweet gift from Heaven, my Mary — a dark-eyed, soft thing. What word can tell how my heart swells with love and pride — she is truly dear.'[71]

It had been a difficult childbirth, lasting some twenty-four hours, and both Agnes' and the baby's lives had been in 'great danger. . . . My baby was born on . . . February 8th at 15 past 3. Her first cry seemed to bring me to life — the effect of it was truly surprising — a rush of life seemed to come to me — and a kind of wild exultant joy.'[72]

Yet Agnes' convalescence was slow; it was nine weeks before she was able to go even as far as St. Alban's. There, she said, she was in a 'cold, dull frame' all through the service and this feeling persisted. Was it because of her own lack of strength or was she already secretly worried about her child, trying to hide from herself the already evident fact that there was something abnormal about Mary? During the next month she felt aimless, weary and dissatisfied, unable to accomplish much. Late in April she wrote, 'My baby is sweet, and bright and well. My dear, dear little child. I have read nothing today — my heart is cold and dull — I seem to be waiting for something — perhaps it is for light.'[73]

On May 1, 1869, Agnes admitted to her diary the greatest sorrow a mother can ever know: that her child would never develop normally.

> The day has been stamped with the world's greatest seal — it is graven, I think, with the word 'disappointment'. Perhaps yesterday was one of the saddest times of my life — let it pass — let it die — only teach me, Heavenly Father to see the lesson it was destined to teach, and while I learn it to do so cheerfully.[1]

If ever Agnes had need of her faith, it was when she learned the truth about Mary. The only child she would ever have was a victim of hydrocephalus — water on the brain. She would live, but never be normal. She would never be able to walk except possibly haltingly and with support, never be able to run and play, never be able to look after herself. She might not be able to learn to speak — indeed, her capacity for all kinds of mental development was uncertain. Her life expectancy was short (although it turned out that she outlived both her parents).

John A., and perhaps Agnes, had almost certainly guessed the truth within the first few months of Mary's life, even if they had tried to hide it from themselves. The baby made such slow progress, and her enlarged head was a clear indication of the problem. By late April, there could be no doubt about her abnormality, and doctors quickly diagnosed her condition. There would be other doctors, other opinions sought, but, in the end, the answers were the same. For both parents, the sorrow was intense. Agnes did not, could not, express her thoughts even on the pages of her diary, and, for some six months, she did not write a word there. When she did write again, in November, she was in a thoughtfully sad mood:

> What has happened with me since this day last year when I sat writing — as I sit now — in my big Diary? Wonderfully little — and yet wonderfully much.

Outwardly all is nearly the same except that my darling child's smile brightens my home — but in my heart I feel that much is totally different. I ought to be wiser for I have suffered keenly in mind since I last wrote here. Only One who knows all our hearts can tell how keenly and painfully or how for long weeks and months all was gloom and disappointment.[2]

Adding to Agnes' sorrow by autumn was her realization that, just when she needed her husband most, she could not count on him for support. Broken by his own suffering over Mary's condition and by worry over his personal finances and his debts in Kingston, which he was now told totalled some $79,000, he had begun to drink heavily again. It had been well over a year since he had done any but social drinking, and Agnes had been hoping that he was going to be able to conquer this weakness. In the back of her mind, however, had been the fear that such bouts were almost certain to recur, and although she had thought she would be able to cope with them, she now discovered that such was not the case. In her disappointment, she reacted with less tact than she had hoped to be able to muster, and then had to admit to her diary that 'I was over-confident, vain and presumptious in my sense of power. I fancied I could do much and I failed signally.'[3]

As always, however, John A. managed to snap out of his drinking to attend to the demands of politics. One less item in his peck of troubles was Nova Scotia. In January, 1869, Agnes had arranged a dinner party especially for Howe and was so jubilant at his having been won over to the idea of Confederation that she could write:

I have never seen my husband in such cheery moods. . . I feel gloriously proud and thankful at his having 'won' in Nova Scotia — hardly a year ago one of the leading men from there. . . told me in seriousness and some dismay that the 'country' meaning Nova Scotia was in a state of complete rebellion, that it needed but one false or nasty move to kindle a flame that might lead to very important and very disastrous consequences — No less than a necessity for calling out the troops.[4]

By the time Parliament opened in April, 1869, John A.'s dream of a country from 'sea to sea' appeared to have a chance of becoming reality. Nova Scotia had accepted the fact of Confederation and Howe had even accepted the Presidency of the Privy Council. It was with optimism that the Prime Minister noted that Prince Edward Island looked ready to join and that Newfoundland could be next. Then he could see the West fitting into the picture: Rupert's Land had recently been purchased by the Dominion from the Hudson's Bay Company;[5] there was the ill-defined area known as the Northwest Territories and, finally, British Columbia would come in as the last piece of the puzzle.

If this dream were to be realized, it was necessary to act quickly before the Americans moved into the West, and, in Rupert's Land, things were already in some turmoil. In anticipation of its transfer to the Dominion, surveyors had descended upon the territory, arousing the fears of its Métis residents. The latter soon found a champion in that complex half-breed, Louis Riel.

John A. recognized Riel as 'a clever fellow' and suggested to William McDougall, a fellow Father of Confederation who was sent to Fort Garry as Lieutenant-Governor with a waiting brief in late October, 1869, that he 'endeavour to retain him as an officer in your future police. If you do this promptly, it will be a most convincing proof that you are not going to leave the half-breeds out of the law.'[6] McDougall's impetuous nature led him to ignore John A.'s advice to proceed slowly and patiently. In any case, he was prevented from even entering the territory. Riel set up a provisional government in Fort Garry and was not willing to receive the Lieutenant-Governor Designate. There was nothing for McDougall to do but resign and go back to Ottawa.

When Agnes heard about the troubles in the West, she felt she should sympathize with her friend, Jessie McDougall, because of her father's unfortunate experience, but she found her sorrow over Mary's condition kept her from being very generous in her thoughts toward others. This bothered her:

> I hate myself for not being more sorry at Mr. McDougall's failure in the North West. I hate myself for not grieving more for that the whole family are so much distressed and disappointed and so I try to conceal my unkind thoughts and in this — their time of darkness — to be mindful that my life may not be all sunshine.[7]

It was somewhat easier for Agnes to regain her sense of proportion and humour with people whom she did not know as well as she did the McDougalls. Early in January, 1870, she paid a visit to Lady Young at Rideau Hall, whom she found

> tucked up in her big chintz sofa.... We talked of Red River, dinner parties, dress...also we drank tea out of delicious little cups.... Then the dear old Governor came in from his walk. Lady Katherine [Robertson] was being sent home in the Royal Sleigh — so reluctantly I occupied a place in it and feeling horribly democratic on its warm cushions, and after being handed out with much dignity by a 'Jeames' of much self-possession went off through the moonlight to my husband's office to walk home with him.[8]

Agnes, as always, enjoyed those walks home with John A. and they were one way of keeping an eye on him during the troubled winter of

1869-70. She knew how he felt about Mary; she was aware of the financial straits they were in; and she realized that the explosive situation in the West alone was enough to bring on another relapse like that of last November. Riel's entrenched position at Fort Garry, rumours of Fenian aid to the Métis and increased American interest in the area had finally forced him to call out troops. By the spring of 1870, a military expedition under the command of Colonel Wolseley reached Fort Garry. Unexpectedly, Riel fled, and the Government acted quickly to solidify its position. On May 2, 1870, a Bill was presented to the House of Commons for the setting up of the Province of Manitoba.

Agnes did what she could during these tense months to look after her husband. But she could not be with him all the time, and, if the *Globe* is to be trusted, he reached out for some port — and then some more — to get him through the early part of May. When the Manitoba Bill was introduced, Sir Stafford Northcote, Governor of the Hudson's Bay Company, who was an interested onlooker in the House, thought that John A. seemed feeble and ill.

John A. *was* ill — almost fatally so. Just four days later, he collapsed in his office. Hewitt, whose office was next door and who had likely assured Agnes that he would keep as watchful an eye as possible on his brother-in-law, rushed in when he heard John A. making strange noises. There he found the Prime Minister lying on the floor in great pain, the result of having passed a gall-stone of unusual size. He was too weak to be moved to his home, and it was decided to convert his office into a sick-room. Agnes was on the scene immediately, and, when she got over the initial shock, characteristically she devoted all her time and attention to her husband during his illness. Six long weeks she watched over him, at times not knowing if he could recover. One day, the story goes, not knowing what else to do, she took a whisky flask and rubbed some of its contents on his face and chest. John A., not surprisingly, whispered, 'Oh, do that again. It seems to do me good.'[9]

At last the doctors pronounced him on the road to recovery and granted him permission to travel to the seashore, where he was sure he would feel better. The place he chose was Prince Edward Island, and he was accompanied by the entire family — Agnes, little Mary, Theodora and Hewitt — plus his physician, Dr. Grant, and an entourage of nurses, secretaries and maids. Soon after they sailed from Montreal on the government steamer *Druid*, John A. began to feel better, but even after a week's trip he was still too weak to walk ashore at Charlottetown.

The party took up residence at Falconwood, a secluded house on the banks of the Hillsborough River. The place had been prepared for them only days before, and such was its state of disrepair that one wonders why it was chosen, unless it was the only available house large enough to accommodate the group. It was quiet, however, and in the peace of its large grounds, John A. rested and regained his strength. He used the unusual free time to catch up on his reading. Agnes often sat near by, checking the pages of the *Invalid's Cook Book,* which she had bought at Durie's book shop in Ottawa just after her husband became ill, and which was of great use during his convalescence. She also had some new novels with her; although John A. had earlier suggested that she read something a bit more substantial, she had been through too much in the past year and needed some sort of release.

During this period, Agnes and the staff kept Ottawa informed by letter and by telegram of the Prime Minister's progress. One person who was following his recuperation with great interest was Prince Arthur, Duke of Connaught, who had been spending some months in Canada. Before returning to England, he wrote John A., saying how pleased he was to hear that '. . . you are so much better. Your illness has been a very long and tedious one. . . . With kindest regards to Lady Macdonald, to whom we all ought to be indebted for the great care she has taken of you in your illness.'[10]

This acknowledgement of Agnes' constant care and of the heavy task she had borne in the supervision of her husband's recuperation was typical of the sentiments of friends and acquaintances. For Agnes, it was enough to see that, day by day, John A. was improving. By the middle of September, he was well enough to go back to Ottawa.

The return to the capital posed another problem of housing for Agnes. She had made the Quadrilateral into a satisfactory home for over three years, but it had never been an ideal situation for her household and now seemed less and less suitable. Mary and her nurse required more space than was readily available, and there were continuing problems with the drains. Agnes was determined to get her family moved to larger and more healthful surroundings. Happily, their friend, Thomas Reynolds, was not using his house on the Ottawa River for a time, and they were able to move into Earnscliffe in the autumn of 1870. It was a case of love at first sight, but Agnes could not immediately write her impressions of the house for, as she admitted, 'I, really a very careless person indeed [,] mislaid my [diary] key and never wrote a word except in letters all these [eight] months.'[11]

It was not until New Year's Day, 1871, that the diary drew her to its pages once more, and then she did write of Earnscliffe. 'My home is on a cliff, fringed with low trees, the windows in the rear overlook the river. When we came here, two months ago, the waters were broad and blue. Now they are all frozen and snow-covered. It is a stern picture now, all frosty, bound for winter.'[12]

Snug inside the house the Macdonalds were happy. Young Hugh John was up from Toronto for the holidays, and he went with his stepmother to the midnight service on New Year's Eve. As they went out the drive, Agnes wrote, 'We looked back... over the thin, low-limbed hemlock evergreens to the pretty, irregular grey stone house which is now my home. The windows with their large panes, glowing with lamp light, looked so cozy — and then my heart warmed with gratitude to the giver of my many home blessings.'[13]

New Year's Day was on Sunday that year, and Agnes was filled with gratitude as she watched Theodora and John A. returning arm-in-arm from the morning service at St. Alban's. 'Could my heart but be thankful', she rejoiced, 'that they were both spared to me, when only last May, all human hope that my husband's life would be spared seemed to have passed away.'[14]

Agnes' usual New Year's reception was not given until Monday, January 2, that year, and 'What a bustling day this has been!', she wrote when, at last, the house was free of guests.

All the fires blazing and crackling, the house in its best order, all the servants important and in a hurry and I in my best black velveteen gown, receiving New Year's visitors! The house was thronged from noon till dinner time, with men of all ages, sorts and styles. Some 130 in all — some merely shook hands or bowed, exchanged a few commonplaces about the weather, but the larger part lunched at a continually replenished table in the dining room and wished me and mine all the happiness of the New Year between mouthfuls of hot oyster soup or sips of sherry.[15]

The only thing that spoiled an otherwise perfect day was that 'Sir John... ordered a Council! I had set my heart on having him with me and lo! he went away before one single caller had rung the doorbell.... He only came in at dinner time.'[16] Even then he had not finished his day's work. Before he could enjoy any of the leftover soup and sherry, he was called to Rideau Hall where the Governor-General informed him that a Joint Commission was to meet in Washington to discuss the complex problem of international fishing grounds. Canada was being asked to name its delegate, and there was really no one but John A. Before the end of February, 1871, he was on his way to Washington with Agnes by his side.

Agnes' decision to accompany him was not made easily. Her thoughts were never far from her child. Yet, as she noted early in January, 'I think this American fishery question bothers Sir John. I suppose it is a ticklish question as Brother Sam may show fight. I wonder Sir John can stand against all this work and worry.'[17] Surely he should not go alone in his present state of health. After weighing her choices, Agnes decided that

Mary, whose condition was stable, could safely be left in the care of her nurse, while her own place was definitely with her husband. Possibly, too, she felt it was a good time to get away from Ottawa. By late February, the northern winter was definitely beginning to drag and there had been days in January which Agnes remembered all too vividly:

> Snowing all morning, and all afternoon too but then it blew as well and the drifts flew perpendicularly past our high exposed windows. 'More fires' is our war cry, our watchword, our hourly, nay momently entreaty. Joe piles up small trees in the furnace and logs in the stove and Olivene (whose shoes the cold weather seems to keep down at the heel to my great distress) flaps about all day long with a coal scuttle![18]

It must have been a relief to get to Washington where spring was already in the air.

As the Conference delegates assembled, Agnes discovered that one of the British group was a cousin, Montague Bernard, whom she had not seen since her wedding. She must have thought that John A. would have an ally here, but as the talks developed, she and her husband discovered that kinship goes only so deep.

The weeks in Washington were a rest for Agnes, who, although she had many parties to attend, had not the work of organizing them or running a busy household. For John A., it was another matter. It was a frustrating, tiring period for him. He was playing a new role, for it was the first time the Dominion had ever participated in such a conference on equal terms. As many a future Canadian statesman would find himself, John A. was squeezed by both the British and the Americans — expected to give in to one, to appease the other. It was not an easy game to play, and he came away with a series of half measures. The only thing he was pleased about was that he had extracted, he devoutly hoped, the promise of some money from England to build a railroad to British Columbia.

Railroad money, however, was important to John A. then, as it would be for many years. While he had struggled in Washington, the Commons, after months of hard debate, had set the terms of British Columbia's entry into the Dominion. They included a pledge that the federal government would build a railroad to connect the five existing provinces with the new western one. This was a bold promise. Granted that the Canadian government had to act quickly to secure the western province before the Americans moved up the coast, granted that a through rail link was part of the 'sea to sea' dream, yet the very thought of actually promising to build such a railroad was almost overwhelming. It was a long route, a hard route, and thus, a very expensive route, estimated at more than a hundred million dollars. Before the Canadian

Pacific Railway was finished, years later, the toll would be heavy, not only in dollars but in heartache, and John A. — and thus Agnes — would suffer much.

After this aggravating winter and worrisome spring, John A. and Agnes agreed that what the family needed most was a good holiday by the sea. He suggested Rivière du Loup, where he had vacationed when Quebec City had been the capital of United Canada. Agnes knew the general area from her own days in the city on the cliff, and they had stopped in it last summer on their way down to Prince Edward Island. Its healthful atmosphere had appealed to her then; she was sure a summer spent there would be very pleasant, and she hoped the fresh sea breezes might benefit Mary. They rented a house in the St. Patrick area of the small town, thus establishing a pattern that would last for many years.

Rivière du Loup was already a popular spot for summer homes among certain groups of prestigious Canadian society. When Lord Monck was Governor-General, he had vacationed there several times in a simple, old farmhouse, and his family had liked the spot so well that they had persuaded many of their Quebec City friends to join them.[19] Some of these people had built their own summer houses in the area, but when the Macdonald family arrived in 1871, John A. could point out to Agnes that the quiet little town had not been changed too much by these visitors. Had he had any reservations as to whether or not Agnes would like it, his mind was put at rest at once. She enjoyed it so much that she was to spend many happy summers there over the next twenty years, and, much later, when she lived on the French and Italian Rivieras, she would remember, with touching nostalgia, her vacations in the little, unsophisticated resort on the St. Lawrence.

In 1871 the Macdonalds had little over a month there before they had to go back to Ottawa. John A. knew he had his work cut out for him — keeping the British aware of the need for a railway loan. Agnes, too, had a task waiting — organizing yet another move for their large household. Thomas Reynolds was back from England and, not unnaturally, wished to live in his own house, Earnscliffe. The Macdonalds moved out with regret, but luckily, they found a suitable house back in Sandy Hill at 194 Chapel Street. This was familiar territory to them, not far from the Quadrilateral, their first Ottawa home, and it had the advantage of being nearer St. Alban's Church than Earnscliffe. This was a relief to Agnes, more for her mother's sake than for her own. While the church did play an important part in Agnes' life, it was even more essential to Theodora, who now had few responsibilities or interests. True, she was concerned about her granddaughter, but there was little she could do for Mary except to sit with her at times. Backgammon with Hewitt or John A. and reading with Agnes were among her few other activities besides those relating to the church. Now it would be easier for her to attend, even during the winter months, when the streets were icy or snow-covered, since one of the servants, or Agnes herself, could accompany her down the few blocks.

Their little church was in need of help at this time. When it had been built, the decision had been taken that it should be a free-seat church, but no one had considered the effect of that decision on the length of time it would take to pay off the capital costs. At the end of 1871, there was still $5,000 owing, on which high interest rates had to be paid. Yet the Rector had long taken a firm stand about money-raising schemes, such as bazaars:

> I took the ground, that real believers in Christ and His Church should give directly to Him, the love of Christ sustaining them. They should do this without the amusement of a Fancy Bazaar with its lotteries and feminine attractions, as well as without the inducement of having a return for the money expended. 'To give to the Lord' meant a free gift, not the price of a cushion or a toy, a picture or an article. . . much less a gambling transaction.[20]

Agnes and Theodora had no less faith than Reverend Bedford-Jones but they saw the juxtaposition of religious and practical matters somewhat differently. (Agnes had earlier written that she thought church squabbles as to whether or not pew rents should be paid were 'most disastrous' and that the congregation should 'pray for unity'.[21]) They believed the congregation could work in unison to do something about the debt on their church. Years ago, when she had lived in Barrie, Agnes had seen her mother and the other ladies organize bazaars in aid of their little church, Trinity Anglican. The same could be done for St. Alban's, despite the Rector's views. During the summer of 1872, he had to be out of the country for a time, and, while he was away, some of the parishioners, who were more practical-minded than he, banded together to help their church. When he returned, late in the year, he found that there was nothing he could do to stop their combined efforts. The result was that: 'Under the patronage of Lady Macdonald then at the height of her own and her husband's political popularity, and owing to her zeal and efforts, Senators and Members vied in opening their purses. I never went near the bazaar, but the debt of $5000 was paid!'[22]

The Macdonalds' personal financial affairs were also put in order during this time. When John A. had been so ill in 1870, some of his friends had become aware, for the first time, of his grave money problems, and they had decided to do something about it. After informal discussions, they had put forward a solid proposal, dated late October of that year. The initiative had been taken by David Macpherson of Toronto, an old friend of John A.'s, who thought it 'unjust, but . . . nevertheless true, that an honest Canadian Minister of State cannot support and educate a family upon his official income alone. . . . [John A.] relinquished the profits of his profession . . . and, in the service of his country became not a richer but a poorer man.'[23] Macpherson continued, pointing out that, since John A.'s services had been broadly national in scope, persons in many parts of the Dominion would 'desire to join in recognizing his great service to the State, his pure patriotism, his brilliant talents, his generous nature.'[24]

The plan of a testimonial fund worked. By early April, 1872, John A.'s loyal friends had collected and invested the sum of $67,500 'for the benefit of himself, his admirable and devoted wife, and his children'[25], as Macpherson had suggested when first proposing the fund. For the first time in years the Prime Minister of Canada could meet his bills when due.

It was as well that the Macdonalds had some sunshine in their private lives at that time because building of the Canadian Pacific Railway was leading them into troubled years. The problems were both financial and political and completely intermingled. It was not just a question of obtaining backing — John A. had begun that fight, with some success, when he was in Washington in early winter 1871. While he was on that trip, however, the planning had taken a very unwise turn that was to lead to serious trouble. As Agnes later explained in a magazine article, the decision had then been made to

build the road through the agency of an incorporated company supplemented by Government aid. I think Sir John regretted this, and would fain have had the railway constructed as a Government work; but his boldness was not to be communicated, and those in charge of the ship in his absence had judged the concession best.[26]

Faced with this *fait accompli*, John A. had to select the right company and that was difficult indeed. Bids to form a company came in fast: one from David Macpherson, the organizer of the testimonial fund; another from Hugh Allan, of the family Agnes liked so much that she once referred to them as the 'good Allans'.[27] One was from Toronto, the other from Montreal. Each was in a position of some delicacy because of his personal relationship with John A. and Agnes. The Government urged amalgamation of the two possible companies, but there was stubbornness on both sides, and by the time of the federal election in July, 1872, no progress had been made in reaching an agreement, with either or both of the bidders.

For this election, John A. planned his strategy carefully. It was not only a question of winning his own riding but of keeping his Government in power. He chose Toronto as a convenient headquarters for his planned tours into the eastern and central parts of the province, and he and Agnes moved into the Queen's Hotel for a long, hot and expensive few weeks. The campaign was bitter. The Opposition's main tactic was to discredit the Government's policies and John A. as their architect. It was years before Agnes wrote of this, but, when she did, she remembered well their cries to the effect that

> [John A.] had sold Canada in the Washington Treaty to curry favour with England. He had given away her fisheries, made a bad bargain all round, and was now filling up the measure of his iniquities by committing her to an entirely new impossible undertaking! A railway line which no one ever could or would build, an entirely ridiculous project which pretended to carry engines, carriages, baggage cars and traffic across inaccessible mountains blocked by snow for half the year, through terrible gorges dense with gigantic timber and impassible scrub, and through rocks miles in extent which dynamite itself would have little effect on![28]

Laugh as John A. and Agnes might over some of the Opposition's extravagant statements, she could see that he was, nevertheless, taking them seriously. He knew better than she just how easily voters can become frightened, especially if they think that their pocketbooks may be involved, and he stumped the province as never before.

Because of the staggered electoral system in use at the time, John A.'s riding of Kingston was won on August 1, and he was then free to devote his energies towards helping out in constituencies where the voting took place later. His aid was needed badly. Cries for help were coming from across the province. Some of the requests were for money, and John A. obtained it. Although he apparently did so without too much difficulty, it was this financial aid that was to cost his career dearly.

Earlier in the campaign, he had discussed funds with Cartier. There seemed to be little hope of filling Ontario's Conservative 'kitty' from sources within that Reform-minded province, so John A. asked his old friend to try to obtain financial help in Montreal. Cartier was successful in his appeal, and contributions were forwarded to Ontario, among them one from Hugh Allan. It was $45,000 — not a large sum for so rich a man — and was put, with the rest, on deposit in the Merchant's Bank of Canada. After John A.'s own election, when panic set in among late-voting ridings, he used this money — and wired for more. In the heat of the campaign, not too much attention was paid to the fact that the extra money had come from Allan, a contender for the railway charter.

All the election results were not in until late August, and then it was seen that the Conservative Government remained in power, but with less strength than before.[29] It faced rough months with the railway question still not settled, and John A.'s telegram for more money from Quebec was on record, waiting to provide explosive 'proof' during the Pacific Scandal that would rock the entire country before long.

In March, 1872, in one of her increasingly rare entries in her diary, Agnes had written:

> I think Jimmy (the clock) is saying 'Write on, write on'! He was wound up yesterday and his dear old tick is brave and strong — so I obey him and take up my pen — Fourteen months since I last wrote on these pages, and almost all things continue the same — My home treasures well and happy, health and prosperity, success and satisfaction still vouchsafed to us — one and all.[30]

One year later, when the Spring Session opened in March, 1873, Agnes would have been the first to admit that the rosy picture she had painted had changed its hue. All things did *not* continue the same. The summer of the election had been an agonizing time for her. She had left Mary so as to be with John A., and she had watched him, without an opportunity for a holiday, subjected to so much pressure. It was the same in the autumn, as he went off, wearily, for yet more rounds of talks with Macpherson and Allan, still trying to convince them to form an amalgamated company to build the railway. There were times then when Agnes knew her husband had been drinking, but he kept on at the task which, by November, even he had to admit was impossible. There would not be any amalgamation, and the charter went to Allan on condition that he divest himself of his American financial backers. Before these financiers bowed out, however, John A. was beaten by allegations that Allan's contributions to the 1872 election expenses had been his way of buying the charter. It was further claimed that John A. had, knowingly, sold out to Allan.

The one person who had nothing to say on the scandal in 1873 was Agnes. The whole thing was undoubtedly too painful for her to discuss even in her diary at the time, and it was not until 1886, when the railway was at last completed that she could write her husband had

> come to see the darling dream of his heart — a railway from ocean to ocean.... During seventeen years, in and out of Parliament, he had battled...through discouragement, obloquy and reverses, and with a strong patience all his own, had bided his time until, as the years went on, men, resolute like himself, had risen to take the aid his Government were determined to offer for the development of this vast territory by the completion of this railway.[31]

In 1873 she could not have written in so dispassionate a manner, but she followed the events in the House that spring very closely.

Another lady who was also keeping an eye on things was Lady Dufferin, wife of the new Governor-General who had arrived in the summer of 1872. Protocol prevented her husband from attending the Commons, but there was nothing to keep her from being present and reporting the sittings back to Rideau Hall. She described the breaking of the scandal in her diary:

Tuesday, 8th — I went to the House as a scrimmage was expected.... The Opposition had asked for a Committee to inquire into the conduct of members of the Government, accusing them of bribery. They lost and then the Government asked for the same Committee, saying they courted inquiry.[32]

By May, the Committee of Inquiry had accomplished nothing, and it was decided that the House should adjourn until August 13, by which time there would surely be some report to put before the Members. Agnes must have known that she was in for a hard period, but she did not know just how bad it was going to be. The family went down to Rivière du Loup, but politics intruded constantly, resulting in John A.'s turning more and more to drink as a palliative. He was trying to blot out not only the Opposition's allegations, but also his sorrow over the recent death of his old friend and colleague, Cartier.[33] In his mind the two events seem to have been inextricably linked, and his grief was great. This was well known by the Opposition, who saw in John A.'s actions at the time a chance to discredit him further:

On the afternoon of the 5th of August, Lady Macdonald received an ambiguously worded telegram of inquiry from a friend, as to the state of her husband's health. A few minutes later another came, followed by more of mysterious import, all hinting of something apparently too dreadful for expression.[34]

According to Joseph Pope, then John A.'s Private Secretary, Agnes took these telegrams to her husband, who was, like herself, at a loss to understand them. Had they read the Opposition papers of the previous day, they would have seen a report that John A., in total despair over his political and personal problems, had made a suicide attempt. He had, allegedly, jumped off the pier at Rivière du Loup; he had been rescued, they said, but was 'in a precarious condition'. John A.'s answer to this rumour, according to Pope, was to send telegrams to his friends assuring them that he 'was never better in his life'.

What had happened? Historians disagree. Somewhere between the rumour and the truth, however, is the fact that a lot of heavy drinking had gone on during much of the Summer Recess and that the Governor-

General had felt it necessary to report the Prime Minister's condition to the Colonial Office in London.[35]

By mid-August, John A. was back in Ottawa for the report of the Committee, Agnes firmly at his side. Still the delays in the findings continued; there was no concensus and the Committee was replaced by a Royal Commission which was mandated to report to the Governor-General before the next Session in late October. It set to work immediately, and, although many of the witnesses were maddeningly vague and forgetful, Lord Dufferin had the report in his hands a few days before the House met on October 23.

Again, Agnes did not, probably could not, write of what happened next, but Lady Dufferin did; it was easier for her to be somewhat more objective.

> We dressed for the 'opening' before lunch — low gowns, feathers and diamonds, uniforms or evening coats — and at 2.30 set off in carriages. . . . The Senate Chamber was full; numbers of ladies on the floor, and crowds of people in the galleries. D. read the speech in French and in English.[36]

The drafting of this speech had been difficult for John A. Part of it dealt with the fact that the Commission's report was to be put before the House; another announced that the railway charter was to be surrendered for lack of funds. The two issues which had, for so long, plagued the Prime Minister were now at a head, and yet he seemed strangely reluctant to speak, strangely unaware that anything was wrong. As the debate on the Speech went on, it was clear that many Conservatives were deserting John A. Still he did not speak. Why was he waiting? It was hard to understand. Lady Dufferin kept her husband informed:

> Tuesday, 28th (Oct) — I went to the House today and remained till 11 p.m. I heard Sir Francis Hincks, Mr. McDonald of Picton and a Mr. Glass. It is supposed that Mr. Blake and Sir John Macdonald are waiting for each other.[37]

It was November 3 before John A. spoke, making one of the most important speeches of his political career to the packed House, to Lady Dufferin, to Agnes who was watching fearfully, knowing the amount of alcohol he was then consuming, and to the waiting country. Soon Agnes must have been filled with pride, but it was Lady Dufferin who reported that

> [Sir John] spoke for five hours, making a very fine speech, full of power, lively and forcible to the end. He did not fail in the slightest degree while speaking,

but when he sat down he was completely exhausted, and his voice was quite gone. Mr. Blake got up after him.[38]

Tuesday, 4th. I did not hear Mr. Blake. He spoke five hours too.[39]

It was obvious where the Vice-Regal sentiment lay.

What Agnes thought on the momentous occasion of John A.'s address is not known, but, despite the support of the Dufferins and many others,[40] it must have been evident that her husand's 'lively and forcible' speech was only a temporary gain in a losing battle. The final blow was struck when the Member for Selkirk, Manitoba, Donald Smith, said that, in all conscience, he could not stand by the actions of the Prime Minister. True, it was only one more defection, but there had already been so many. In John A.'s opinion, there was no point in hanging onto office.

On November 5, Lady Dufferin drove in to Ottawa. She had fully expected to hear the speeches and see the Division, but at the Office,

> I was told that Sir John was with the Governor-General. Soon we saw Colonel Fletcher taking Mr. Mckenzie [sic] to His Excellency. Of course we guessed that he had been 'sent for'.... We took our places in the House, and Sir John got up and briefly announced that the Government had resigned. The announcement was heard in perfect silence.[41]

Since Agnes had not gone to the House that day, she first heard the news when John A. came home. She thought him a little early and was surprised that he went directly to his room. On going to see if anything was the matter, she was quietly informed,

> 'Well, that's got along with.' 'What do you mean?', said she. [He replied] 'Why, the Government has resigned', and arraying himself in his dressing-gown and slippers, and picking up two or three books from a table close by, 'It's a relief to be out of it', he added as he stretched himself on the bed, opened a volume and began to read, intimating that he did not wish to be disturbed.[42]

Agnes must have had mixed feelings about the Conservative Government's fall from power in November, 1873. On the one hand, it was a personal defeat for her husband and meant at least a temporary halt to his dreams of building a strong Dominion from sea to sea — dreams that she had come to share and cherish. On the other hand, it gave her the chance to get down off the pedestal on which the wife of the Prime Minister must, inevitably, live. This role, with its demands on her time and energy, its access to the inner circle of power and its constant requirements of a public face had sometimes afforded her delight and wonder, but, more often, feelings of inadequacy, guilt, fear and, occasionally, outright annoyance. The fact that she had had to learn to play 'a great Premier's wife' simultaneously with learning to be the wife of a complex, sometimes difficult man whom she admired and adored made it no easier.

In short, Agnes' experience over a six-year period might almost have been summed up prophetically in her diary entry for January 1, 1870. She described how, on her way to Midnight Service, she had

> looked up at the closed windows [of the Quadrilateral], so unsuggestive and gloomy as it seemed in the dim moonlight and thought of the many days of storm and sunshine that I had seen under that roof. I thought of the sins and the struggles, the joys and the sorrows — the pleasure and the pain — that I had known there.[1]

At that time Agnes had also remarked that she felt 'cheered and hopeful and happy'.[2] At the end of 1873, as she entered a new phase of life, she may have had the same sentiments. She was determined to put her memories of pain and sorrow behind her as she faced this new period. She had the advantage of now understanding herself better than before and, in so doing, could better understand others, show more patience, act with more tolerance. As for her husband's changed status, she could see that he seemed not the least concerned about it, even though she had often heard him say, during the 1872 election, that he needed five more years to complete the building of the Dominion.[3] He just took up his reading in a very quiet but determined manner and from this, Agnes took her cue. She would accept John A.'s defeat without railing and use her new-found time as usefully as possible.

Not that she had to give up her interest in politics or attendance at debates. John A. was still leader of the Opposition, and she could be quite useful to him in the House. As his first biographer was to say of her, 'No one was quicker to note the appearance of a new member and to take the measure of his parliamentary figure. She would take in every word uttered in a new member's maiden speech and could gauge with an instinct almost equal to Sir John's the manner of man he was.'[4]

Indeed, John A. noted that it was rather pleasant to be in Opposition except for one thing — sitting on the other side of the House meant he could no longer get a good view of Agnes in the Gallery and he missed her reactions to the proceedings. (She had reportedly 'learned the deaf and dumb alphabet, and [in times past] occasionally she might be seen telegraphing to Sir John from the gallery by this means'.[5])

There was also still entertaining for Agnes to do, as wife of the leader of the Opposition and as a continuing close friend of Governor-General Dufferin and his wife. But her social schedule was not as onerous as it had been in the past, partly because of the change in her role, partly because the new Mackenzie government was marked by a change in style. As Lady Dufferin noted after she and her husband entertained some of the new ministers, 'I am trying to become a Grit, and I can't quite manage it. It takes me as much time as the outside edge backwards[6].... I sat between Mr. Mckenzie [sic] and Mr. Cartwright. I like them both and the latter is very talkative and pleasant. Mr. Mckenzie [sic] is very straightforward and nice.'[7] This could well be called damning with faint praise, but Lady Dufferin was not the only Ottawa hostess to note that the dour, righteous Scot was no replacement for the convivial Macdonald.

One thing Agnes could — and did — do with her increased freedom was to devote more time to Mary. Too often since the birth of this flawed, delicate infant, Agnes had had to decide whether her place was at the side of her child or her husband. Now all three could be together more often and the parents had more time to do what little they could for this much-loved daughter.

The tragedy of Mary's condition was intensified by the fondness both her parents had for children in general. J. Pennington Macpherson, John A.'s nephew by his first marriage, would later recall that the statesman, while a young student, had often gone to the Macpherson house to play

1. Lady Monck, wife of the Governor-General of British North America and then Canada, 1861-1868.

2. Sir Samuel L. Tilley, the New Brunswick supporter of confederation.

3. George Brown, the old opponent.

4. Agnes in 1868, soon after her marriage.

5. Earnscliffe.

6. Agnes and her baby daughter Mary, June 1869.

7. The anteroom in Earnscliffe added by Macdonald for his private secretary.

8. Agnes and Mrs. Samuel Tilley, January 1870.

9. Hugh John, Macdonald's son, in 1871.

10. The drawing room at Earnscliffe.

11. Lady Dufferin, wife of the
Governor-General 1872-1878.

12. Princess Louise, 1879.

13. Agnes in 1878.

14. Agnes firing the first shot at the old firing ranges on the Rideau.

15. D'Alton McCarthy, M.P. Simcoe North, Ont.

16. Agnes as she looked in May of 1881.

17. Theatricals at Rideau Hall in 1880.

18. Later in 1881 she posed for a somewhat less austere portrait.

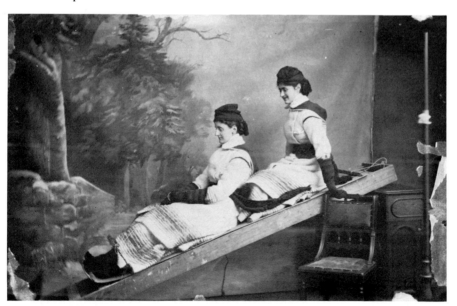

19. On a mock-toboggan, Lady Landsdowne and Lady Florence Anson indulge in a photographic frivolity.

20. Agnes in 1885 in a studio portrait.

21. Agnes with the Macdonald party visiting Port Arthur, Ontario, in 1886.

22. Two views of the Macdonald cabin at Banff.

23. Agnes fishing at Nipisquit River, New Brunswick, with Robert Leckie and his wife, Sarah, in 1886.

24. Lady Maud Landsdowne, in 1888.

25. Emma Albani.

26. A favourite corner of Sir John's at Earnscliffe. The wheelchair is daughter Mary's.

27. Macdonald as he appeared shortly before his collapse in 1891.

28. Macdonald's study at Earnscliffe.

29. Agnes with Mrs. Mary Fitzgibbon
(Lally Bernard), in 1891.

30. Lady Stanley of Preston.

31. Agnes (now Baroness Macdonald of Earn-scliffe) with Mary in 1893.

32. Sir John S.D. Thompson, Prime Minister 1892-1894.

33. Sir Charles Tupper.

34. Hugh John Macdonald with his wife Agnes Gertrude and son John Alexander.

35. A formal studio portrait of Agnes.

with his sister-in-law's little children. Another biographer noted: 'A friend of his in Kingston remembers seeing him toss his silk hat back on his head and get down in the street to play marbles with some little boys.'[8] Yet, even when John A. became a father for the first time, he had had to miss so much of Hugh John's childhood because of the demands of politics and the difficulties he faced, first with an ailing wife and then as a widower. He loved his son dearly, but duty had dictated his priorities and he simply was not able to see much of the boy.

Agnes, too, was drawn to children and vice versa. When she had lived in Barrie, as a young lady, the Patton's little girl, Lulu, had been particularly fond of her. Over a year after the Bernards left, Mrs. Patton wrote Theodora that

Lulu often says she wishes Mrs. Bernard and *Annes* would come back again.... She has asked me two or three times if I thought you and *Annes* would have any little girl in *Ebec* to tell stories to. The idea seems to distress her very much.[9]

But Agnes did not have any little girls in Quebec or any relatives' children to lavish attention on in those years. Her only nieces, Richard's daughters, Dora and May, lived in Barrie, and since their father had died so young, they were naturally much closer to their mother's family than to the Bernards.

From the period after the Bernards moved to Toronto, there is evidence that Agnes created a strong bond with at least one of her Sunday School pupils there, a bond that endured and surfaced after John A.'s death in 1891. For a few moments then, Agnes' sad thoughts were distracted by the contents of one of her letters of condolence:

Years ago you may remember having in your Sunday School class in Toronto a little girl named Fannie Spink. She has never forgotten...nor can she ever forget the Miss Bernard who tried so hard to make a good girl of her.[10]

For parents such as these, Mary's hydrocephalic condition must have been not only a shock but a terrible disappointment. At first it had been a hard struggle just to keep her alive. Even when she had survived her first year and a half, her hold on life was tenuous. The trip to Prince Edward Island, after John A.'s grave illness in 1870, was especially hard on her, and at times her parents had doubted that she would survive it. As John A. wrote to his sister Margaret:

Agnes has kept you and will keep you posted as to poor little baby. Baby has had a hard time of it but if we get her home safely, I have more hopes of her than I have had.[11]

And as late as 1874, she would be the object of solicitude from summer neighbours in Riviére du Loup. Charles Thibeault, a permanent resident of the town, wrote then to John A.:

s'il vous plâit me donner des nouvelles du petit bébé car nous avons su qu'il était malade.[12]

The sad truth, which both parents knew all too well, was that they could never expect too much of Mary. But they loved her tenderly, played with her, told her stories even when they had no way of knowing whether or not she could understand them.

Gradually Mary's general health improved somewhat and she did begin to develop, although very, very slowly. By the time she was seven, she was a big girl, but very clumsy and making no progress at walking alone. Her parents tried some orthopaedic 'instruments' to see if they *might* enable her to walk without support. These very complicated braces were designed, the manufacturer said, to help in cases of knock-knees, bow-legs, hip diseases, paralysis and club foot. What would they do for Mary? Nothing, and she was destined to spend her days in a wheelchair despite all her parents' efforts.

Other aspects of Mary's development — or lack of it — are less clear, partly because no one seems to have retained records, partly because both her parents, well in advance of their time, were determined to treat her as much as possible as a child of ordinary physical and mental capabilities. In 1873, when she was four-and-a-half, John A. sent her a charming note at Rivière du Loup, a letter made more touching by the realization that it was written from Ottawa only days after his supposed 'suicide'. Depressed or not, harried by politics or not, he made it appear as if his only thought was about his little girl's return from the cottage.

My dearest Mary

You must know that your kind Mama and I are very anxious to see you and Granny again. We have just put a new carpet in your room and got everything ready for you.

The garden looks lovely just now...there are some fine melons.... You must pick them for dinner and feed the chickens with the rind. You remember that Mama cut my hair and made me look like a cropped donkey. It has grown quite long again. When you come home you must not pull it too hard.

I intend to have some new stories for you when you come in the morning into Papa's bed and cuddle him up....

...and so goodbye my pet and come home soon to your loving papa.

John A.[13]

By 1877 it was Mary's turn to write to John A. In a letter which is marked as verbatim dictation, the little eight-year-old said:

My dear Father   Toronto, October 12, 1877

I hope you are quite well. Your wife Agnes sends her love. She did not tell me to say so but I am sure she would if she knew it.

.... Dear Father, when are you coming back? I hope you will be back very soon.... The house seems so dull and lonely without you and I miss my evening stories very much....

Your affectionate Baboo and daughter.

Mary Macdonald.

Oh! What a scrimmage I've made. I forgot to say anything about my old hen. Sarah is well and chirpy as ever. That's all.[14]

This letter and many like it raise the question of how much verbal communication Mary ever attained. The notation of 'verbatim dictation' suggests that, unlike many hydrocephalics, she did learn to speak rather well. Yet, as late as 1906, her mother wrote she could not 'speak more than a few words and those very badly'.[15] Clearly, she did learn to communicate with at least those close to her, but when and to what extent may never be known.

No matter what was the exact state of Mary's advancement in November, 1873, after her father's defeat in the House, Agnes must have rejoiced in the certainty that she would now have more time to spend with her crippled child and be free to supervise her treatments and education more closely.

Another thing Agnes found she had more time to do was to keep up with her reading. She had never gone back to her Tuesday reading group after Mary's birth, but had continued to read, as always, fitting it in as best she could. As John A.'s biographer, Biggar, noted, 'She might be seen during the session going about the Library. . . or sitting on the bare steps of the Senate entrance reading a book.'[16] She also tried to find time to read aloud to Theodora and to the servants, but best of all were those quiet Sunday evenings when John A. read to her in front of her dressing-room fire. While she took the greatest pleasure in this, she sometimes felt a bit guilty, especially if he had been working hard during the week; one night, after he had been reading *Lockesley Hall,* she wrote in her diary, 'I would not listen any more tho' his dear voice was sweetest music to my ears.'[17]

Agnes' taste in reading was quite broad, especially after John A. started suggesting books to her, many about statesmen, soon after their marriage. One thing she did not especially like were popular, risqué novels. *Cometh Up As A Flower,* for example, she found to be

> . . . a decidedly objectionable book. . . . Of all things I hate the fashionable delineation of passion in novels à la mode. The scene in *Cometh Up* especially Nellie's last interview with her lover when, herself a wife, she tells him how dearly she loves him and how she wishes never to leave him, is . . . coarse and vulgar. It is all flippant mischief and I do not like it![18]

While Agnes deplored this kind of writing by 'authors, authoresses in particular who seem to think it necessary to write something very startling or very bad',[19] she was also critical of some autobiographies. With a healthy sense of humour, she commented on some of these writers, wondering if they were always as fine as they portrayed themselves. One such author, a Mrs. Schimmel-Pennick, she said, 'must have been very tired of being sensible from her very babyhood!.'[20] Despite her impatience with pretentious piety, however, she continued her youthful habit of reading religious books on the Sabbath and apparently found inspiration in many of them.

This new, quieter period in Agnes' life was soon marked by another great change — the very sudden death of her mother on February 26, 1875. Agnes was, most unfortunately, out of town with John A. at the time, but by chance, Reverend Bedford-Jones happened to be on hand. Both he and Hewitt knew what a shock the news would be to Agnes and they

> arranged that telegrams should be sent at an interval of two hours, one announcing the alarming illness and the other the fatal end. The stupid operator sent the second message first! It came that day to Lady Macdonald who had been with a gay party at Niagara, when she was seated at dinner with her host, Mr. Henry O'Brien. The shock was awful. I went to meet her at Prescott and brought her to Ottawa next morning. For a time we feared she would have permanently lost her reason.[21]

Almost the last entry in Agnes' spasmodically kept diary details Hewitt's account of their mother's death. It was not until March 14 that she could bring herself to write, and then, with the sad memory of Theodora's burial uppermost in mind, she said, 'She had been resting 12 days — I have lived with her blessed and saintly memory and I am better. I have let no one come home — no one — who can fill her place? It is Sunday — a grey chill March Sunday —'.[22]

Yet, while Agnes suffered in solitude, she could take great personal joy and some measure of consolation in one event: John A. made his First Communion in the Anglican Church. On the evening of March 1, a private funeral service had been held for Theodora, a service attended by all the household. After it was over, the Rector asked to speak with John A. Did he suggest that John A. become a communicant to comfort the sorrowing Agnes? It would appear so, but as the Rector wrote: 'What passed between us must be sacred.... As we parted at a late hour he held my hand and only said "Thank you Doctor." '[23]

On the following morning a home service of Holy Communion was already planned. In front of an improvised altar, Agnes knelt near Hewitt and Hugh John — and yet the service did not start. As the Reverend Bedford-Jones recounted:

> Col. Bernard turned to his sister and asked 'What are we waiting for?' She hurriedly replied, 'Sir John'. The Colonel gave a start evidently taken by surprise. But in a moment or two Sir John came in and knelt beside his wife, having in his hand a small Altar Manual. It was a most solemn and affecting service. I could scarcely speak the words as I delivered the sacred elements into the open hand of Canada's Premier, himself moved to tears and kneeling upright with his eyes closed in most fervent prayer.[24]

After the service, when the Rector had put away the vessels and linen, John A. was waiting for him with the invitation: 'Come Doctor, I have been waiting for you to join me at breakfast; come along, and keep me company'.[25]

To Agnes, it was natural that the two men should keep each other company. They had often done so during summers at Rivière du Loup, where, taking long walks over the hills, they had had many discussions of a religious nature. John A. was, as the Rector was a little surprised to discover,

> a well read theologian.... He took much interest in the religious controversies that were then agitating the Church of England and he read everything on the subject. ...we discussed the Eucharistic Controversy; and having brought with me the last new book on the subject, 'Notitia Eucharistica'...Sir John very gladly accepted the loan of the volume and, after reading it, gave me an admirable criticism as to its merits. At the same time he requited my loan by the gift of a very valuable collection of essays by the most learned divines, edited by Dr. Weir and Dr. Maclagan, the present Archbishop of York.[26]

Clearly, for John A. as for Agnes, the period after November, 1873, was one in which he finally had the leisure to rethink his life and reorganize his priorities. Not that his life was without pressures — political and financial. Now that he was no longer Prime Minister, his salary was reduced, but his household expenses continued to rise, especially because of the cost of attempting to provide a near-normal life for Mary. The 1871 Testimonial Fund had given him some $4,000 interest annually, but he needed to increase his income further. The obvious way was to give some attention to his long-neglected law firm, which had moved to Toronto earlier in 1873.[27]

For much of 1874 and early 1875, John A. travelled back and forth between Ottawa and Toronto. Occasionally Agnes went with him, but, by the months after Theodora's death, husband and wife had had enough. Too often they were separated, with John A. in Toronto and Agnes, now bereft of Theodora's company, in Ottawa with Mary. When they were in Rivière du Loup in the summer of 1875, they talked over the situation and decided to move the family to Toronto. For nearly a year after the move, they rented a pleasant, roomy house, set in spacious grounds in a quiet neighbourhood on Sherbourne Street, from their friend, T.C. Patteson, of the *Mail*. John A., however, had his eye on another house, an impressive residence, only a few years old, at 63 St. George Street;[28] he finally bought it in the spring of 1876. It was a new building, but even so it required alterations to adapt it to the Macdonalds' special needs, and Agnes spent the spring supervising the work of carpenters and painters. In early May she organized yet another move, but once they were settled, the family found that the house was ideal.

One important factor in the Macdonalds' decision to move to Toronto had been a desire to be closer to Hugh John. Father and son had seen each other only at intervals since Isabella's death, and John A. often felt that the role of 'visiting parent' was a highly unsatisfactory one. His second marriage had not really improved the situation. Hugh was already seventeen at the time, only fourteen years younger than Agnes, who, for years past, had had little contact with young people. Not since her days in Barrie had she lived close to youth, and Hugh John was no mere youth — he was her step-son. In those first days of feeling her way into a totally new life, she had been unsure how to approach the young man when he visited during school holidays. Certainly, she had welcomed him warmly, even if she had not been sure how to react: 'So glad to see the dear old boy. I love him if only for his likeness to my husband'.[29]

During that visit, she had even tried giving a little party for him, but, for the new hostess, the entertaining of teenagers had proved no easier then than it is now. The party, she thought, 'was very stupid. I could do nothing to promote gaiety myself.... Sir John was charming, however, and we could never have done without him.'[30]

Later, her step-son became 'Hughie' to her, but her uncertainty still showed up in her diary, uncertainty as to whether or not her feelings were more of concern than of 'motherly' love: 'Hughie is here — our good, steady going dear old Hugh, one cannot help respecting and loving him.

John's both fond and proud of him but the boy has been brought up necessarily much away from his father.'[31]

In 1870 Hugh had gone even further away — west with the Wolseley Expedition. On his return, he had lived in Ottawa briefly with John A. and Agnes, but in 1872, when he was called to the bar, he had gone off again — this time to Toronto, to join his father's law firm. So, when John A. and Agnes also moved to Toronto, they had hopes of establishing a closer relationship with Hugh than holiday visits could ever give, but they were doomed to disappointment. By 1875 Hugh wished to marry, but John A. did not approve of his choice. Jean King was a widow, a little older than Hugh and a Roman Catholic. John A. felt she was not the right wife for Hugh and he made this known in the strongest terms. The atmosphere between father and son became very strained and ended in Hugh's leaving the firm and moving to Kingston, with Jean as his bride.

Luckily, the rupture was not to last long. Agnes had nothing to say in this, for she never interfered in the Macdonald family's affairs. Perhaps she felt John A. had been so good to her own family that she did not feel it right to make any comment, although, at times, she must have wished with all her heart to do so. Certainly, from the time of her marriage, Agnes saw that the Macdonalds all leaned on John A. heavily. In some ways this was similar to her own mother's dependence on Hewitt, but in John A.'s case, his responsibility went beyond providing guidance to a widowed mother, and extended to his sisters, Louisa and Margaret, even after Margaret's marriage. Both constantly sought his advice, not only on financial matters, but on any perplexing question. Where should they live, how should they manage the details of their affairs? At times, they even asked for money, which Agnes must have thought hardly fair when John A.'s own finances were in such a precarious state, and yet they had always depended on him. Margaret's husband, the Professor, also made requests, although his were mostly for professional reasons. The Observatory at Queen's was in need of support and what could John A. do towards obtaining funds?

The timing of the Macdonald family's requests also probably struck Agnes as occasionally almost ludicrous. Shortly after her marriage, when John A. was deep in the final stages of seeing the British North America Act passed, one of his commissions was to buy garden seeds for the Professor and get them to Canada in time for the early planting. Just after the 1873 fall of the Macdonald Government, John A. even had to advise Margaret on how to keep a maid: 'Say to the girl "Now your wages are so & so. If we get on well together & I find you with me on say 1 June next, I will make you a present of say $10 (or any other sum.)". . .Try this plan.'[32]

Somehow, Agnes apparently managed to avoid comment. The only time she ever seems to have offered any advice to the Kingston relatives was in the spring of 1875. Margaret had been ill during the winter, and Agnes, worried about her living out at Heathfield, some miles from Kingston, suggested that the Williamsons and Louisa, who lived with them, go to a good boarding house in town for the coming winter. Despite John A.'s agreement, this advice was not taken. Margaret died in the spring of 1876, and only then did the Professor and Louisa consent to leave Heathfield. John A. and the Professor carried on a long correspondence about erecting a suitable tombstone for Margaret. When a decision was finally taken, it was, naturally, John A. who paid.

Margaret's death affected John A. in another, more serious way — although only temporarily. It reminded him that he was almost sixty years old and increased his resolve to free himself from the stress of politics. Two-and-a-half years earlier, at the time of the Pacific Scandal, he had made up his mind to retire from politics for good. Then, as on previous occasions, he had been persuaded that his departure would mean the complete collapse of a badly shaken party, so he had stayed on, although hinting that his doing so was only a temporary measure. During the Sessions of 1874 and 1875, he had held aloof, finding being in Opposition first relaxing and then, possibly, rather boring. In the spring of 1876, shaken by Margaret's death, he determined that he would leave the political arena for younger men and concentrate on his law practice.

Agnes must have had her doubts about this resolve. She had been his wife for long enough to know that, in truth, he was no nearer to quitting than he had ever been. Politics had been his life for too long for him to think seriously of any other full-time vocation. For years he had come to grips with Canada's problems, and she knew that it must be frustrating for him to see Mackenzie (who had been and still was, in the opinion of many, a good stone mason but not a builder of a Dominion) making so little progress. He was not even a good Cabinet maker, John A. observed early in 1874 when the new Prime Minister was having difficulty in putting together his first Cabinet.

By the spring of 1876, even as Agnes was planning her garden for the fine, new home in Toronto, John A. saw that he must get back into the political ring. The Mackenzie Government had sown disharmony in so many segments of Canadian society while its positive accomplishments had been so few. The question was only how to make his comeback?

The answer came in the form of an invitation to speak on behalf of candidates for bye-elections at two political rallies in early July. The form of the rallies — political picnics, which were something new — seemed ideal to him. What could be pleasanter than spending some time in a shady park, talking to potential Conservative supporters while enjoying the best of good food and drink?

The first picnic was at Uxbridge, north-east of Toronto, on Dominion

Day, 1876. The holiday mood infected the three or four hundred supporters who accompanied John A. and Agnes from Toronto by train. From the station, they all walked to the park to the beat of two brass bands. And the picnic! The tables were piled high with every imaginable delicacy; there was lemonade and plenty of wine. John A. was in his element, moving from table to table.

As Agnes saw him move from group to group, so effortlessly, so happily, she must have been certain that the die was cast, that it would not be long before her husband's life — and, therefore, hers — was once more centred on Ottawa. What were her thoughts on this occasion? There is no record of them, but they must have been very mixed. Surely she felt pride in seeing John A. regain his old verve, obviously because he was back in his proper element. Surely, too, there was disappointment; she had just finished settling the family into a very fine, comfortable home — were they to have to think of leaving it already? On the other hand, Agnes may have missed the Ottawa scene more than she had thought she would. Her whole married life from 1867 to 1875 had been spent where she could be an avid observer of the political scene from her Gallery seat. On the few occasions, such as the Uxbridge picnic, when she again found herself in the realm of politics, she probably realized how much a part of her own life it had become. It was going to be like that again, she was convinced, and she was quite right.

The two bye-elections were won as a result of John A.'s picnic appearances, and he was asked to speak on behalf of every Conservative candidate in the rash of bye-elections held that summer.[33] By the end of 1876, as a result of his trips, Mackenzie's majority had been reduced by fourteen seats.

The Macdonald family supported John A.'s re-emergence in the political arena as joyfully as did the people and Conservative politicians. The Professor wrote to say how sorry he was that he and Louisa could not have gone to a rally-picnic at Belleville, but Louisa had become ill at the last minute. Hugh, too, never one to hold a grudge against his father, wrote to offer his humble and hearty congratulations. Agnes stood at John A.'s side as often as possible. Since there was clearly no time for a family summer vacation in Rivière du Loup, she took Mary and the nurses down to Coburg. There, her little girl could be out of the Toronto heat, and she had access to easy transportation for joining her husband as he travelled from picnic to picnic.

The trips continued throughout most of the following year, finishing in late October, 1877, with a triumphant rally in Hamilton. There, a local paper recounted,

Among the incidents of the march, the most touching was the presentation of a bunch of flowers to Lady Macdonald by six small children. . . . On the platform Lady Macdonald was the recipient of a second gift and in this instance the donors were adults. Mr. Clark, a working-man, on behalf of the working-men of the city, presented the lady with a gold necklace and pendant and a very handsome piece of jewellery it seemed to be.[34]

Possibly in order to save her husband's voice, which Agnes was very worried to find hoarse from fatigue, she summoned up enough courage to say her own 'thank you' in what John A. later referred to as quite a nice speech. She had come a long way from the time in 1868 when the 'good people of Kingston' had given her a piano and although she had read a reply of thanks, she had admitted that '. . . if I had not been half dead with nervousness, I should have been quite delighted with myself'.[35] Even in 1872, when the Toronto Trades Assembly had presented Agnes with a fine gold casket, she had not been ready to face the large audience, and it had been John A. who replied on her behalf, using the opportunity for witty political comment: 'I am a working man myself. . . and then I think I am a practical mechanic. If you look at the Confederation Act. . . you will see that I am a pretty good joiner; and as for Cabinet-making. . . I have had much experience.'[36]

Now Agnes was ready, and so was John A. When the House opened in February, 1878, it was clear to all that nothing was being done there, no legislation was being passed. Something would have to happen to get the country out of this state of inaction. By September, 1878, it had happened: an election had been fought and easily won by the Conservatives. John A. was back at his old trade of Cabinet maker, and Agnes was packing up, once more.

The Macdonalds packed to return to Ottawa in triumph in the fall of
1878, but Agnes found it very hard to leave 63 St. George Street. She had
lavished time and attention on this house they had lived in for two short
years. Now, just when the garden was responding to her care and the
trees were showing signs of growth, she had to leave. How many times
must they move? Could they never stay in one place more than a few
years?

Back in Ottawa, the Macdonalds were lucky in finding a large stone
house on Laurier Avenue East for rent. Here, in Stadacona Hall, Agnes
was able to make a home which suited their needs very well: it was large
enough for the entertaining that would again play an essential part in
their lives; there was some space that she could have converted into
offices for John A. and his staff; and the fact that it was in the familiar
neighbourhood of Sandy Hill was very satisfying. Agnes, by this time,
was becoming more and more expert at getting her family settled in the
shortest possible time. Too, the size of the household had shrunk:
Theodora was missing from the always close family, and Hewitt had, for
some years, been living in an apartment of his own. (Indeed, by 1878, he
was hardly ever in Ottawa, since he had retired a year or two earlier and
taken to spending most of the year in a warmer climate.)

As Agnes went about all the chores involved in moving back to
Ottawa, she must have deplored the fact that her return was more or less
coinciding with the Dufferins' departure from Rideau Hall. When the
Macdonalds arrived in the capital, Lady Dufferin and the children had
already gone and one of the Governor-General's last public acts was
swearing in John A. as Prime Minister on October 17, 1878. John A. and
Agnes had enjoyed an easy relationship with this young, out-going Vice-
Regal couple, who had been such a contrast to their predecessors, the
Youngs. From Lady Dufferin's arrival, in 1872, Agnes had found her
visits to Rideau Hall were no longer stifled by the atmosphere there.
Lady Dufferin did not lie about on chintz-covered sofas in hyacinth-

scented, overheated rooms, but was very active.

The diaries of both women suggest a genuine friendship grew up between them, and during the years before John A. and Agnes moved to Toronto, there had been much interchange between the occupants of Rideau Hall and those of the house on Chapel Street. Besides sharing many political problems and formal social occasions, the Macdonald and Dufferin households had come together for many informal pleasures. One had been tobogganing — that winter sport which Agnes had so enjoyed as a young lady in Quebec. Of course, as the wife of the Prime Minister she was too dignified to participate in it any more, but she could be an interested observer. During her earliest days in Ottawa, after a luncheon with the Moncks, she had gone out with her hostess to watch a toboggan party which was 'a rather picturesque sight. The dresses, too, are more or less picturesque spots of crimson, scarlet, purple, blue [which] show up well on a white surrounding and as Lady Monck and I stood on the bank above the sounds of merry talking and laughter came pleasantly up.'[1] When the Dufferins had been at Rideau Hall, the sport had reappeared with even greater gusto. Whether or not Agnes ever had the joy of another ride down a snowy slope is not known, but she certainly had plenty of opportunity to be an envious on-looker in the Vice-Regal grounds.

Mary, too, had often shared in Rideau Hall's entertainments, at least those held indoors. When Agnes and Mary had joined John A. in Ottawa for the 1877-78 Session, Agnes had been so delighted that Mary could go, once more, to see the Dufferin children, assisted by the children of the ADC's, putting on their annual plays. Sadly, all that Mary had been able to do was watch, but it had been a pleasure for Agnes to see how much her daughter enjoyed these little presentations. Mary had been able to take an active part, however, in a church bazaar that Lady Dufferin organized in Rideau Hall in the early summer of 1878. Among the various activities, stalls had been set up in the garden, and 'Miss Mary Macdonald sold flowers, and various young ladies had raffle-papers to fill up. Miss Macdonald and Nellie had the principal stall.'[2] (It was undoubtedly only with the help of the Dufferin's daughter, Nellie, that Mary could have managed to do this little charity work.)

With such pleasant memories of the Dufferins, Agnes, like most of Ottawa society, must have been somewhat apprehensive about their successors. The new Governor-General was the Marquis of Lorne; Canadians had no concern about him, but his wife might be a different story. She was the Princess Louise, Marchioness of Lorne, and the daughter of Queen Victoria. After Victoria was widowed, rumour had it that she had become a cold, difficult person who insisted on protocol as a cushion against the world. What would her daughter be like? Would the limited society of Ottawa have to adjust to a new pattern at Rideau Hall? Was it all to change from the open, friendly tenure of the Dufferins?

Ottawans were kept in suspense for a few weeks while Princess Louise was doing just as Agnes was doing – seeing to the arrangements of her new home. They were given their first glimpse of the Princess as she drove through the snowy streets of the capital on her way to the opening of Parliament on February 13, 1879. Agnes had long since stopped keeping her diary, so it is not known how she first reacted to Princess Louise, but soon she, like everyone else, found out that life in and around Rideau Hall was not going to change. The Lorne theatricals may have lacked a little of the verve that had been typical of the talented Dufferins, but the new Governor-General and his royal wife were as enthusiastic about winter sports as were their predecessors. They tobogganed and skated (with or without guests) as the Dufferins had done, and later they, too, enjoyed salmon fishing in New Brunswick. All in all, they turned out to be less formidable than had been expected and Ottawa could relax!

The Session of 1879 was busy but productive. John A., back as Prime Minister with strong Commons support, was working to accomplish his two overwhelming desires. He wished to see the C.P.R. completed as soon as possible and he wanted to put into effect the National Policy[3] that he had long advocated. When he had selected his Cabinet in 1878, he proved that he was, indeed, a 'good Cabinet-maker'. Charles Tupper, long-time confederate of John A. and a staunch supporter of the railway, became Minister of Public Works, where he could use his reputation as a staunch supporter of the railway. Tilley, as Minister of Finance, would introduce new tariff regulations to bring in part of the money needed to build the line. John A. served as his own Minister of the Interior; his role there was to encourage the settlement of the West. Without a large increase in inhabitants to hold the country beyond Winnipeg, there would be no economic justification for the railway at all. The three strong men who had worked together for so long were now united in the biggest scheme since Confederation. And they knew that, if the money could be found, it was generally a popular scheme. Indeed, persons, like the Dufferins, who had travelled to British Columbia in the previous year or two reported that settlers already in the West had become angry with the Mackenzie Government's failure to push ahead with the promised project that would unite the country physically.[4]

Planning, which went forward very well under John A.'s new government, was one thing, but money was another. No one supposed that any tax scheme could support such a huge undertaking. So, in the summer of 1879, John A. made plans for a trip to England, where he hoped, among other things, to 'sell' the British Government on the idea of the projected line being a safe route to the British colonies in the Orient.

The trip was not to be all work; indeed much social activity was planned, for Agnes was going, too. It would be the couple's first visit to England since 1867 and there was great excitement as preparations were made. First of all, Mary's summer had to be worked out. The doctors did not think it safe for her to make the long voyage, so she was taken down to the cottage where, as her father wrote Louisa, 'She is much better at R. du Loup where she has Sarah and Oswald, two very good women with her and Miss Reynolds next door.'[5]

After getting her daughter settled, Agnes sailed to England, but alone. John A. had cholera and had to remain in his bed in Ottawa for a couple of weeks until he was fit to travel. By August 4, however, he was with Agnes in Batt's Hotel on Dover Street, London.

Throughout the visit, John A. and Agnes combined business and pleasure as often as possible. On their first weekend together, they accepted an invitation from Sir John and Lady Rose to Losely Park, their home in Surrey. It was ten years since Sir John had left Canadian politics to enter a British banking house, but Agnes had memories of her first impressions of Charlotte Rose. As a bride, Agnes had not approved of her, remarking once, '[She] has a cosy yet cutting smile — she is really good I know, but somehow seems worldly',[6] and again 'she is so clever but her stories savor of such worldliness that I feel she is dangerous.'[7] At that time, it had only been at John A.'s insistence that Agnes had consented to invite Mrs. Rose to the Quadrilateral. Many years and much suffering had softened Agnes, and she now found that she very much enjoyed her weekend at Losely Park.

Indeed, Agnes enjoyed almost everything on this trip — seeing the places she had not seen for over twelve years, meeting her old friends and, especially, being reunited with her cousins, Annie Broome and Louisa Scott, both of whom happened to be in London for a time. There was much to catch up on, especially with Annie, who had had many adventures since their last meeting. Her husband's sheep farming venture in New Zealand had not succeeded, and they had returned to London in 1869, where Annie had tried her hand at many things, including expanding her work as a writer and taking on the post of Lady Superintendent of the National School of Cookery. Then her husband became restless once more and in 1875 they had moved to Natal. In 1879, they, like Agnes, were probably home on a visit.

It was interesting for John A. to see Agnes with her 'two charming cousins.... The three are very alike and standing together make a very distingué group', he wrote to his sister, Louisa. 'Agnes has been enjoying herself immensely.'[8] He also told his sister that 'It would amuse you to see how Agnes swells it & I like to see it.'[9] He was very possibly pleased to see how much Agnes had changed since their days in London in 1867. Then, although she had been socially at ease, she had been a rather harsh-judging member of society. Now she had changed into a more sophisticated person herself and was able to adapt to the demands on her time and his with more good grace — and with evident enjoyment.

There were many occasions for Agnes to 'swell it'. Besides the weekend with the Roses, the Macdonalds were invited to

> . . . stay with the Earl of Carnarvon. . . at Highclere Castle, one of the swellest places in England. We intend to go to Mr. Bouveries, son of the Earl of Radnor and instead of sailing from Liverpool shall go to Ireland and sail from Londonderry. This will enable us to spend a few days between Lord Monck's and Lord Dufferin's. . . . We intend to visit Lady Lisgar at Bosworth Park.[10]

Not all of these invitations could be accepted because of changes in John A.'s schedule. For one thing, there was a summons from Queen Victoria, bidding him to go down to Osborne, on the Isle of Wight, to be sworn in as a Privy Councillor in formal recognition of the role he had played in the 1871 Washington Conference. Agnes spent the day in London, and John A., now the Right Honourable, was back in time for dinner with her and her cousins.

In between business meetings and country weekends, John A. and Agnes attended the theatre and went to church. 'St. Paul's in the morning, St. Alban's, High Holborn in the evening with Agnes, who also went to Westminster Abbey at 3 p.m.',[11] read John A.'s diary for August 24. They also spent some time in the shops. Agnes seems to have kept her personal expenditures rather modest; the only extant bill is for a 'Reduced Silk French Model Dress at 28½ gns. [plus some gloves and ribbons].'[12] Assuredly she did buy more clothes, but her main purchases were for the house. For the first time in years, the family finances were on a firm footing and she could indulge in new dinner-ware and crystal.

It was just as well that Agnes had such an enjoyable summer, for during the fall she became seriously worried about John A.'s health. In England he had seemed fine and in good spirits, but now she began to wonder if he had completely recovered from the summer's cholera attack. He kept going, but the winter was very busy, socially and politically. Under the strain, he collapsed one Sunday during the morning service at St. Alban's. His doctor offered no great comfort or advice on the illness, saying John A. was just suffering from old age. Remembering how much he had enjoyed London, Agnes suggested he try the recuperative powers of another trip.

This time it did not work. He did too much business in England, and although, on his return, he assured his family that he did feel much better, he was still not in good health. By December, 1880, when the House opened early, John A. was not well enough to attend. On orders of Dr. Grant and at Agnes' insistence, he was keeping very quiet. During the Session, Agnes became her husband's 'ears', reporting the happenings in the House to him as wives of the Governors-General had always done for their husbands. She was well prepared to fill this role for, from the beginning, she had often watched the debates from the Gallery, no matter how heated the argument. (There is only one record of her having broken the decorum expected of her there. During the 1878 Session, she had been annoyed by a debacle over the choice of a new Speaker and, reportedly, 'stamped her foot angrily and exclaimed aloud, 'Did ever any person see such tactics!'[13] She was usually able to keep her peace, at least until she got outside the House, but, that one time, she had apparently become so wrapped up in the heated debate that she let her emotions take over.)

Despite all the efforts of Agnes and others to spare John A., when Parliament prorogued late in March, 1881, he was more or less broken down. Some days he was well enough to go to the office; others, Agnes felt she had to insist he must remain at home and let the Cabinet come to him.

Throughout these months, Agnes became more and more disenchanted with the advice given by Dr. Grant, who did not seem able to diagnose John A.'s illness and who, she felt, had a depressing effect on his patient, always finding some new symptom that suggested another complaint. A family conference was called, which both Louisa and Hugh attended. When Louisa saw her brother, she was shocked. 'I never saw John looking what I call old until this time. His hair is getting quite grey',[14] she told a concerned Professor Williamson. In fact, she thought that if the doctor told John A. he was too weak, he would just give up. After the family discussion, Louisa and Hugh supported Agnes in a decision that John A. should go back to England and seek other medical advice there.

John A. agreed, reluctantly, and Agnes called on Hewitt to accompany her and her ailing husband to London. If the worst happened, if John A. did not get better, she would have need of her brother's support. Hewitt would also be good company for John A. if, as was to be hoped, he would soon feel better in the English atmosphere but would have to take life a bit easy all the same. Perhaps in this same eventuality, and, possibly, to provide herself with some female company, Agnes invited her nineteen-year-old niece, May Bernard, to join the party.

By late May, 1881, they were established, once more, in Batt's Hotel, and soon they had the opinion of an English doctor, who diagnosed John A.'s condition as being catarrh of the stomach and a touch of gout. Agnes was relieved to learn that if her husband paid strict attention to his diet and got plenty of rest, he should soon improve.

It did not prove easy for her to insist on these instructions being obeyed. As soon as John A. was feeling better, he started holding discussions with British colleagues, and, to save him from this, Agnes and Hewitt began to look for a place somewhat less accessible than the hotel. Soon they found what they were sure was a suitable house in Upper Norwood, on the outskirts of London, near the Crystal Palace, where they envisaged John A. taking leisurely strolls in the grounds. They all moved out there, and for a short time John A. was co-operative. Then the invitations began to come in. They could not refuse a luncheon invitation from Princess Louise, who was in England for the summer. Neither could they turn down a dinner invitation from the Duke of Argyll, the father of Lord Lorne. Soon they were back in the social whirl, going to dinners, to the theatre, to garden parties and to State functions. They took trips to Canterbury, to Tunbridge Wells, and to other near-by centres of historic interest, and, in late July, they went to Wimbledon to congratulate the victorious Canadian Rifle Team.

John A.'s health did not suffer from this renewed activity, and Agnes was so relieved that she did not try to restrain his social life. She, herself, was busily making up for her abstemious behaviour in 1879 when she had shopped only for the house. This time, soon after they arrived in London, she began to replenish her wardrobe. She went to Harris and Toms for a pair of French corsets and a black straw hat trimmed with white lace, as her first purchases, and then she added several new dresses as occasions for them arose. She shopped, too, for her young niece. Aunt Agnes saw to it that May had a suitable wardrobe for the new society into which she was being introduced on this, her first trip to England. The shop on Cavendish Square produced dresses for day and evening, hats and feathers, bonnets, gloves, shoes and even the stylish 'dress improver' for the nineteen-year-old. Finally, there was only one more purchase needed — a tin-lined packing case to hold these new clothes,[15] and then the whole family was off back to Canada, all feeling better and happier for the trip.

When they got back to Stadacona Hall, there was the usual work awaiting them. As always in these years, much of John A.'s work was connected with the settlement of the West and the railroad. The great project was now moving ahead, with a company and some money (though never enough) backing it. John A.'s appeal for funds from the British Government in 1879 had been ill-timed, for it had been preparing for an election and he had only been able to obtain a note from Disraeli expressing interest. When John A. had returned to England the following year, theoretically for a rest, Disraeli was no longer in power, but discussions with Gladstone's Liberal Government had yielded a firm promise of financial backing. By October, 1880, a company had been formed with George Stephen as President. Stephen was a successful entrepreneur, a man of drive who accomplished what he set out to do, and John A. had so much confidence in him that the surprised delegates to a convention in November, 1881, heard the Prime Minister say the line would be completed in five years, not the ten promised British Columbia earlier.

The great project, however, made constant demands on John A.'s time and political skills. There was frequent uncertainty about railway finances, about whether or not the agreement with Stephen was the best that could have been worked out, about whether or not sufficient settlers could be enticed to western Canada. Years later Agnes was to write that John A. had told her, 'After Confederation. . . it was relatively plain sailing'. In retrospect, she continued, this period looked to her more like 'very difficult navigation in very troubled waters'.[16]

With a husband who was sixty-seven years old but determined to carry on political activities in troubled waters, Agnes searched for ways to make his life as easy as possible. They had neither the time nor money to go to England each summer, and even when they did go there, they also had to rent a house in Rivière du Loup so Mary could have her holiday, too. The time had come, Agnes thought, to buy a house of their own in the St. Lawrence resort. John A. might go down more often if he knew that he had his own office set up there, and it would be much easier for him to combine a little rest with the work he always brought on holidays if he were in his own home and not having to adjust to one rented place after another. So, in 1882, Agnes bought a large, rambling cottage from a Joseph Chouinard; today it is still referred to as the Macdonald House.[17] When Agnes bought it, the house was given the name of Les Rochers, apt because of its location among the crags that dot that pine-covered area beside the St. Lawrence. It was the very type of summer house that invites repose, with wide, open porches to sit on during the day and a large sitting room where a wood fire could blaze away when the evenings became chilly. The property was large enought to allow the residents good walks under the pines, yet it was only a short stroll down to the river to the salt-water bathing which Agnes, in particular, so much enjoyed.

Mary became very fond of the house. Sometimes she was carried down to the shore but, as a rule, she was content to sit in her chair on the big porch and watch the river traffic. Some member of the family was nearly always there to keep her company, sometimes more than one. When John A. was in residence, he spent part of each day in his miniature office, attending to business with his Secretary, but he also made time for reading and walking. In the evenings one or another of the neighbours would drop in. Not too long ago, an old resident of Rivière du Loup searched his memory of the days when the Macdonalds lived at Les Rochers and recalled: 'Sir John worked all morning, read or rested in the afternoon and several evenings a week would watch Lady Macdonald enjoying a game of bezique with Mr. (later Sir Henry) Bate and his wife. But Sir John never touched a card.'[18] (The old-timer seems to have forgotten that John A.'s favourite game was Patience, which always rested his mind, as Agnes had discovered.) On Sunday mornings, the Macdonald family could be found in the front pew of the community's little Anglican Church, and Agnes often helped with its bazaars, just as she did at St. Alban's in Ottawa. How pleased Agnes must have been to see that her plan really was working — John A. was relaxing more, and the family was able to spend more time together.

One family member who was missing in 1882 was Hugh. When his father and Agnes had returned to Ottawa in 1878, John A. had suggested that his son move back from Kingston to take on the work of the Toronto law office. Hugh, as always, now that time had healed the rift caused by his marriage to Jean King, had been ready to oblige his father. The young couple had moved into the house on St. George Street and had had three happy years there before Jean's sudden death in 1881. Like his father, he had had but short-lived happiness in his first marriage. Like his father, too, he was left with a small child — Daisy, who was then only four years old. The little girl was to spend much time with John A. and Agnes throughout her youth, in both Ottawa and Rivière du Loup, and often served as a companion to Mary.

In his desire to escape the sad environs of Toronto, Hugh, in 1882, took the advice of the mid-century American journalist who said 'Go west, young man, and grow up with the country'. He was not alone; some 20,000 young men of Ontario were lured beyond Winnipeg that year by the promise of fortunes to be made as the C.P.R. opened up the area. Hugh went not to speculate in land but to open a law office.

In the winter of 1883, Hugh came back East on a visit and stopped off in Toronto. When he reached Ottawa, his father and Agnes found he had brought along a guest and news for his family: he was going to remarry. His fiancée was Gertrude Vankoughnet, and she and her family were no strangers to the Macdonalds. In fact, during the 1850s when John A. and Isabella had lived in Toronto, young Hugh had often been sent to play in the Vankoughnet home and Gertrude's uncle, Philip Vankoughnet, had been an old friend and a colleague of John A.'s. So, this time, there was no family opposition to Hugh's choice. From Ottawa, Hugh went to Kingston to introduce Gertrude to Louisa and the Professor and, in advance of this visit, John A. wrote them, saying, 'Hugh will go up in a few days. . . . His intended is with us, an exceedingly nice girl. We are much pleased with her.'[19]

Another happy change came for the Macdonalds in 1882, although it began by looking like another worry. While they were down at Rivière du Loup, the owners of Stadacona Hall sent down a list of repairs they were willing to carry out. It was clear from this extensive list that the building was not in very good condition, but the disappointing part of the letter was that the owners had decided not to build the extra room that the Macdonalds had requested. Since they were obviously not going to get the additional space they felt they needed in the house on Laurier Avenue East, they began to consider other possibilities. The solution to their problem came surprisingly easily. Their friend Thomas Reynolds had died two years previously and his house, Earnscliffe, which had been their favourite Ottawa home, became available. In 1882, they bought it. Many years later, Agnes admitted that she had

> begged Sir John very hard before he would buy it. He was always thinking of me and a possible future without him and did not want to diminish his savings, by putting it into property.
>
> But I did want him to have a really nice comfortable home & *coaxed hard* & had the great satisfaction of knowing that he thoroughly liked & enjoyed the place. . . . It was a very wise purchase, made a delightful home for us.[20]

Agnes now had her family comfortably housed in both Rivière du Loup and Ottawa and surely she deserved a little peace in which to enjoy this new state of affairs. She didn't get it. In a renewed attempt to sow disharmony in Canada, 'yellow' newspapers in the United States carried a series of slanderous attacks not on John A. but on Agnes. The vicious rumours referred back to an incident in 1879 when Governor-General Lorne and John A. had supposedly disagreed over a ruling on a provincial matter.[21] Even then, these papers had circulated stories that Agnes had, in some way, been disrespectful to Princess Louise because of the 'disagreement'. At that time, John A. had written Lord Lorne to ask his advice as to whether or not a denial should be made, and Lorne's reply had been 'Certainly, if it is worth while to contradict such reports. There is no foundation whatever for the statements made.'[22] John A. had apparently felt, however, that it was better to ignore the rumour-mongers. In 1882, the stories reappeared, now claiming that relations between the two women were so bad that Princess Louise had been driven out of the country (she was on a trip to Bermuda at the time). Agnes was so upset that John A. wrote to Colonel de Winton, an A.D.C. at Government House, to express Agnes' and his concern. Soon he had not only a reply from Colonel de Winton, but a letter from Princess Louise, who wrote:

H.M.S. Dido, January 25, 1883

Dear Sir John.

I have been waiting to write to you ever since I saw those ill-natured articles in the papers against Lady Macdonald and myself, but His Excellency thought as they were such preposterous inventions I should leave it alone. Now, that you have written to Col. de Winton, I cannot help sending you a few lines, having received so much kindness from you and Lady Macdonald ever since I first came to Canada, and I have learned to look upon you both as friends that I made out there. It is, therefore, most annoying to me that such stories should have been circulated. To invent that I had a misunderstanding with your wife vexes me beyond measure.

You must know in how many ways I admire Lady Macdonald and think her a worthy example to every wife. . . .

Believe me, with kind remembrances to Lady Macdonald,

Yours very sincerely,

Louise[23]

When Joseph Pope wrote his biography of John A. in 1893, he published this letter in full, as well as the Prime Minister's reply:

Stadacona Hall, Ottawa, February 20, 1883

Madam,

I am honoured by the receipt of your gracious note, and can assure Your Royal Highness that I gratefully appreciate its kind condescension.

Your high position, while it does not altogether shield you from the base attacks of a degraded press, renders them powerless for harm and your Royal Highness can afford to treat them with the contempt they deserve. It is otherwise with Lady Macdonald, who has already proofs that these baseless calumnies have been widely disseminated and that some people have been willing to believe them simply because she happens to be my wife.

Lady Macdonald feels especially aggrieved at the imputation cast upon her of having failed in respect and duty towards your Royal Highness, from whom she has received such unvarying kindness. Both she and I are, however, more than compensated for the annoyance by the gracious letter sent us by Col. de Winton and we hope in good time to have the opportunity of personally tendering you our best thanks.

John A. Macdonald[24]

In publishing these two letters, Pope noted that he did so 'to illustrate the character of the relations which existed between Her Royal Highness and Sir John Macdonald during the whole period of Lord Lorne's administration in Canada.'[25] Furthermore, Pope, who had been John A.'s Private Secretary during part of Lorne's term of office, positively asserted that 'the relations between Government House and Earnscliffe were of the most friendly character during the whole period. Had there been the slightest truth in the story, it is incredible that such relations could have existed.'[26]

Had the letters been made public at the time they were written, Agnes might have been saved a lot of future grief, for the falsehood occasionally resurfaced to plague her the rest of her life.[27] In 1883, however, nothing more was said about the matter, and both John A. and Agnes were content in knowing, even if privately, that Princess Louise and Lord Lorne were as astonished as they that people could be so gullible as to believe such inventions.

Some months after this exchange of letters took place, Lord Lorne's five-year tour of duty in Canada came to an end. The new Governor-General, the Marquis of Lansdowne, was, like his predecessor, a comparatively young man, but John A. was feeling old. He was also conscious of the fact that he seemed to be surrounded by old men at a time when the affairs of Canada needed young blood. As early as the mid-1870s, he had given thought as to who should inherit his own mantle, and his attention had been caught by a young lawyer from Barrie, Dalton McCarthy. That McCarthy was also married to Agnes' sister-in-law, Richard's widow, had nothing to do with John A.'s choice of the young man. Agnes had learned long before not to intervene on behalf of friends or relatives. John A. had made it clear to her, within a few months of their marriage, that this was not done, and there is no evidence that she ever again had to write what her diary of December 1, 1868, recorded:

> A sad scene today — it is extremely painful being asked to beg John to interfere in getting places for my friends — especially for those I love and value. He is so just that I know it is distressing to be asked for what he does not think it right to give — and yet, I cannot refuse to do all in my power — legitimately for my good friends, those who in days gone by and in different circumstances were so good to me.[28]

In 1883, John A. tried to start 'grooming' the young McCarthy by offering him the post of Minister of Justice, but McCarthy refused, as he did, again, in 1884. His reasons were the same each time: he had a large family to support and the salary of a cabinet minister was not adequate. He would remain a Member of the House but had to be free to carry on his law practice.

John A. was disappointed in this; he was also not feeling well. His stomach was bothering him, and home remedies were not helping. Agnes, still suspicious of Dr. Grant, sent her husband to see a Montreal doctor whose 'prescription' was the old one: an overseas holiday. In early October, 1884, Agnes saw John A. off to London, and there he began, as always, to feel stronger.

While John A. was in England, Agnes did some travelling in Canada. For some time the couple had been worried about Louisa, whose health was beginning to fail. In order to keep John A. informed on his sister's condition, Agnes went to Kingston to see for herself, and what she saw was hardly encouraging. Her sister-in-law had obviously not benefitted from a summer holiday in Old Orchard Beach, and Agnes could not be reassuring when she next wrote to John A. Agnes also used the opportunity to renew her contacts with the few Bernard relatives she still had in Barrie. May was the only one of her two nieces she had seen for some time, and she was interested in seeing how Richard's other daughter was getting along. Dora had married a Barrie lawyer, Frank Pepler, in 1881, and by now there were babies to be seen, too. Earlier, Agnes had invited Dora and her husband to come to Ottawa for a visit, but the young mother had explained:

> to run away in the midst of work and daily duties would be a very bad thing
> for young people like us. The autumn is always a very busy time with women
> as well as men. I have to arrange a comfortable night nursery for the children,
> to see to their winter clothing, get up stores, put in double windows. I am so
> sorry. There is nothing I would have liked better.[29]

So, on her trip, Agnes stopped in Toronto, then continued to Barrie to see the young Peplers.

In late November, when Agnes and John A. were reunited after their journeys, one of the first items on their agenda was a large Conservative demonstration in Toronto, marking the occasion of his fortieth anniversary as a politician. Some 40,000 persons gathered for this great testimonial, and when John A. appeared on the platform at the Grand Opera House,

> [it] was the occasion of indescribable enthusiasm. The vast audience cheered
> itself hoarse, hats were thrown up, delegates rose in their seats, the banners
> from the dress circle fluttered, while. . . the fair ladies in the boxes waved their
> handkerchiefs. . . . The cheering was again and again taken up. . . . The tiger
> was given in due course.[30]

A few weeks later, there was another gala celebration, this one in Montreal, to mark John A.'s seventieth birthday. (Agnes had been in on the plans for it; G.A. Drummond, a Montreal banker and businessman, had asked her co-operation when John A. was away in London.) Montreal seems to have tried to outdo Toronto in the splendour of its festivities. From the moment Sir John and Agnes arrived on the evening of January 12, 1885, 'The City was in a blaze of illumination, and the enthusiasm never for a moment flagged. Sir John, Lady Macdonald and party were escorted through the streets by a torchlight procession. . . . The splendid dining-room of the Windsor was crowded to its utmost capacity.'[31]

John A.'s speech, possibly one of his best, began by reminding the audience that it had been in Montreal he began his political career and that it now gave him great pleasure to 'see. . . the population without distinction of race, or I might say of politics, surging along the streets of this magnificent city to show that even if they could not give [me] their political support, they appreciated the honest and earnest exertions of a public man.'[32] In closing, he reminded his audience that he had reached his three score years and ten and had nearly run his course. When there were the expected cries of 'No! No!', he quickly reassured them, and, giving credit where credit was surely due, added, 'Here I am, strong for my years. . . and, thanks to a kind providence and thanks to the great care of a good wife — (loud and enthusiastic cheering, the whole audience rising) — I feel as old Adam said, like a lusty winter, frosty but kindly.'[33]

To Agnes, these displays of warmth towards her husband must have seemed a fitting expression of gratitude for some of the many trials endured during those forty years, seventeen of which she had shared as his wife. John A.'s words of praise for her support and care must have warmed her heart.

He was not alone in recognizing the importance of her role. During the Toronto celebration, for example, she was unaware that, in the audience, Nicholas Flood Davin[34] was busily composing a sonnet about her:

Ah! dearer far than star a Queen may dower,
And dearer than the people's loud acclaim,
A noble woman's welcome and the power
Her touch can give whose life is void of blame.
We build men statues; did but Justice speak
She'd say: Do likewise for those gentler lives
Who, hid away from public gaze, but seek
The selfless guerdon won by faithful wives —
To do all one can do, all patience can,
And be the day star of the work-worn, weary man.[35]

Agnes' reactions to these lines are unknown, which is possibly just as well as far as their poetical style is concerned. It is to be hoped, though, that she realized the justification behind Davin's tribute. She had begun her seventeen years of married life with so many doubts as to her capabilities, so many qualms as to her own worth. Now, in 1884, through a series of compromises with herself and her world, she was at peace with her life. She had even accepted the fact that her only child was to be a life-long invalid. The important thing was that, for some time, she had enjoyed great personal happiness as John A.'s wife and that, as always, she felt great pride in him as a consummate politician.

While Agnes had beamed with justifiable pride as she saw how warmly her husband had been received in the capitals of both English and French Canada, she knew, as well as he, that there were many battles yet to come and that he would fight them to the end. The Montreal and Toronto commemorative celebrations had been exciting tributes, but their euphoria could not hide the challenges that lay before him in early 1885. The times were not good: the boom of even three years earlier was over, and, in spite of what John A. had said — or left unsaid — in Montreal, Dominion-Provincial relations were steadily worsening. Foreign relations, too, were causing concern, with the United States fishery question once more at the top of the list, while, at home, the C.P.R. was still coming cap-in-hand. The railway was by now so near completion that it must not die for lack of funds, and yet it seemed to some that John A. was 'making haste slowly'. John A. himself knew exactly what he was doing, and Agnes noted that 'step by step, here a little and there a little in his own peculiar light good-humoured way. . .',[1] John A. was handling the situation. As always, he had his own strategy.

One of his projects in early 1885 was to get a Franchise Bill passed. He had introduced it into two other Parliaments, without success, but by July, 1885, it was finally accepted after a hard debate. Agnes must have been glad to see the last of it, and this raises an interesting point, for it extended the rights of only male citizens.[2] During the 1880s there was limited agitation from some Canadian women seeking political equality with their husbands, brothers and fathers, but Agnes was not of this persuasion. Indeed, she had very definite views on women being too interested in politics. It was all right to be a spectator, it was all right to play a supportive role, but to become an active participant was going too far, she thought.

In March, 1868, for example, after a dinner party in Ottawa, she wrote in her diary:

the talk at dinner very bright and after very chatty. Politics, of course, but not too much. Sandfield [Macdonald] says he likes politically inclined women. I do in great moderation but too much of anything approaching too much is out of most women's sphere. If a woman gives too much attention to politics, I think she becomes too violent a partisan and is apt to ride her hobby to death and then a softening influence is needed — which we ought to try and spread.[3]

A few months later, she wrote that she did not wish to become too political even in her reading, adding, 'so few women are clever, consistent and intriguing enough to make useful use of political knowledge and bias and when they are too amateur in it, they are bores — or make mischief — so it seems to me.'[4] In her opinion, which was quite typical of her time, it was better to be, as Davin had written of her during the Toronto celebrations, 'the day star of the workworn, weary, man'.[5]

In the summer of 1885, Agnes' 'work-worn, weary man' was primarily concerned about the Northwest. The promise he had made in 1881 that the railway would go through in five years, not ten, had seemed likely to be fulfilled. Indeed, during the banquet in Toronto in the previous December, a telegram had been received which read:

December 18, 1884. End of Track B.C. Ten days ago the first crossing of the Columbia River was effected, and ere this reaches you the iron horse will be eleven miles further west, and it is now beyond a doubt that a junction will be effected with construction. . . from the Pacific early in October next.[6]

Soon after, however, George Stephen, the company head in whom John A. had so much faith, had run into trouble and called out for more financial aid, which he feared might come too late to help.

Then the unexpected happened. In July, 1884, Riel had re-entered the picture. This time he had moved into the Prince Albert area, where his own people, the Métis, had already given the Lieutenant-Governor of the Northwest Territories, Edgar Dewdney, cause to keep a sharp eye on their actions. To start with, Riel had, seemingly, only advocated that the Métis seek a legal solution to their cry that they were being deprived of their lands.[7] Soon, however, rumours began to come out of the West to the effect that Riel was demanding huge sums as personal recompense for past injustices, and was representing himself as the new David who, after years of exile, had come back to lead his people. Members of the Riel family claim that the true story of their famous relative has yet to be written; certainly, it is hard to find an unbiased account of what happened in the Northwest in 1885.

Whatever the truth about Riel's goals, he managed to stir up the Métis, then virtually retired, leaving his cousin, Gabriel Dumont, to lead the warring half-breeds and Indians. In March, 1885, the Federal Government had to send out a force of some 3,500 men to counter the rebellion. Although they were poorly equipped and, for the most part, poorly trained, they managed to put down the insurrection within two months of their arrival in the Northwest. Dumont fled to the United States, but Riel was taken prisoner and, on May 23, entered a prison cell in a Regina jail, a dejected figure, failed by his God and his fellow men. It was only a matter of time before he would be hanged.

One of the ironies of this strange, bitter incident is that had it not occurred, the final funding of the C.P.R. would probably have been still further delayed. Canada's westward expansion had always been helped in the most curious ways, by pressures from without and from within. When the troops were sent to Saskatchewan, the existing lines of the C.P.R. were used to get them there. This, John A. thought, was a powerful argument for the usefulness of the line and the need to pay for the completion that was within reach. Despite what must have been Agnes' many injunctions to avoid overtiring himself, he pursued his quest of financial aid with all the power he could muster, despite the delaying tactics of the Opposition. Finally, he succeeded in getting help from the English banking firm, Baring, which guaranteed a new C.P.R. bond issue, and the work could be speeded on to its conclusion. On November 7, 1885, the final spike was driven — not a gold one but a plain iron one like all the rest that had been put into place during the years and years of hard struggle when little more than the faith of the Conservative Prime Minister had kept the project alive.

Ironically, it was not that man of faith and vision who drove that last spike, but one of his enemies, Donald Smith, the man whose lack of support for John A. had brought down the Conservative Government at the time of the Pacific Scandal, the man whom John A. had called, after a quarrel on the floor of the House in 1878, 'the biggest liar I ever met'.[8] Agnes may or may not have heard this exchange in person, but years later, thirty years later, when Donald Smith, then Lord Strathcona and one of her greatest friends, was advising her on matters of personal finance, she wrote to Pope saying, 'How strange the wheel of life goes round! That the day is here in which Donald Smith is such a kind friend to me.'[9]

In 1885, Donald Smith was no kind personal friend to either Agnes or John A. Yet, the Prime Minister would have had to agree that, without Smith's financial support for the railway in 1884, when he had pledged even his household goods, the project would have faltered and the final 1885 bond issue would never have been raised. (Smith's actions were motivated out of gratitude, not to John A., but to Canada, where he was in the way of making a fortune. Another factor, undoubtedly, was that the builder of the line, George Stephen, was his cousin.)

It was not by plan, however, that Smith drove in the last spike. By an ironic twist of fate, *finis* was being written to the building of the C.P.R. and to the Riel Rebellion almost simultaneously. Public opinion was running so high on the latter situation that Governor-General Landsdowne, who had been in the West and had been expected to officiate at the simple ceremony at Craigellachie, British Columbia, was forced to rush back to Ottawa. John A. could not leave the capital for the same reason. Some directors of the railroad were in Craigellachie, however, and, by common consent, Donald Smith, being the eldest director present at the site, was given the honour of bringing down the hammer that signified the completion of the line.[10]

Across the land, public attention was concentrated more on the Riel case than on the C.P.R. Riel's appeal for clemency (on the grounds of diminished responsibility) had been dismissed by the Queen, and the decision of the Canadian Cabinet had been that he should be hanged. That sentence was carried out on November 16, 1885. It happened so close to the driving of the last spike in the C.P.R. that the latter event was obscured. An occasion of great national joy was overshadowed by one that aroused the passions of Quebec, which was largely in sympathy with the late Métis leader. The Federal Government feared that it was in for lively times in its relations with that province.

John A. accepted this possibility, and, although he made no concession, he did not let it influence his plans to go to England for a holiday, leaving in late November. He would normally have sailed from either Montreal or Quebec City, but instead he chose to go from the remote port of Rimouski. This kept him well away from potential trouble areas and, also, allowed him to have the company of his wife and daughter part of the way. Agnes and Mary were off for a little trip of their own into the Maritimes, and, as soon as they saw John A. safely on board ship, their path turned south in the comfort of a private railroad car. (The C.P.R. put a car at Agnes' disposal for this and the many subsequent trips she was to make in Canada.)

After Mary got back to Ottawa, she wrote about this trip to her father, who was still in England:

> We had a lovely trip after we left you. We were down at Halifax and St. John. . . . Have you seen Her Majesty the Queen? Do you remember what you told me last year about kissing her hand?
>
> It is very cold here now. I suppose it is not so cold in England? What are you going to do on Christmas Day? I will miss you very much.[11]

At the close of her letter, which was written just before Christmas, Mary added, 'Mamma is away just now and how long she is going to stay I do not know.'[12] Agnes was indeed away, fulfilling a long-awaited dream. For years she had wanted to see the Rockies and the West Coast. Lord and Lady Dufferin's reports of their trip there in 1877 and, more recently, stories told by Lord Lansdowne, who had travelled all the way to the Pacific on Canadian soil, had further whetted her enthusiasm for seeing the area for herself. Now that her husband's vision of the C.P.R. was reality, she could no longer wait.

Before leaving, she had to make arrangements for Mary's care, which, as always, included provision for her social life, especially during the holiday period. Christmas Day itself would be spent with the family of some of the household servants. John A.'s birthday, which was always a day of celebration for the Macdonalds, whether he was there or not, involved special plans, which show that Agnes was no longer treating her daughter as a child but as a young lady. Neither parent would be back in time to share January 11 with Mary, so, as Agnes later wrote to her sister-in-law, Louisa, '[Mary] gave a little ball in honour of her father's birthday & had over 80 guests. No children this time for she is so nearly 17! I arranged all her plans before I left for the North West, sent out the invitations & asked two ladies to help Mary receive.'[13]

With the knowledge that Mary was being looked after and that John A. was enjoying himself in England, casting off some of the cares of office, Agnes was able to enjoy her own trip fully. It seems to have been an unqualified success. After she and John A. were both back home, she wrote Louisa:

As for me I have been to the summit of the Canadian Rocky Mountains by C.P.R.... It was by far the most interesting and delightful trip I ever made in my life. I asked Judge & Mrs. Brooks[14] to go as my guests & took a butler & maid & we had besides a car porter who is also cook.... We started off quietly, very few had any idea I was going away at all....

We were absent 16 days and nights, spent 2 days & 2 nights at Winnipeg, two more at Canmore (in the mountains) & half a day & night at Port Arthur & travelled all the rest. Every day was a pleasure & a new interest....

The C.P.R. were ever so good to me. Mr. Van Horne[15] said I might go where I liked.... Altogether it was too delightful.

What astonished me was the comfort & ease of the railway, its strict punctuality, its quiet & prompt management & its little motion. We read, played games, wrote letters, all generally with great ease & this on a line far away in an almost uninhabited country & in depth of a Canadian winter....

Ottawa seems so dull & tame & stupid & *old* after that wonderful new western world with its breadth & length & clear air & wonderfully exhilirating atmosphere that always seems to lure me on!...

We were only 500 miles from the Pacific but I had to hurry homeward to meet Sir John....

It has done me ever so much good. I feel a new person. Constantly nursing the sick & housekeeping in Ottawa for a large household & looking after all sorts of things daily for almost two years *is* fatiguing. . . .

Goodnight dear Aunt Lou. . . . Sir John is sound asleep or he would send a lot of love.[16]

Agnes' verbal account of the trip and what it was like to have actually seen the Rockies must have been equally enthusiastic, for she told Louisa that John A. was '. . . quite pleased with my visit to the west & shall never rest till he too goes!'[17]

John A. did want very much to see that part of Canada which he had previously 'seen' only on surveyors' and engineers' maps and charts and through Agnes' eyes, but he had to wait six months before he could make the trip. Then he was able to have it serve two purposes: satisfying his own curiosity and serving as a campaign trail — all the way from Ottawa to Vancouver — for the elections planned for the winter of 1887.

On July 6, Agnes wrote to C.P.R. General Manager Van Horne to confirm the plans for this historic trip: 'According to your kind permission given some time ago, Sir John and I hope to leave by the Saturday night's train for the Pacific coast. I am so delighted about it that I can think of nothing else.'[18] In order to be keeping their arrangements as much as secret as possible, Agnes wrote across the front page of this letter, 'As usual our plans are private, and, Of course, by regular train'.[19]

It was July 10 before the Prime Minister's party got away. They had missed the first passenger service from Montreal to the western terminus at Port Moody by only a few days, but, in John A.'s opinion, this was an advantage. Their train could make a 'whistle stop' whenever he felt it politically expedient to do so; they were not just among the group of officials on the first 'run'.

This trip gave Agnes a wonderful opportunity to try her hand at writing once more. The intermittent diary entries had long since ceased and, apparently, so had the occasional 'scribbling' she had referred to in them. (None of this writing exists today, and it may not have included much of literary value.) There had been long 'stories' to Aunt Mary Mayne in Dublin, and, after her Nova Scotia trip in the summer of 1868, Agnes had noted in her diary, 'I have written six close sheets of letter to dear Mrs._____ who, I know, will like my long Nova Scotian story.'[20] Apart from these detailed accounts of her life and travels, written to family or friends, there had been at least one time when Agnes had had an idea for a story. Thinking it out one night, before falling asleep, she had told the plot to John A., who, apparently, had not been enthusiastic, for 'he wanted to know if the title ["Wasted"] would apply to the reader's time!'[21] Thus rebuffed, she had put away her pen except for family letters. Now she would take it up again.

As with the diary she had started at the beginning of her married life, so it would be with her account of the 1886 trip to the West: both were records of new experiences, exciting and stimulating. The differences between the two attempts at writing are interesting and suggestive. Her diary entries had been kept under lock, and even then she had admitted self-censorship. Now she wrote openly, uncurbed by John A.'s position. And she wrote for publication — her report of this trip, 'By Car and by Cowcatcher', was printed by *Murray's Magazine* in London and was so successful that, for the next few years, Agnes became a regular contributor to that periodical. It seems that, at last, Agnes felt free to express herself, for she wrote under her own name for a magazine that would, she knew, be read not only in England but also in Canada.

Joseph Pope, in his capacity as Private Secretary, went along on the trip, and he, too, wrote about it but, in his diary, not for publication,[22] so his account is more concerned with plain facts. In his precise manner, he tells us that 'Our party consisted of Sir John and Lady Macdonald, Fred White,[23] George Johnson of the *Mail* staff, myself, and two servants — old Ben Chilton, Sir John's man, and a maid.'[24]

Through Agnes' description, which has more detail and warmth, it is possible to share in her impressions and the thrills from the moment the Special (for they could not go by regular train) '. . . glided out among the soft shadows of a summer night. . . bearing us westward'.[25]

Agnes, although so excited that she could think of nothing but the fact of going on the trip, nevertheless acted 'in capacity of general manager, [giving] particular care to hampers and grocery lists [while] others of the party have selected new books, illustrated papers, maps, games, and embroidery, mindful that for at least three weeks during our absence we shall have no home but the railway car.'[26]

If their life in a railway car would necessarily be somewhat limited, at least they had very special accommodation. It was the *Jamaica,* the same car in which Agnes and Mary had made their Maritime trip late in 1885, and it now

> presented a very homelike effect. Baskets of flowers stood on narrow tables, already heaped with books and newspapers; comforting sofas lined her polished sides, and wide arm-chairs stood on either side of the entrance-doors. . . all somewhat resembling the cabin of a fine ship, everything being as richly coloured and effective as black walnut and gilding could make it.
> Eighty feet over all, and wide in proportion.[27]

As the train sped through the dark night, Agnes had time to reminisce about this 'wonderful line' which had first been talked of so many years ago, when the 'idea was generally laughed at'. As she lay there, lulled by the gentle motion and by the surprising fact that the railway had survived all its battles, she recalled:

> Politicians quarrelled over it, speculators shook their heads, engineers doubted it, and railway authorities expostulated against it. The scheme broke up one Government, embarrassed another, set everybody by the ears.... The road would be too dangerous, too difficult, too costly...but, above all, it was quite impossible!... A few very very wealthy men whose lives might have been easily spent in that fashionable pleasure-seeking so common to so many of their class, faced the situation, formed a Company, took the Charter, and set to work. Before anyone had time to think much about it, the line was finished.[28]

Before Agnes had time to think further about the railway and its struggle for life, she fell asleep, to be awakened in the morning by the sound of running water. Looking out, she saw 'the great uplands thickly timbered...against the pink morning sky.... Fuel for all time covers great rounded hills that rise in endless succession; forest trees of..., pine hemlock and cedar.'[29]

They had reached North Bay, which Agnes had seen in the previous January. Already, she could observe, many changes had taken place, but, for the most part, the land was rough and many areas offered little but rock and scrub. The settlers who had moved into the region lived in the crude shelters which the navvies had used during the construction of the line. There were a few isolated stations, too, where 'we chatted with the railway officials, who dwell in stately seclusion.... One of these, a jolly-faced Englishman, was most agreeable. He welcomed me as if I were an old friend; talked "primrose" politics,[30] showed me his wife's pictures and became quite confidential.... I offered him a *Graphic*.'[31]

Until the train reached Port Arthur, there was no 'business' to attend to, so Agnes used the opportunity to introduce her prospective readers to some of the party. Her description of the travellers was more graphic than Pope's simple list:

> First then comes our 'Brother-in-law' [John A.][32] a very well known personage in Canada, who is taking this trip for a 'special' purpose. He has come to see the realization of the darling dream of his heart.... No happier hours had come to him, I think, than these, as he sits thoughtful in the *Jamaica*, looking on the varied scenes through which we pass.... Next comes the 'Comptroller' [Fred White, Comptroller of the North West Mounted Police.]...Then the Secretary—best of men; never absent from his post, furnished not only with every good quality, but also with the loveliest writing cases...red memorandum books...the latest style in elastic bands, and the sweetest thing in pens![33]

At Port Arthur, 'a very pretty little town', they were impressed by the variety of minerals shown them and by the information that the Province of Ontario was selling this richly endowed land for the equivalent of eight shillings an acre! When Agnes heard this, she proposed that they simply stay in Port Arthur and all become miners — an offer not taken up, she said, by the Chief who was 'in grave and earnest talk with a large circle of welcoming friends'.

During the next night they passed into Manitoba and by early morning were in Winnipeg, 'a new, smart, handsome, busy town. . . . We steam into the station amid loud and ringing cheers, for this is the Chief's first visit. . . . Then follows a long interval of handshaking. . . after which we drive to Government House.'[34]

Both Agnes and Pope, in their very different styles were impressed by Winnipeg. She called it 'a prodigy among cities', and he wrote that he had not expected to find so great a development: 'It is excellently paved from end to end with wooden blocks and is a long street of exceptional width (138 feet) lighted with electricity and furnished with all the appliances of modern civilization, including a first-rate line of street cars.'[35]

The Macdonalds and their party enjoyed a two day stop-over in Winnipeg, as guests of Lieutenant-Governor J.C. Aikin and his wife. This gave the Prime Minister a chance to discuss Manitoba's concern over railway monopolies,[36] and they were taken for a side trip, on the South Western Railway, to Boisevan, where Agnes remarked on the beauties of the valley of the Pembina. John A., she noted, was

busy from morning to night. . . adding in every possible way, to his store of knowledge about the country and its necessities, the people and their requirements.[37]

Their original idea had been to get to the West coast as quickly as possible and stop at the towns along the route on the return trip, but it was not always politic to adhere to this plan. News of the Chief's trip, naturally, preceeded them and many impromptu stops had to be made. In spite of these welcoming parties along the line, they made good time to Regina, where they had a pleasant visit as guests of the Dewdneys at Government House. The residence charmed Agnes very much, a long, low building with pretty, small rooms 'so fresh-looking and pretty, full of flowers, pictures and dainty things'. Regina itself Agnes dubbed the 'baby Capital of the North-West Territories', and she was thrilled to watch a division of the North West Mounted Police returning from duty at Prince Albert, some 250 miles away. A colourful sight they must have been in their bright red coats as they '. . . rode compactly together, and wheeled into a low enclosure of the Police fort.'[38] The Macdonalds' stay in Regina was busier than they had planned, for each day arrived a constant stream of visitors, anxious to meet John A. Both English settlers and Indians came and if any story had two sides, the Prime Minister heard both!

Before the party left Regina, Agnes had time to write a letter of thanks to Van Horne, telling him how their trip was going and John A.'s reactions to it.

[Even] the weather, which has been so hot — has joined everything else in being specially good to us.... I do not think any of us have suffered any inconvenience from the heat....

Sir John is really very well, and thoroughly enjoys the change, being so full of interest about everything & everybody.

I am obliged to be a little selfish and troublesome at times, in trying to induce him to spare himself & his many friends to see the necessity of his doing so — but so far, Sir John is well 'up' to his work, as well as to his play, & will, I hope continue to be so.

It is *all* most interesting — if so to me, how much more to Sir John who has so long worked & planned & hoped for this wide country & tried to the best of his abilities to shape her destinies aright.... I am very impatient to see the mountains & all the kind greetings — the clappings — the bouquets & the pleasant words do not turn my eyes away from the distant Selkirks & that Pacific sea, which I have so long set my heart on, that Sir John should behold via the C.P.R.![39]

But before John A. could see the Rockies, he had more work to do. When the party left Regina, it was joined by Lieutenant-Governor Dewdney, who also held the post of Indian Commissioner for the Territories, and whose presence John A. thought would be desirable during the talks he had scheduled to take place with Chief Crowfoot of the Blackfoot tribe. As the train sped across the 350 miles of prairie towards Gleichen, in what was to become Alberta, the two men planned a joint approach to the Indian chief.

When Pope's help as Secretary was not needed, he took time to study the 'strange and novel sight' of the landscape through which they were passing:

Imagine a boundless plain, perfectly level, covered with short wavy grass, not a tree or a bush of any kind.... The buffalo had disappeared some years before, but every now and then one could perceive their bones bleaching on the prairie.... In 1882 there were 100,000 skins sold in St. Paul, and in 1883 just four.[40]

As they approached Gleichen, some fifty miles east of Calgary, Agnes observed that they could feel they were already in the foothills, already climbing slightly. She also noticed something that she had not been able to see the previous January when the ground had been covered with snow: 'Large fires have passed over much of the prairie we look upon, leaving great tracts black and bare.'[41] It was to discuss these fires, the disappearance of the buffalo which Pope had noted, and other matters, that John A. was preparing to meet Crowfoot on the following morning.

By about 6:00 a.m., it was possible to tell that the Indians were approaching the 'Special', which had been on a siding during the night. Agnes could hear

the soft rapid tread of many moccassined feet passing near our car. It was a pretty sight to look at soon afterwards as we watched them coming, mounted and in gala dress, tearing across open prairie in the early sunshine. . . . On the slopes round the station and cars hundreds of men were already grouped. . . . A few were smoking slowly. . . . All sat listless [with the air of] a rather bored nonchalance. . . . In an hour all was ready for the Conference to begin. The Lieutenant-Governor, the Chief, and the ladies had seats on a low platform. . . . Before them the Blackfeet sat massed. . . all minor chiefs in war-paint and feathers. Head-Chief Crowfoot being in mourning for his adopted son Poundmaker[42] wore nether garments of greyish tweed, a flannel shirt, a wide felt hat, and a large brown blanket.[43]

Dewdney explained to the Indians that the Chief was on his way to the sea but had stopped on purpose to 'know the mind of his red brothers'. As Pope said, what was bothering them was that

their people were originally happy and free with plenty of food at all times, that the white man had come in, taken their land, killed off their buffalo, thus depriving them of their means to live. . . . Crowfoot went on to protest his loyalty, . . . and, Sir John. . . provided a banquet for the occasion together with the presents of pipes, tea, and tobacco.[44]

Crowfoot brought up the subject of the burned tracts of land and asked John A. what the Government was going to do about this damage done by the 'fire-waggons'. Agnes described the intensity of the scene for her readers: When 'Our Brother-in-Law' answered, he spoke very calmly and was closely scrutinized by Crowfoot as if he would read his very soul.'[45] John A. tried, she said, to explain to the Indians that the railroad was doing much good and that the damage, except in the dry season, was relatively small. Urging the Indians to try to help themselves, he said that they must 'dig and plant and sow like white men, to get good crops. . . .

White men worked hard for their food and clothing and expected the Indians to do the same. . . . The Government had already given seed and grain and farming implements; the reserve was fine, rich land; they must work and till it.'⁴⁶

These arguments were not understood and so were reiterated until, Agnes said, 'By this time, I for one, was dreadfully hungry — nearly midday, and nothing yet but a cup of tea. With much satisfaction, I observed signs of approaching end to the Conference.'⁴⁷

But it was not all over. A sham war-dance was put on for the entertainment of the visitors, and, during a lull in this, Chief Crowfoot's wife was presented to Agnes.

> I made her a little gift. . . . She bade me welcome. . . [and] scanning with something of disdain, my plain travelling dress and dusty appearance, she enquired if I were not a great 'chief lady'. I assured her I was but a humble individual brought to the prairies only to look after the travelling comforts of my lord and master.⁴⁸

In case any of her readers should think the trip was simply for pleasure, Agnes jotted down the activities of a 'sample day'; nothing could be further from a holiday schedule!

> Beginning with the Blackfeet Conference at Gleichen, from 6 a.m. till noon, we then had fifty miles to travel to Calgary; a reception on arriving there; a long drive; a review of the Mounted Police; addresses in the Town Hall; an hour for visitors in the car; the ceremony of laying a foundation stone; another long drive; more speeches, and to wind up, towards morning, two hours at a large 'Social' or Church entertainment, where, on a carpeted platform in a big highly decorated skating-rink (converted by its summer-flooring of boards into a fine ballroom) we drank tea, listened to music, and were made welcome by new friends, so kind and cordial, that it seemed almost ungrateful to admit that we were very tired.⁴⁹

With such a schedule, it must have been particularly galling as they prepared to sleep, near dawn, to hear someone outside their car remark that he 'guessed them Canada folk had about enough of it!'

The Rockies started to come into view soon after the train left Calgary, but, in Agnes' opinion, it took a frustratingly long time to get into them. A single peak would appear and all on board would rush to see it — only to have it disappear from sight. There were 'great mountain shoulders, half-misty, half-defined, with occasional gleams of snowy peaks far away before us like kisses on the morning sky.'⁵⁰ Finally, the train did penetrate the mountain range and the party 'gloried in its endless new vistas as the line wended its way around what looked, from a distance, like impenetrable barriers, to further progress.'[51]

Past Banff, the climb was more sustained, and, finally, they were so high that they could look down on the trees, which, from the height of the train, did not seem to Agnes to have any base. 'This conveyed to me an idea of our elevation, and it was delightful to think of oneself as hidden away among those solitary mountains. . . all the troubles and worries of life left in noisy bustling cities far away!'[52]

From Calgary to Laggan Agnes travelled in the car of the engine, accompanied, as she said, by a 'victimized official'. She had, thus, an excellent view, and being of an inquisitive nature, asked many questions about the engines, boilers, signals, etc., the answers to which might 'come in handy some day'. She told her readers she 'even ventured to whistle "caution" at a "crossing". . . but the Chief's quick ear had detected a falter, and. . . he sent a peremptory message, desiring me "not to play tricks." '[53]

At Laggan Station, still some distance from the summit, they got out to examine the big 'mountain engine' which was necessary for both ascending and descending steep grades. It was then and there that Agnes had what seemed to her an even better idea of where to seat herself for the rest of the journey. 'from the instant my eyes rested on the broad shining surface of [the engine's] buffer-beam and cowcatcher. . . I decided to travel there and nowhere else for the remaining 600 miles of the journey!'[54]

The idea of the Prime Minister's wife riding the cowcatcher caused the crew no little consternation. What was she going to sit on, for example? This question she answered for them by choosing an empty candle-box, which she then placed on the buffer beam. The next thing to do was to have Agnes obtain John A.'s permission. When she approached him:

> The Chief, seated on a low chair on the rear platform of the car, with a rug over his knees and a magazine in his hand, looked very comfortable and content. Hearing my request. . . he pronounced the idea 'rather ridiculous', then remembered it was dangerous as well, and finally asked if I was sure I could hold on. Before the words were well out of his lips, and taking permission for granted by the question, I was again standing by the cowcatcher. . . and asking to be helped on.[55]

At least some members of the Prime Minister's staff were as nonplussed as the crew by Agnes' unorthodox choice. Pope, for one, did not approve and wrote of Lady Macdonald's 'characteristic imprudence'. (As there was never any other mention of Agnes being imprudent, it seems more likely that he meant 'impulsive', for she was that.) One reason for their objections may have been that the younger gentlemen of the party —

Fred White, George Johnson or Pope himself — had to take turns sitting with her in this exposed position, and at least Pope seemed to feel that she was asking a bit much.

On the last morning of the cowcatcher trip, Pope had reason to be upset. The danger that cattle might be on the track was ever-present, but on this particular day it was a number of young pigs that appeared just in front of the train. All except one managed to get out of harm's way, but that one was hit by the train and Pope declared that it passed between his body and the post he was holding. Had either of the passengers on the cowcatcher been hit by the animal, the impact could have been fatal. Pope rightly decided that this mode of transportation was not for him: 'I have not ridden on a cowcatcher since.'[56] Agnes was aware of the possible danger of her exposed position but much less worried about it. On that morning, she wrote, she was admiring the scenery when 'There was a squeak, a flash of something near, and away we went.... The Secretary averred that the body had struck him in passing; but as I shut my eyes tightly as soon as the pigs appeared, I cannot bear testimony to the fact.'[57]

The ride on the cowcatcher gave Agnes too much pleasure to leave room for fears. 'Enthroned on a candle-box with a soft felt hat well over the eyes, and a linen carriage-cover tucked around me from waist to foot...', she turned to the Superintendent who shared her 'peril' and decided that some word of comfort was necessary for him: 'This is *lovely, quite lovely;* I shall travel on this cowcatcher from summit to sea.' The poor Superintendent only surveys me with solemn and resigned surprise. "I-suppose-you-will", he says slowly.'[58]

When the summit was passed and the rivers began to flow westward down towards the Pacific, the steam was shut off and the brakes put on. The sixty-ton engine glided into the pass of the Kicking Horse River, making a descent of 2,800 feet in only twelve miles.

With a firm right hand grasping the iron stanchion, and my feet planted on the buffer-beam, there was not a yard of that descent in which I faltered for a moment.... There is glory and brightness and beauty everywhere, and I laugh aloud on the cowcatcher, just because it is all so delightful....
Halted at Palliser, The Chief and his friends walked up to...make a morning call. I felt a little 'superior' and was rather condescending. Somewhat flushed with excitement but still anxious to be polite, I asked 'would the Chief step up and take a drive'? To the horror of the bystanders, he carelessly consented.... There was general consternation among our little group of friends... — the Chief rushing through the flats of the Columbia on a cowcatcher!... It is a comfort to the other occupant of the buffer to find someone else wilful.[59]

John A. did not ride the cowcatcher long, but some of the rest of the time he did sit on the end platform of the *Jamaica*. Along these parts of the way, there were still construction gangs at work, and, as news of the approach of the 'Special' reached the workers, they gathered to give the Chief a warm welcome. They stood in small groups wherever they could get a good vantage point — sometimes on the top of railway cars or in angles of rocks; they were even to be seen in overhanging trees.

Many of the workers in this part of the country were Chinese. Although Agnes noted that their persons and the condition of their campsites were extremely neat, she found them an extraordinary sight.

These Chinese navvies, all ridiculously alike in form and feature, wearing queer little blue-and-white gowns, baggy trousers, wooden shoes, and thick flat straw hats, give a foreign air to the scene. Standing mute, wide-eyed and expressionless, their shovels all held at the same angle, . . . they had a curious effect, as of some mechanical apparatus with an awful semblance of humanity. And yet we know theirs is the oldest civilization in the known world! How fortunate it is that all nations do not express civilization in the same way![60]

The wife of a public figure could not write such a statement today, yet it would not have seemed unusual or racist to Agnes' contemporaries. Chinese were not seen in any numbers in the East, and her comment was one that any lady of the day, except possibly one from British Columbia (where Chinese were already numerous), might have been expected to make. Indeed, in her acceptance of the idea that these people had a civilization, albeit one she did not appreciate, she showed a somewhat unusual awareness of other *mores*. Perhaps this was in some part a legacy from her youth in the multi-racial, if unconsciously racist, society of Jamaica.

The route to the Pacific, through the valley of the Eagle River, wound through cedar forests 'gemmed' with blue lakes before they entered the immense valley on the other side of the Gold Range. On this part of the line, there were many tunnels, some of them wet. Agnes, by now the sole occupant of the cowcatcher, was provided with an umbrella and a waterproof. When they emerged from one such tunnel, they saw a party of young English sportsmen, standing and looking in understandable amazement at the sight

of a lady, bareheaded and with an umbrella, seated in front of an engine, at the mouth of a tunnel in the Gold Range of British Columbia! I am sorely afraid I laughed outright at the blank amazement. . . and longed to tell them what fun it was; but not being 'introduced, you know', contented myself with acknowledging their presence with a solemn little bow — which was quite irresistible under the circumstances![61]

From time to time, the Superintendents who accompanied the *Jamaica* were changed, and one exhausted a dictionary of entreaties in trying to persuade Agnes to come inside. Seeing it was useless, *he* retired in some indignation, to his private car. As she said: 'I am perfectly aware it is exceedingly dangerous, . . . but the wild spell of the moment is strong upon me, and I sit watching the stars gleam out over the mountain crests and the foam flash white 150 feet below, with a moved and swelling heart!'[62] It was only when there seemed to be danger of a landslide that Agnes could be persuaded to ride inside.

But the days during which the wife of the Prime Minister could see the West while seated on a candle-box were fast coming to an end. They were approaching Port Moody, the western terminus of the railway, and some formality was expected by the inhabitants of this little town. John A. was to make a little speech there from the back platform of the *Jamaica,* and rebel though she had been on the trip, Agnes knew she would be expected to appear at her husband's side in a clean dress, without ash on her face and with her hat firmly in place. Undoubtedly she was proud to stand beside John A. at that moment, but it was Pope who said it for her:

> I could not help feeling what an exultant moment it must have been for [the Prime Minister]. His chief opponent had left on record his belief that all the resources of the British Empire could not build the road in ten years. Here it was built. . . in less than half that time. It was no paper road, this. . . . Here, lapping his feet were the waters of the Pacific Ocean.[63]

From Port Moody, the Macdonald party crossed over to Victoria. After a stay there of three weeks, they began their homeward journey. By August 30, they were back in Earnscliffe, which must have seemed tame after the excitement of the summer months, but it was time to take up, once more, the realities of the official side of their lives. There was much in the offing. During the trip, when frequent 'whistle-stops' had been made, the coming federal election had evidently been much in the Prime Minister's thoughts. Now there were provincial political considerations as well. Fall elections had been called in Quebec and Manitoba, and, in the midst of plans as to the date of the federal election, Ontario suddenly announced that its voters would go to the polls in mid-November.

So John A. had some six months of hard campaigning ahead of him. Hardly had he unpacked from the trip west before he was off on a tour of Ontario, sometimes with Agnes along in an effort to see that he did not overwork. By late October, after the date for the federal election had been set for February 22, 1887, John A. stepped up his travels as he fought a campaign which Pope thought was '. . . the hardest fought of all

Sir John's electoral contests of which I had personal knowledge'.[64] After Christmas, Agnes scarcely saw her husband as he travelled in either the *Jamaica* or its sister car, the *Ottawa*, ending up in Kingston, where he again won his seat.

Agnes continued her 'scribbling' during and after the election, apparently expanding her sights from travel adventures (which were commonly written by 'lady authors' of the day) to political commentaries (which were not). There is no absolute proof of this, but several unsigned articles in *Murray's Magazine* during the next two years are very much in Agnes' style and reveal inside knowledge of the Macdonald government.[65] One describes the election of 1887 as

> the most hotly contested, the most exciting, and the most interesting altogether.... The Macdonald Government had held the reins for eight consecutive years, had met with a fair share of success in the results of their administration, and were, as Governments go, popular...their opponents loudly declared that they were certain of shipwreck.[66]

Yet, as the article said, 'the cheery old combattant at the head of Canada's affairs seemed to take things easily, and gave no sign of distress. Time, too, brought him revenge.'[67] With a majority of about thirty seats in the new Parliament, John A. was ready to carry on.

Because of the date of the election, the House did not sit until the middle of April and, necessarily, carried on its work later into the summer than was usual. Les Rochers was advertised for rent, and Agnes remained in Ottawa with John A. through those hot, boring weeks described in her pungent style in another *Murray's Magazine* article:

> the unlucky M.P.'s...sat patiently through hot days and nights in a chamber built mainly with an eye to winter requirements, and in an atmosphere so oppressive and exhausting that it is not surprising the Government had not energy enough to propose anything of great importance, and that the Opposition was too languid to show much fight.
>
> It is true that cricketers from both sides met daily in a friendly game [in front of the buildings]...and perhaps this also had something to do with the serenity that reigned within....
>
> Very early in the day the leader of the Opposition gave up altogether, laid his arms on his desk, his head on his arms, and took no further interest in the proceedings.[68]

The Leader of the Government, however, was not asleep, although he seems to have been in the minority. The writer said:

> I counted four pages asleep at once round the steps of a chair in which the

Speaker had gone to bed. Five members in one row lay back snoring peacefully; in the next, one was making a sketch with ink on a reclining sleeper's bald and shiny crown; while another dropped ice water into his neighbour's left ear.[69]

The Members did rouse themselves from time to time, mainly to discuss Manitoba's threat to construct a rail line to link up with the United States. To the Conservative Government, this looked like suicide, since it would encourage traffic to move north and south, not east and west as an independent Canada wished, but no action was taken.

All in all, it was not a productive Session, and it finally came to an end in June when

> The Governor-General, after three hard months' labour at balls, parliamentary dinners, sliding, parties, concerts and plays, varied by writing despatches about the pig-headedness of American politicians on the Fishery question, must have rejoiced when his Ministers asked him to prorogue. Certain it is that His Excellency jumped out of the horrors of a tightly fitting uniform and into a homespun travelling suit and was off for his salmon waters up the Cascapedia almost before the last cannon's boom died away in the hot evening air.[70]

If Agnes were, indeed, the writer of this article, she was not wasting time envying the Governor-General. She, too, was off for a two-week fishing holiday in New Brunswick, as soon as she had met her official obligations for the closing of Parliament and that summer's celebration of Queen Victoria's Jubilee.

In 1887, Queen Victoria had been on the British throne for fifty years, an event which was celebrated throughout the Empire on June 21. For months, Canada, the first of the colonies to gain a degree of independence, had been talking of nothing but how to mark this great day properly, especially since there had been some criticism of the way the public seemed more and more inclined to treat the Queen's birthday as a private holiday, rather than an official celebration.

While contemporary newspapers are short on information as to exactly what the general Canadian citizenry did on Jubilee Day, they do record its observation at Rideau Hall, both by a dinner on the eve of the anniversary and an 'At Home' given by the Governor-General and Lady Lansdowne on the afternoon of the great day itself. Agnes was at the dinner, but she apparently felt that was sufficient official celebration. On June 21 she was well away on a long-planned trip to the salmon streams of the Restigouche River in northern New Brunswick.

Indeed, Agnes must have left the capital the minute she changed her clothes after the Vice-Regal dinner party, since by Jubilee morning, she was in the *Jamaica,* on a siding near Rivière du Loup, waiting while her party assembled. As her guests, she had invited the Robert Leckies and the Edward Brooks, of the Eastern Townships. Unfortunately Mrs. Leckie had to remain at home with her new baby,[1] but the rest of the party were soon off on a holiday that Agnes was to describe in detail for the readers of *Murray's Magazine.*

The trip did not begin auspiciously. It would normally have taken them only a few hours to get to the Restigouche, but a heavy rain held them captive in the railway car for over a day and a half. They were impatient to be off and found the waiting 'not exactly festive. Still we all tried to be delightful, played games, read novels and old newspapers',[2] and watched the clouds for signs of clearing. After the party finally reached the river, the journey continued in a scow,

60 feet long and 9 wide, with square ends, and in the middle a long tent-like cabin made of canvas stretched on rough boards, with a door at each end; within, a table, four camp-stools, and our baggage neatly piled; astern, outside, a heap of boxes and bales containing provisions and tents; towing behind, our three canoes; forward, bundles of hay for our three steeds, who, harnessed with ropes and attached to a 60-foot cable, now came splashing forward above their knees in water, and took up a position ahead, the left horse ridden by a large weather-beaten man in waterproof leggings and a shady hat. Well forward on the scow stood two tall young men armed with long iron-tipped poles, and a very wide rudder . . . was managed by a bushy whiskered giant, whom we called the Pilot. The rest of our party consisted of six canoe-guides and a cook.[3]

It was, as Agnes thought, 'a novel mode of conveyance' but it was great fun and the party passed the time with stories and laughter. They did not forget the Jubilee and, to mark the occasion, named their scow the 'Empress of India'.

It was not an easy trip; the high water and the many logs in the river made it necessary, at times, to put the horses, cable and all, on board the scow.

When the horses were passengers, we were close together, and on very confidential terms. Indeed Bell and Jean ate wet oats by turn out of the deal box in which, when they had refreshed themselves, I hid my opera-glass, notebook and novel, to keep them dry.[4]

Floating logs and high water were not the only impediments to the party's progress. They were overtaken by another heavy rain storm and sought shelter in a small, near-by house known to one of the guides. The family in this shanty were 'most kind, and it was speedily settled that we ladies might sleep in the parlour if necessary, and the gentlemen would stay on the scow.'[5] Even though it meant sleeping on the bare floor, Agnes thought the incident the

greatest possible fun. . . . In two minutes I was sound asleep. At three, next morning, I was awakened by my friend's voice. . . . [She] had been unable to sleep a moment. 'The floor is lively with insects', she assured me — 'very dirty, and very horrible'. I felt convinced she was right, yet the absurdity of the situation so overcame me that. . . I fell into fits of immoderate laughter. It was contagious, and especially to one of so gay a heart. She laughed too. Peal after peal echoed through that silent cottage. To stop was impossible.[6]

As Agnes said, the Micmac guides must have thought them quite mad, but it was impossible to explain that it was not 'a custom among palefaces to fall into hysterics at daybreak, especially during times of trial and discomfort.'[7]

Laughter brought them luck, it seems, and early in the morning they were able to proceed, although with difficulty. The pilot informed them that he could not navigate the rain-swollen river as far as their intended destination, the mouth of the Patepedia River, but, as fate would have it, they met an old friend of Agnes' who invited them to stay at his Lodge at Indian Brook. It seemed wise to accept, partly in view of the condition of the river, partly in view of the warnings they had been given of insects in great number if they proceeded. '"You'll be ate up", [said the pilot,] "ate up if you go to Pattymejaw. This is the best place — stay here; you'll be ate up, I tell you, Missis, if you camp at Pattymejaw."'[8] They were encouraged to stay, too, by the Superintendent[9] who owned the waters and who, good fisherman that he was, offered to instruct the novices in the party.

The following day, after a breakfast of hot beans eaten off a tin plate, the Prime Minister's wife set out to learn how to cast. Dressed in a loose grey dress, still damp from the previous night's shower, and an old straw hat with a mosquito veil tightly fastened by elastic to keep out sandflies and mosquitoes, she entered her canoe and sat on a candle-box which was

> wedged close to a delicate 'thwart'. For a moment, the Restigouche — the camp — the Indians, faded away, and once more swift memory [took] me tearing across the delicious valleys of the Columbia, and below the snowy summits of the Rockies, on the never-to-be-forgotten Cowcatcher of the C.P.R. . . . [It is] clearly my fate to enjoy life most of all when seated on an empty candle-box.[10]

Eventually she had to come back to the present and remember that she was supposed to be learning to cast. That was, she discovered, more difficult than she had expected, even with an experienced teacher, and not until she had had the disappointment of seeing many salmon get away was she eventually successful. Suppressing a 'frenzied giggle', she followed instructions and, after an hour of struggle, landed a twenty-five-pound fish. As the party went back to camp in the dusk, Agnes wrote, the canoe 'bore a reclining figure, with its head on a candle-box and its eyes on a dead fish, and with a heart so full of deep content and satisfaction that there could be but one answer in her estimation to that unhealthy, but oft-asked question — Is life worth living.'[11]

'Camp', Agnes told her readers, 'was gay that evening' as they sat, chatting, around the campfire and listening to the guides singing. With smudges built on all sides to keep the insect life at a distance, they were to spend many evenings in this pleasant manner. The camp itself was well located, its site being 'unshaded, dry, cool and close to running water'. The party had been cautioned by the 'knowing ones' not to bring too much luggage, and Agnes had complied, managing with only two water-proof bags, the smaller one for her simple wearing apparel, the other packed with 'two pairs of blue blankets, a sheet, bath and pail, all made of india-rubber; a small eider-down pillow, a tiny dressing and writing-case, six coarse towels, three novels, a musquito-net [sic], and a straw-covered bottle full of penny-royal mixed with olive oil, an antidote to flies.'[12]

The novice fishermen worked hard to improve their skills and the thrill of accomplishment at a catch wiped out all previous disappointments. Soon so many fish were caught that there was a problem of keeping them fresh until they could be eaten or sent to Matapedia for onward distribution. This was solved by building a small artificial pool which filled from the river. One evening Agnes added a large fish to this collection and later sent it

> packed in fern leaves and ice to the Chief in Ottawa, who had the effrontery to ask afterwards where that fine salmon had been bought!... This remark was all the more cruel because I had suffered very much over that salmon, and had played him from the bank for an hour, standing, walking, kneeling by turns on hot round stones, with the thermometer at 80 in the shade, no hat on, and just enough flies about my ears, cheeks and throat, to leave wounds, unfelt until the excitement was over.[13]

In spite of this, it was a true holiday. There was time to lie in the hammock for an hour or two at midday, to read, to doze, to think about the afternoon's fishing, but not to think of 'those other deeper troubles that clutch the heart for a lifetime and never quite go — even these brightened in camp because there is no time to talk them over and so make matters worse.'[14] There was time before dinner each day to take a 'dip in some sheltered waters below the island, . . . or better still, under the arching trees at Patepedia where it was exciting fun to venture so dangerously near the rapids that the 'swirl' gripped one's bathinggown, and tried to pluck one off the stones.'[15] By 10:00 p.m. each day, all were asleep on their spruce beds, contented after the day's round of activities.

One 'sorrowful morning', it was all over; it was time to go home. Agnes returned to Ottawa, but after only two weeks there, she travelled once more by train to New Brunswick. This time John A. and Pope were with her, and they spent a month at the Inch Arran House in Dalhousie, a popular tourist hotel of the time. The salmon river lay just outside the door, but the fishing season was closed and, in any case, this was John A.'s holiday. To him, fishing implied weeks and weeks of hard negotiations with the United States, not a relaxing sport. So they spent their time quietly in the area, only once moving further afield — to visit the Tilleys' summer home at St. Andrews. By early September they were back at Earnscliffe again, but Agnes' travels were not over yet; she had to repack and leave almost immediately for Banff, where Mary had spent the summer.

The development of Banff as a resort can be at least partially credited to Agnes. When she and John A. had made their trip west the previous year, Agnes had written to Van Horne from Banff, remarking on its beautiful setting, pointing out that it had sulphur springs which the Indians had long ago discovered to have great medicinal value, and commenting on her disappointment that there was, as yet, *no* accommodation:

> May I venture to beg in the interests of my countrymen and countrywomen that the C.P.R. authorities will secure the best of these 'water privileges' & proceed to build a Sanatorium which will then be *really* done & *really* managed & *really* useful to all of us?[16]

This remark had not fallen on deaf ears, for, by the spring of 1887, the Banff Springs Hotel was under construction, and nearby, facing the Bow River, a twenty-by-forty-foot log cabin was being built for the Macdonalds' use.[17] Its full-length verandah would be a fine place, Agnes may have thought, for Mary to sit during the day, while in the evenings and on wet days, a large stone fireplace would provide warmth and cheer for the occupants of the cottage.

Agnes had been delighted to learn of the construction of the cottage and, possibly, had had it in mind as a place for Mary to spend the summer of 1887, a summer that, from the opening of the Session on April 13, had promised to be very busy:

> With the Session and Easter comes the Season to Ottawa, to continue with more or less Parliamentary excitement, social festivity at Government House, and hospitality everywhere until the guns fire at Prorogation.[18]

Agnes had known all this would mean a great deal of work for her and much strain on John A., then seventy-two years old, even if they were able to slip in trips to New Brunswick. It would be better for all concerned, Agnes had likely thought, if she were to take Mary to the peaceful, healthful atmosphere of Banff. It may have been too early for the cottage to be ready, but, in any case, Agnes and John A. had decided to have their daughter try the healing powers of the waters, and by early April, Agnes had taken Mary and her attendants to the springs.

As soon as she had settled her daughter, Agnes had returned to Ottawa to be of whatever help she could be to John A. There, she confided in a letter to Louisa how relieved she felt about her arrangements for Mary:

'during the session the house is always full and busy.... I shall always try to get her [Mary] away for the session for she does not do well here unless she can be with me & have all her quiet comforts as usual. This is impossible during the session.'[19]

As early as the end of May, the news from Banff made Agnes certain that she had done the right thing. Mrs. Dewdney, wife of the Lieutenant-Governor of the Northwest Territories, had spent a few days with Mary and written Agnes of her daughter's improvement. 'Especially she dwelt on Mary's face being so healthy and smiling. She was using her right hand to do her felt work.'[20] To make Mary's enjoyment more complete, Agnes sent out a large tent for her to sit in during the day, should she wish a change of view.

In 1887, Mary was eighteen and a prisoner of her wheelchair, a condition which would never be changed. There was so little that could be done for her. The very nature of her condition implies brain damage as well as physical retardation. At that time, little was known about treatment; even today, despite improved diagnosis, the advice often given the parents of a hydrocephalic child is do exactly what John A. and Agnes did — to make their child's life as pleasant as possible, offering as many diversions and amusements as they can devise, and expect very little improvement.

Yet Mary's parents, while following their common sense, had continued to seek medical advice, hoping, always hoping for a miracle. The orthopedic shoes and braces with which she had been fitted some years earlier had been of little help, except to give her some measure of support. In 1880, Agnes had taken her to New York for treatment. Later, when Princess Louise had been at Government House, she had suggested Swedish massage from a specialist she had brought with her to Canada, and Mary did try this form of theraphy, both then, and later, from an Ottawa doctor trained in the technique. Nothing helped very much, and, from time to time, Mary was allowed to be free of all treatments, which Agnes could see she found irksome.

In Mary's teens, it must have been particularly difficult to accept the fact that she could join in her friends' fun only from her wheelchair. John A., especially, tried to soften the blows. One time, as the guests were preparing to leave at the end of a dance which Mary had given, he quietly persuaded them to stay a little longer. 'When they resumed the dance, he leaned over his child's chair and said, "You see, Mary, they want a little more of your society and a little dancing by the way".'[21]

If John A. occasionally over-compensated by indulging his little 'Baboo', as he sometimes called Mary, it was left up to Agnes to be the disciplinarian, and she wrote of this to Louisa in 1887: 'I have tried to teach Mary what my mother tried to teach me, that she must do, or have done, what is best for her and for others and not grumble & she has perfect faith in our plans for her.'[22]

Whether because of her mother's teachings or not, Mary seems to have inspired quite genuine love in almost everyone who came in contact with her. Her half-brother, Hugh, summed it up nicely in a letter to the Professor in 1889: 'She is a gentle amiable girl and no one who sees much of her can help being fond of her.'[23]

Hugh, who had firm convictions about Mary's condition, preceded this remark with some shrewd insights into her development during these years of late adolescence. During the summer of 1888, he had spent some time with his father, Agnes and Mary and concluded that:

[Mary's] mind was developing and that she was becoming more of a woman and less of a child than she had heretofore been, although in many respects she was still very childish. This, however, is accounted for by the fact that both my father and mother generally treat her as a child and that her companions, when not people well advanced in life, are as a rule much younger than herself.[24]

For that summer of 1888, Mary chose to remain in the east, possibly because she had found the previous summer in Banff too far away from the rest of the family and the waters of the sulphur springs had not proved beneficial to her; possibly because she knew Hugh and his family were going to be in the East for an extended holiday and she had become very fond of his daughter, Daisy, who passed a good deal of time in Ottawa and Rivière du Loup. Indeed, since the railroad had been completed, Hugh's entire family (which now included a step-brother for little Daisy, John Alexander, born in 1884) had moved back and forth from Winnipeg to the East with some regularity.

The needs of visitors, family and others, invalid daughter and overworked husband were all in Agnes' mind when, in late 1888, she was finally able to have some alterations made to Earnscliffe. These changes should have been made before they first moved in, but she had been so happy at convincing John A. to buy the house that she had not pressed him to have the work done then. Now, however, some repairs could not be put off any longer (there was dry rot in the woodwork), and it seemed a good time to have structural changes made, as well. A new dining-room was added, the original converted into a library for John A., and two smaller offices were arranged, one for John A. and one for Pope. Very likely at Agnes's insistence, two cunningly devised escape routes were also built, ways by which John A. could slip out of the house and avoid unwanted callers. And a verandah was added at the back facing the river, a spot of special interest to Mary, who could spend many hours there in her wheel chair, but also a place of enjoyment for all the family.

The family moved back into the renovated house in December, 1888, but it was another month before the painters and carpenters had completed the finishing touches and Agnes could begin to show off Earnscliffe to her friends, something which John A. said she never tired of doing. His part of the work, the payment of $7,000 of bills, would soon follow.

The paint was scarcely dry, in February, 1889, when the Macdonalds had a distinguished house guest in the person of the famous singer, Emma Albani, who was a Canadian, although she had become known on the Continent. A large At Home was arranged for Madame Albani and her husband, and Mary was able to attend this, although she could not manage the concert the famous singer gave in Ottawa. So that her daughter would not feel left out, Agnes asked Madame Albani to sing for Mary's birthday, a performance that charmed the girl.

Agnes' thoughtfulness extended beyond her own immediate family circle and important guests such as Madame Albani. In the spring of 1889, it was an old lady from Kingston who benefited from her kindness. Eliza Grimason, a friend of John A.'s in his youth and a staunch political supporter always, had her greatest dream fulfilled when she was able to go to Ottawa for the opening of the 1889 Session. Agnes took the elderly lady into the Speaker's Gallery and, later, showed her around the house and grounds at Earnscliffe. Back home in Kingston, Mrs. Grimason, in her strong Irish brogue, related her trip to her friends:

> They do have a lovely place, all their town, down there by the Rye-do. The house has a lovely slate roof like they have in England, and beautiful grounds, and everyting in style, an' a man to wait on the dure. Lady Macdonald kapes her own cow an' hins, and they make their own butter, man dear. They have two fine cows and six servants.[25]

The friends in Kingston were also given an appreciation of Agnes herself:

> She's a very plain woman is Lady Macdonald — not good lookin' — but oh, she's the fine eddication, and that's where she gets the best of thim. Why, I heard her talkin' Frinch to a carpenter workin' about the house. It's her fine eddication that makes her so nice, and she takes such good care o'Him. And if I went back there today she would make as much of me as if I was the richest woman in the country.[26]

Mrs. Grimason shrewdly noted what remained Agnes' prime concern, 'what good care she take o'Him', but she also noticed the large amount of mail that arrived at Earnscliffe: 'as thrue as I tell ye there was the full of that for thim' (holding out her apron).[27]

Most of this mail was for John A. and there was really so little that Agnes could do to protect her husband from the cares and work of his office. In his farewell note in the summer of 1888, Lord Lansdowne had wished John A. 'as much happiness as is compatible with a servitude from which your country will, I suspect, not allow you to emancipate yourself.'[28] His words had proven prophetic. While the Manitoba railway issue had been resolved[29] even before Lord Landsdowne left Canada, the question of economic relations between Canada and the United States kept reappearing. By the end of the Session of 1888, the return of good times to Canadian business temporarily shelved the idea of actual commercial union with the States, but John A. continued to be much plagued by what was going on south of the border, by all the cries from businessmen on both sides of it for economic integration (which he was sure would end in the loss of Canadian political independence) and by all the old difference between the two counties.

Some of John A.'s work was of a lighter nature, as Emma Albani recalled in her autobiography with some amusement:

One evening in the middle of dinner. . . Sir John was called out and he asked my husband to go with him. It turned out that he had promised the people to open a new ice slide, and would not disappoint them. They drove two or three miles and were then put into toboggans and shot across the Ottawa River in the dark, Sir John in the first one and my husband following in another.[30]

This new slide was at the Oshkosh Toboggan Club, of which Sir John was the honorary patron; tobogganing and skating had not lost their appeal for the residents of Ottawa. Successive Governors-General entertained their guests in this manner, and the Stanleys, who had succeeded the Lansdownes a few months earlier, were no exception. They were, possibly, trying too hard to fit into Canadian society, John A. confided in a letter to George Stephen: '[They] are working hard to make themselves popular and are succeeding but *entre nous* are making themselves far too cheap & therein causing disadvantageous comparisons to be drawn by our upper classes between them and the Lansdownes.'[31]

Whether or not the Stanleys were cheapening themselves, they would have had to put on quite a show to match the one their predecessors had staged one December. It was of such magnificence that Agnes had to write about it for *Murray's Magazine*.

An annual midnight fête at Government House about Christmas time is par-ticularly attractive, if the weather be fine and the cold not extreme. Then the little valley and the dark sleeping woods around flush crimson in the glare of two enormous bonfires, near which the 'music' sits with circled stands on the snow. Engine headlights, placed at intervals, pour their white shafts of dazzle far and wide. Thousands of Chinese lanthorns glow in the air, and suspended on wires, in double rows encircle each crowded rink, outline also both slide and stairway, and dance in vistas under the purple night sky. Great is the fun and merriment, for all the world is there. Those who themselves take no active part in the sports sit in a much-windowed building overlooking the grounds, and watch the swift gleam of many shining skates, or the flight of descending tobogans [sic] as they dart — a flash of light and colour — across the snowy landscape, for sometimes the foremost sitter holds aloft a blazing torch which throws a line of fire over her red and blue companions. Presently rockets, Roman candles, and lights orange, green and blue, dazzle through the air, and as they fade out, a belt of dark wood is seen spanned with a contrivance in gas jets wishing all there present. . . a Merry Christmas and a Happy New Year.[32]

Was Agnes, herself, one of those who took 'no active part in the sports' but sat watching and remembering the days when, still a young lady, she tobogganed at Montmorency? It is quite possible, since it seems that the only times she dared to be herself were those like the trips on the cow-catcher and salmon fishing, when she was far away from the restrictive standards set by Ottawa society, which dared to criticize even the Stanleys for their behaviour.

In the autumn of 1890, Agnes saw another opportunity to take a trip to the West. She wanted to get away from Ottawa for a time; John A. was immersed in the problems of the Bering Sea fisheries,[33] and she was suffering from a neuralgia attack which left her so weak that she did not think she could be of any use to her husband. Perhaps she also hoped (quite correctly, as time would prove) that a journey would give her material for another magazine article. She later told her readers that she felt overdue for a rest, away from politics and her own responsibilities: 'The winter had been changeable, festive and busy; the summer given up to seaside and social cares; August divided between efforts at cheerful conversation and sitting in the sunshine with fingers pressed to an aching eyebrow.'[34]

According to her article, getting away was not as easy as she had hoped. John A.'s energies were drained and his temper worn thin by two Parliamentary Sessions which had dealt unsuccessfully with the economic situation and the eternal fisheries problem. When Agnes broached the idea of a trip, saying she had to go away to search for a remedy for her aching eyebrow, he seems to have been out of sympathy and, reportedly, said he thought it 'frivolous and unnecessary, adding that his grand-mother. . . had never complained of neuralgia, or asked for change and rest.'[35] This reference to his most superior grandmother did not satisfy Agnes, and, deaf to his suggestion that a round of household duties

128

might be just the thing to take her mind off her distress, she said she informed him 'that routine of all things was most distressing to my particular brand of neuralgia, while household accounts brought on severe spasms, and the sight of a butcher's boy was fatal.'[36]

At one point, Agnes said she thought she had lost her case. 'The Chief, taking up an awful looking pile of blue-lined paper, ostentatiously labelled "Behring [sic] Sea Matters", pointed to the library door and, with a polite smile, asked if I would be good enough to leave the room?'.[37] Possibly it was the sight of the detested word 'Behring Sea' that strengthened Agnes' resolve to make the trip and she began to plead eloquently, she said. This time, she was successful. '"You may go if you like", said he with gentle resignation, born of fifty years of parliamentary practice; and as I began to develop into gratitude he took up a new article on the McKinley Bill,[38] and with decision, ordered me out of the room.'[39]

Agnes soon invited a friend to join her, and, in a few days, the little party was heading west on the *Earnscliffe* 'in a vague, pleasant sort of way for Winnipeg, on the prairies, Calgary, in the ranch country, Banff, in the Rocky Mountains, Glacier, in the Selkirk Range, and Vancouver, on the Pacific Coast'."[40]

Agnes did not actually go all the way to the Pacific. She had been there more than once, so she remained at the Banff Spring's Hotel, a place of quiet beauty so late in the season, while her friends continued westwards. After several rest-filled days, during which she sketched and explored Lake Louise, the Hot Springs, the Bow River and Devil's Lake, the party returned and began its journey home to Ottawa amid plans for a trip to northern Saskatchewan the next autumn.[41]

Such a trip, however, was one Agnes was never able to make. An election was to be called for early 1891. It would not only prove to be John A.'s last but would bring on his final illness and death. Agnes would be a widow by next autumn and things such as journeys to northern Saskatchewan would not even enter her mind.

The election was called for March 5, 1891, but John A. had begun his preparations as early as September with a speaking tour of the Maritimes. Indeed, in some ways, his entire life had been a preparation for this campaign since its main theme was annexation, into which American policy seemed to be trying to starve Canada. Despite his age, despite his failing health, despite the efforts of Agnes, Pope and all those closest to him, the man who had dreamed and created the Dominion was not to be restrained in such an election battle. He moved to Toronto where, as usual, he set up his headquarters from which he was soon travelling to make out-of-town speeches. To Pope, who accompanied his Chief, it was all too much:

Every day presented fresh difficulties. Sometimes he was so weak that I dared not trouble him. . . . His Kingston supporters, however, worked like Trojans, and re-elected him by a thumping majority, which gratified him exceedingly. On the eve of the election day, he rallied sufficiently to leave Kingston for Ottawa where he took to his bed, and so did I.[42]

On the day of the election, John A. had a special wire installed to Earnscliffe in order to keep up with the returns, but he had worn himself too thin. Apart from showing some interest in his own success, that of Hugh (who was running in a Winnipeg riding) and the re-elections of old friends, he did not seem to care much what the final outcome was. While Agnes could rejoice for him that he and his party did win, that he had succeeded in keeping a united Empire, she could not then say what Pope was to quote her as saying six years later: 'I, who can speak with something like authority on this point, declare that I do not think any man's mind could be more fully possessed of an overwhelming strong principle than was this man's on this principle.'[43]

Even more than Pope, Agnes had witnessed what the latter described as the 'fever, the struggles, hopes and fears, disappointments and successes, joys and sorrows, anxieties and rewards of those long busy years'.[44] After the election of 1891, she was more concerned about John A.'s health than about his 'overwhelming strong principle' with regard to keeping Canada in the Empire. It was evident to her that her husband's political struggles were coming to an end. The struggle ahead would be for his life.

From the terrible night before the election, when John A. returned to Ottawa from Kingston too ill even to argue that he did not wish to go to bed, Agnes never moved far from his side. She attempted to convince him that he would recover, but she did not believe it. True, she had seen him recover from illness before, even from his attack of 1870 when nearly everyone had given up hope, but now he was an old man — seventy-seven years old — and he was simply worn out. She knew there was nothing she could do but be with him and make his last few weeks or months as peaceful as possible.

For two weeks she managed to keep him quiet and, for the next month, endeavoured to hold the world at bay, insisting on plenty of rest and some hours on the sunny terrace facing the river. By the end of April, he did seem better, and he was able to attend the Opening of Parliament and enjoy the proud moment of entering the House with Hugh, with the son who might carry on the Macdonald name in political circles.

From the opening of the Session, John A. worked with his customary dedication, but, on May 12, Pope noticed a slight change in the Chief's speech: he had had his first stroke, although a slight one. John A. did not allow Agnes to be told, since it would worry her and since she would un- doubtedly insist on his giving up some of his work. He was determined to stick to his normal routine and was able to do so for another few days. On May 23, he even insisted that Agnes give one of their regular Saturday dinner parties. Agnes tried to cancel it that night when she met him at the gate, after a Cabinet meeting that had lasted until six, and saw how alarmingly tired he was, but he was not to be persuaded. The party went on as usual and John A. played the genial host as always, but during the night of May 27, he had another stroke, one that it was not possible to hide from Agnes. Awakened by his call, she found that, while he could still talk, movement of the left side of his body was affected. This paralysis soon wore off almost completely, and, during the following day, John A. was able to work with Pope on parliamentary matters. He also signed some papers relative to his estate, for he knew that time was run- ning out. Indeed it was. On the 29th, he suffered another stroke, which affected the right side of his body. The doctors thought he might live another thirty-six hours.

John A.'s family and friends gathered in Ottawa for his last days, as did the press, both Canadian and foreign, rushing each bulletin from the attendant doctors to the waiting world. Queen Victoria remained in touch with Lord Stanley, who went to Earnscliffe personally, from time to time. Crowds assembled on the lawn — John A.'s friends, fellow parliamentarians and many others who wished to get as close as possible to the dying man. They grew so numerous that, at one point, it was rumoured even the sick-room had been 'invaded', but the *Empire* clearly explained:

> no one had admission to Sir John's sickroom but Lady Macdonald, Mr. and Mrs. Hugh Macdonald, Mrs. Dewdney, Mrs. Fitzgibbon, Miss Marjorie Stuart, Sir John's two secretaries (Messrs. Pope and Baird), Mr. Fred White and Mr. George Sparks. The sickroom is entirely under the control of Dr. Robert Powell, who is never many minutes absent from it, and who is assisted in the actual nursing only by Lady Macdonald and Mr. James Stewart of the Dominion Police force, a valuable man-nurse.... The utmost quiet and regularity are observed.[45]

The newspaper account was not completely accurate because Agnes did, after some consideration, allow the children into the sickroom. The first was Hugh's son, Jack, who had pleaded to see his grandfather. The boy, just six years old, held his grandfather's hand and prattled on, unable to understand why his questions did not receive answers. His presence did, however, seem to elicit some animation in the old man's face, and when Agnes saw this, she thought it might be a good time for

Mary, too, to be admitted to the room.[46] When Mary was brought in, she was reportedly able, by a tenderness and skill that were said to have been pathetic, to discourage Jack from asking any more questions. In a few minutes John A. again lapsed into unconsciousness, and soon it was seen that the end must be near.

It came the evening of June 6, 1891, peacefully and without apparent pain. The *Times* of London reported to the world: '"Sir John Macdonald died 10:15 this evening." [June 6, 1891] So read the last bulletin posted on the gate at Earnscliffe at 25 minutes past 10 last night. The end had come.'[47]

It was an end, too, for Agnes — an end to that part of her life which had found its centre in the great and powerful force, her husband. Alone, without him, she was without direction, lacking a focal point, and her life became merely an existence during which she wandered, searching and not finding any real meaning in her life. She was shortly to term herself 'an exile indeed' as she set out on the restless years of her widowhood, trying first to reconcile herself to life, without John A., in Canada, and moving away on finding this was not the answer.

3
An
Exile
Indeed

10

Agnes' great loss was acknowledged by Lady Stanley when the latter wrote the Queen Victoria, saying '. . . now, poor thing, her all has been taken from her.[1] Knowing that Her Majesty would be interested in some details of the final days of the stateman whom she had admired, Lady Stanley wrote:

> Poor Lady Macdonald never gave up hope till within a few hours of the end. She never left his side, always thinking he would be able to say some last words to her, but they never came, and it was only by the pressure of his hand that she knew he knew she was at his side ready to carry out his slightest wish, as she had always been throughout his life; certainly a more devoted wife could not have been seen. . . . But she is very brave, and, as she writes me word, she will not be weak, as Sir John would not have liked it.[2]

Agnes must often have fallen back on John A.'s desire that she 'not be weak' as she faced the next few days — and years — with friends but almost no family to guide her. (When Mary was told of her father's death, she remarked that she must try to be a comfort to her mother now, instead of a burden.[3]) Scarcely had the sad knell of seventy-six strokes been sounded from the City Hall bell tower before a suitable funeral had to be planned.

Despite her grief and certain desire to suffer privately, Agnes agreed to a state funeral, realizing that there would be many who would wish to pay their last respects and that this should be done with due ceremony. She did not make her own farewell for two more days. Until then the body remained at Earnscliffe, in the new dining room, now become a funeral chamber, for 'the remains. . . to be viewed by members of the sorrowing household and a few personal friends'.[4] On the morning of June 9, a private service was held at the house, conducted by the Reverend J.J. Bogert of St. Alban's, and then it was time for Agnes to let the State take charge.

With the ladies in the family to keep her company, Agnes remained at home while the body was taken to the Senate Chamber, where thousands of mourners filed past the coffin before it was taken to St. Alban's for what Lady Stanley described as a very beautiful and most impressive service. Agnes remained at home, too, while a funeral train went to Kingston, where the citizens of that area paid their last respects to one of their own. Then he was laid in the family burial plot and the nation was left to mourn.

An Ottawa paper commented: 'So far, Lady Macdonald has borne up bravely; but strain upon her endurance has been inconceivably severe.'[5] In London, where there had been many testimonials to the Empire's loss, Lord Lorne wrote, for publication, a touching eulogy in which he referred to Earnscliffe, 'that little house on the edge of the cedar-grown cliff above the swift currents of the Ottawa'.[6] There, now, Agnes sat in the first days of a long and lonely widowhood.

As she sat there, reading the multitude of letters and telegrams that came in each day, she must have felt anything but brave, and the contents of the letters did little to let her forget her sorrow. Yet, she had promised John A. to try to be strong and took her cue from the fact that so many of these letters showed that her husband had been so well-loved. As she wrote to Tupper, late in July, they came 'from *all* parts of the world — many from people I had never seen or heard of & even from little children written in round hand!'[7]

Some were on black-edged paper, others on pages torn from notebooks, still others on letterhead with the official seals of organizations as diverse as the C.P.R., municipalities, Liberal-Conservative Associations, temperance societies, lodges and convents. Although their diversity and testimony must have made Agnes very proud, one cannot help but wonder how much comfort she received from some of their contents. From Government House in Charlottetown came the thought that Agnes must have been under such a strain. From Government House in Manitoba came long pages full of underlined expressions of a most dolorous type. They began with 'Words fail me', and one might have wished they would. Did Agnes have to be reminded that 'Yours is no ordinary bereavement and no ordinary grief — which together with your sensitive and loving nature must intensify your anguish'[8]? Did she need to hear that 'You have been the guiding star for good of *your own* & the country's lost & loved one'[9]? Was it any comfort to be told that 'your value to your dear, sainted husband has been above rubies. . . [that] Canada owes you a debt of gratitude'[10]? Such lugubrious tomes were typical of the late nineteenth century, but it is hard to imagine that they were not occasions for fresh tears.

In early July came a letter with more tactful condolences — and a mark of royal esteem. At the time of John A.'s death, Queen Victoria had written to the Governor-General asking him to convey her grief to Agnes. Now she wrote, personally, to Agnes to reiterate this feeling, and to ask her to accept a title:

Windsor Castle, July 2nd, 1891.

Dear Lady Macdonald,

Though I have not the pleasure of knowing you personally, I am desirious of writing to express what I have already done, my deep sympathy with you in your present deep affliction for the loss of your dear distinguished husband — I wish also to say how truly & sincerely grateful I am for his devoted and faithful services which he rendered for so many years to his Sovereign and this Dominion.

It gives me great pleasure to mark my high sense of Sir John Macdonald's distinguished services by conferring on you a public mark of regard for yourself as well as for him.

Your health has, I trust, not suffered from your long and anxious nursing.

Believe me always,
Yours very sincerely,
Victoria, R.I.[11]

On July 27, 1891, Agnes replied:

I have received with deepest emotion and with feelings of profound gratification the kind letter of sympathy with which Your Majesty has deigned to honour me on the occasion of my great loss and crushing sorrow.

The words of gracious acknowledgment in which Your Majesty is pleased to refer to my beloved husband's long and faithful services and devotion to Your Majesty's Throne and Person are indeed the richest earthly consolation I can ever know, and in gratefully receiving the high mark of favour by which Your Majesty has been pleased further to express this acknowledgment, I beg to convey my profound sense of Your Majesty's goodness to me and to him whose useful and unselfish life has now, in the providence and wisdom of God, been brought to a peaceful close.

With every assurance of renewed devotion and loyalty to Your Majesty and the Empire,

I have the honour to remain

Your Majesty's faithful humble servant,

Agnes Macdonald[12]

Within a few days, Agnes was to become known as Baroness Macdonald of Earnscliffe, a title which was a fitting memorial to John A. Had she been thinking clearly, however, had she not been sunk in her own sorrow and surrounded by evidence of the country's loss, she might have found the courage to refuse this mark of esteem, which she was eventually to find a burden.

Some years before, rumours had circulated that John A. was about to receive a peerage; Agnes had then written Louisa:

You may be sure that he will never take a peerage! It would make us both look ridiculous & tho' we have both been very wicked often, I humbly think we have never been ridiculous! Nothing would distress me more than to see him — that most unfortunate of men — a *very poor Lord*. In no way possible could we live as nobles ought & are expected to do.[13]

Now, in her newly widowed state, however, she felt, as she wrote to Tupper, 'It was very gratifying to me — in addition to the Peerage to receive such a kind letter written by the hand of the Queen herself — I feel it would have pleased Sir John!'[14]

In England, the honour was well received as fitting recognition of John A.'s services to his Queen and country. In Toronto, the *Globe* took a characteristically dim view of the action, the editorial writer expressing the hope that 'the whole business of decorating Canadians with feudal badges which have no more meaning in a modern community than the beads and red ochre of a Cree Indian'[15] would not become a custom. (He was, however, pleased to think that the new leader of the Liberal Party, Wilfred Laurier, would naturally refuse to have anything to do with such nonsense.) Most Canadians, however, were pleased by this posthumous honour shown their fallen leader, and letters and telegrams of congratulations showered upon Agnes when the news became public. Many were from politicians, in witness of their esteem not only for her husband but for herself as well.

By coincidence — and John A. would have appreciated the irony had he lived to read it — the June issue of the *Ladies Home Journal* had brought Canadian and American readers an article on Agnes as part of a series on 'Unknown Wives of Well-known Men'. It had defined very well the role she had played in her husband's life, referring to her as 'The brilliant woman who for nearly twenty-five years has shared with the Premier of Canada — to a degree not common in the case of wives of public men — the toils and triumphs of his arduous and illustrious career.'[16] The writer also said, 'She forms her own opinions about the subjects of the day and never hesitates to express them in clear, concise terms.'[17] Both statements were true, and the second continued to be so for the rest of her long life. A woman who had been at the centre of Canadian political life for nearly a quarter of a century could not be expected to put aside all interest on the day of her husband's death.

Indeed, on the very night of John A.'s death, Agnes had written Lord Stanley 'begging His Excellency, in the interests of Canada and of the Conservative party, to send for Sir Charles Tupper to form the new administration.'[18] Pope, too, thought that Tupper was 'by all odds the man for the occasion... by reason of his experience, energy, courage, resourcefulness and boundless optimism.'[19]

The Governor-General, however, had not sent for Tupper but had asked Sir John Thompson to form a Government. Thompson had been a Minister in the Macdonald Cabinet since 1885, when John A. had brought him in, in search of younger men when the overtures to McCarthy had failed. There was little love lost between Agnes and Thompson, who was known for the satirical nature evidenced in a letter to his wife during the election campaign of 1887:

> the old man... is showing some of the failings of age in being very suspicious. He has had something in his nose against me for a little while past but instead of submitting like the others do I shewed fight and treated him to considerable impudence. I ignored his opinion on a legal question and... I kept up the — — by not speaking to that mole catcher of a wife of his at Gov't. House. Of course the poor old fellow is worried to death but I do not care for him and I am so determined to let him see it that I insult him at every turn.[20]

John A., who had been a master of men for well over forty years, could not have been unaware of Thompson's attitude towards him, and, although he had felt that the Minister of Justice was the man to succeed him, Agnes must have been relieved when Thompson refused. She surely felt it would not have been quite fitting for someone who had treated her husband with such 'impudence' and who would not even speak to her at Government House, to step into the position of Prime Minister. There was also another, more political reason why Agnes felt it would have been wrong for Thompson to have accepted Lord Stanley's request. 'There would have been, I am sure, a stampede of Ontario supporters. It is not so much his religion as the fact of being a pervert.'[21] (She, of course, did not mean to write 'pervert' but 'convert'; Thompson had left the Methodist Church to become a Roman Catholic like his wife.) And in this judgement, she was right: Ontario Protestants would not have been in favour of Thompson holding the highest office in the land.

When it was left to J.J.C. Abbott to take John A.'s place, however, this, too, seemed to Agnes a great error. Abbott was too quiet, too delicate, and too old to take on the post. Comparing him with John A., the widow saw that the country was going to suffer from indecisive leadership, as would the party. On the day of John A.'s funeral, she had received an address of sympathy signed by Dalton McCarthy as Chairman of a

Committee of Members of the Conservative Party in both Houses of Parliament, and in it a note of alarm had been apparent. It had spoken of the loss of their 'loved and respected leader', but pledged that they would not give way to despondency but would 'endeavour to carry on the great work so dear to his heart. . . the consolidation of a united, free and prosperous Canadian nationality. . . in connection with the great Empire'.[22] This had been John A.'s wish for the Party he had guided for so long. It was a wish that Agnes, who had been by his side since 1867, shared fully.

Yet despite her continuing interest in politics, despite the excitement of receiving a peerage, her role and routine had changed abruptly and definitely as soon as John A.'s funeral was over. Worse still, the house on the cliff rattled with memories now that only she and Mary were there. No more did friends drop by for breakfast (which had been, by long custom, the noon meal in the Macdonald home since Agnes felt that unwanted callers who might not have any qualms about interrupting the Prime Minister's luncheon *might* respect the sound of a gong which they were told, if they did not already know, announced the first meal of the day). In the evenings, there were no more of the pleasant half-hours which John A. had set aside as often as possible to be with his daughter before she went to bed. No more did the sound of his voice ring out a little later in the evening as he read aloud amusing passages from the local papers or recounted the events of the day. It was all changed, and Agnes began to feel she could not endure staying at Earnscliffe any longer. Neither could she bear to think of going down to Rivière du Loup; it, too, held too many memories. She had to go somewhere that John A. had never been.

Luckily, she was helped in her need to get away by Van Horne, the C.P.R. manager with whom she had always enjoyed such a pleasant relationship. Soon after John A.'s death, he had written Pope:

I hope Lady Macdonald may be induced to go away from Ottawa for a while. She ought not to remain shut up with her grief. I trust that when a favourable opportunity occurs you will tell her that the *Earnscliffe* will very soon be at her disposal and that if it should be delayed the *Saskatchewan* is always at her service.[23]

This thoughtful gesture was much appreciated by Agnes, and after the worst bustle of John A.'s death was over, she decided to take Mary out to Earnscliffe Cottage at Banff.

Unfortunately she could not get away as soon as she had wished, for before leaving Ottawa, she had to go to into the laborious task of examining her financial situation. Surprisingly, it was not serious. By the middle of July, the details of John A.'s will were made public, and it was soon seen that he was not so badly off as had been thought. As the *Globe* reported: 'In this country a man who has $85,000 salted away, exclusive of a life policy for $15,000 and a gift of $80,000 belonging to his wife. . . is usually regarded as very comfortably off.'[24]

For the period, there is no doubt but that it was a fair amount of money, and the income from it provided Agnes and Mary with sufficient means to live comfortably. From the day that Agnes was left to handle her own affairs, however, her finances were a constant worry to her. As her mother had done when so perplexed by money in her widowhood, so did Agnes: she turned to someone in whom she had confidence. In Agnes' case, it was Pope, who was one of the trustees[25] of the Macdonald estate, and whom she had learned to admire and trust during his eight years as John A.'s Private Secretary, when she saw him almost daily. As she became older and then ill, she would seek his advice with increasing regularity, although, in the end, this relationship would be broken and there would be justifiable bitterness on both sides. For many years, however, he was 'Dear Joe' or 'Dear old Joe' to his late Chief's widow, the person to whom she wrote both as an advisor and as a friend and confidant. It is through their voluminous correspondence that it is possible to follow the life of Agnes during her long widowhood.

During the years after John A.'s death, Pope followed Agnes' restless travels. First, she followed her plan of going to Banff, where she spent some weeks before discovering that, despite its idyllic setting, she could not find peace there. This year even her neuralgia did not go away in its atmosphere, and she sought the air of the Pacific Coast. Nothing helped, and she soon returned to Ottawa. It was difficult to go back to her old home, and it proved especially painful to be in Ottawa while the House was in Session. Meeting old friends made her realize that her role there was finished.

Her place, if she had one, seemed to be with Hewitt, and his plans called for moving to Lakewood, New Jersey, for the winter months. So Agnes spent three weeks in Ottawa preparing Earnscliffe for rental, sorting and packing her belongings and looking after the welfare of her old servants — and then left. She and Mary went south to join Hewitt, thus beginning a pattern she was to follow for the rest of her days. No longer would her 'restless disposition' allow her to spend more than a few months at a time in any one place.

While the hotel in Lakewood was luxurious — and expensive — yet, Agnes confided to Pope, she was often lonesome and homesick. Hewitt was too ill to be much of a companion. In fact he was, she admitted, 'a sad sufferer & the sadness of his condition never seems one instant absent from his mind. If he would only grumble I think he would be better &

140

perhaps forget some of his woes.'[26] But Hewitt did not grumble, nor did Mary, nor, with the exception of this one remark, did Agnes. Their days, she said, were spent quietly: an early morning walk with her paid companion, Miss Peacock, and later on, a 'walk' with Mary and Hewitt, each of them in a wheelchair. Mary spent part of the rest of the day quietly in their rooms, lying in the sun when that was possible. She was, according to her mother, 'better than ever she was & enjoys life thoroughly. Everyone pets & humours her as usual & she is quite the little Queen I hear downstairs.'[27]

As for Agnes herself, she said, 'I live in my own rooms'. Much of each day was spent with Hewitt when 'I read to — and sit with him a great deal.... [He] is I think changed since this sad spring — the shock of which I think he has not recovered. I do all I can to cheer and comfort him.'[28]

There was not, unfortunately, anyone to cheer or comfort Agnes, who, suffering keenly her own loss, needed to be the recipient instead of the giver of solace. How changed she found her situation. A few months previously, she had been at the centre of a busy political and social life in Ottawa. John A.'s biographers, already busily at work, fully acknowledged Agnes' role, both social and political. One even termed her 'the crown' to Sir John's social success. She who could remember the days when, without her husband's presence at a party, nothing seemed to go right, must have been bemused at this glowing praise:

Of the society circle there [i.e. Ottawa], she is voted preeminently the Queen where in every project of social enterprise, she is the first and the last, and no less the favourite of the elderly and demure than of the young folk... so kindly is her nature that she is prodigal both of her time and energy to make everything agreeable.... She seems to be in the social what her husband is in the public sphere.[29]

The same writer did not forget to praise Agnes for her political acumen. '... this gifted lady takes no little interest, and her judgment is said to be scarcely less sound than that of Sir John who, it is whispered, is in the habit of consulting her when he is about to take some important step.,[30]

Small wonder that so many of Agnes' letters to Pope, now that she no longer had an inside track on what was happening in her country, should have been filled with queries and comments on Canadian politics. Very often, during that winter in New Jersey, Agnes' thoughts went, unbidden, back to Ottawa and the happenings there. At the time of the Opening of the House in February, 1892, she confessed to Pope, 'As I took my quiet little stroll... this afternoon at 3 pm. I could not help going in spirit to the old place in the Senate chambers & seeing again the tall figure with its decorations & well known face standing so erect & earnest at his post! I used to watch him — master of them all — with much pride and triumph.'[31]

This memory sparked many others of her early days in Canada and of other Openings in other Canadian capitals. 'One of the first things I remember in Canada is of an "Opening" of the House, the poor little Ontario & Quebec House in Quebec & seeing Sir John, almost a young man then — standing just there to the Governor's right!'[32] She was going through a trying period, and Pope was the only person with whom she felt free to share her thoughts and memories of the past. She had to keep quiet about her loneliness and longing, always, for Mary's and the Colonel's sakes: 'I say nothing about it.... [They] depend on me for their spirits and cheerfulness so I must always be heedful.'[33]

Agnes returned to Canada in the summer of 1892, but with very mixed feelings. After settling Hewitt in a hotel in St. Hilaire, Quebec, where it would be easy for his man servant to take him for outings in his chair, Agnes and Mary went on to Les Rochers. There she found that 'alas! the joy & gladness & pride of our little country home is gone from us & everything is sadly different.... We seem doubly alone without him where every spot is connected with his few holidays — & I see his figure everywhere & hear his voice — But he liked us to be cheerful.'[34]

In an effort to be faithful to John A.'s wish that they be 'cheerful', Agnes invited several of the family to the cottage. Hugh's daughter, Daisy, came and so did Professor Williamson. (The latter was also alone now, for Louisa had died in 1889.) Later in the summer Agnes' niece, May Bernard, who had married Claire Fitzgibbon, an American, joined them. In the early part of September, she and Agnes left the others at the cottage and made a trip into the relatively unfamiliar Lac St. Jean region of Quebec. From Rivière du Loup they went by train to Quebec City and thence north to Roberval, where they stopped over to allow Agnes to do some trout fishing and to take in the wonders of the local hotel, which was not exactly on the tourist route of the day:

[It] is a genuine surprise — There on the banks of this remote lake we found a very large, rather handsome hotel — well fitted, bright with electric light, *capital* attendance & the best bed I have slept in for some years (except the Mount Stephens[35]).

The hotel contains fine bedrooms, a very pretty diningroom-ball room & *theatre*...in all respects first rate — of its kind — no plush of course — but everything *good* & comfortable & such civil people.[36]

From Roberval they travelled by buckboard and pair, thirty-five miles the first day to Hérbertsville and then fifty miles the next to their destination, Chicoutimi. This was no mean feat and suggests that Agnes, when free of the demands and needs of Hewitt and Mary, and in the company of someone young and in good health, was still full of spunk. The return trip was made partly by boat and, all in all, the outing provided Agnes with a welcome diversion before it was time to come to grips with what she should do during the winter months.

She remained at Les Rochers as long as possible, until, as she wrote Professor Williamson, who had already returned to Kingston:

> We are the very last of the Mohicans! Every soul gone but ourselves — all the cottages barred & shuttered & hardly a figure to be seen on the roads. Today, no service. . . . We have had no butcher nor grocer for a fortnight & the post office is nearly closed. . . . We thus find ourselves quite out of season — but I loath giving up the home life and wander away again.[37]

But wander they must. Eastern Canada was cold for Mary in the winter and the thought of going back to Ottawa for more than a day or two at a time was still out of the question. Yet Agnes did not wish to return to New Jersey for another winter: 'I know Sir John would not approve of our spending so much time in the States — You know what a Britisher he always was!',[38] she wrote the Professor. She decided to take Mary to Victoria and have Hewitt accompany them; in the end, however, his doctors would not allow him to make the trip and Agnes and Mary went alone. Perhaps, much as she wished to take care of her brother, she was relieved that he could not be with them for, during the months they had been together in Lakewood, she had found that 'Mary does not prosper when near so great an invalid as her poor Uncle has grown to be. . . . Altogether I felt compelled to come away but it was awfully hard and I feel a wretch about it.'[39]

For the trip West, the C.P.R. once again put a car at Agnes' disposal. After a short stop-over in Winnipeg, where she found Hugh and his family doing well, Agnes and Mary had a week in Banff, living in the car but going to see the cottage, which Agnes renamed Ketotsim. They then headed for the Pacific and settled for the winter in Victoria's Dallas Hotel, a pleasant spot overlooking the sea. Agnes still felt it beyond her strength to manage a house, especially in a situation that led her to write: 'I was afraid of housekeeping. One heard such alarming accounts of bad drainage & Chinaman cooks who say "Chinaman don't like" at the most critical domestic moments & go away (never to return) that very instant!'[40] Obviously Agnes had still not come to terms with the fact that so many of the labour force in the coastal cities were Chinese. Yet, despite her qualms about hiring one of these men of strange appearance, rumoured to be so undependable, she did engage one to push Mary's chair. By so doing she could make a point of demonstrating to Pope that she was trying to be economical: 'I could not possibly get anyone but a Chinaman, horrible as they are [for] 25¢ an hour.'[41]

Despite the pleasant climate and domestic arrangements, Agnes found scant peace in Victoria during the winter of 1892-93. She sought little social life, noting, 'A great many have called & a few I received but I do not think I shall visit any more at all.'[42] For one thing, Mary, who liked Agnes by her side, could not go visiting with her; for another, Agnes did not feel up to starting new friendships.

She did take an interest when the Dewdneys moved to Victoria on his appointment as Lieutenant-Governor of the province. From the hotel to Government House was only a two-mile walk, and for Agnes, who was used to walking five or six miles a day, this was just an easy stroll. For her to have good old friends so close at hand was very comforting, and they managed to meet often. 'The Government House is quite charming — such an English looking place — & dear old house, just the place Mrs. Dewdney will enjoy with a capital big garden & orchard — a pretty conservatory and above all a first rate poultry yard!'[43] In sum, it was the sort of life Agnes had once lived herself. She had had her large houses, her gardens and orchards, she had had her greenhouses, her chickens — even her own cows at one time — but that was all in the past. Life was in the past, as she wrote to Pope, 'My day is over — my little part played & it is time to make room for younger people.'[44] Indeed, her philosophy had become to 'try in my poor way to do what I think Sir John would like until we meet again'.[45]

Aside from her welcome contacts with the Dewdneys and with a few old friends who were also spending some time at the Dallas that winter, Agnes had little distraction from her own sad thoughts other than in reading. For some months past, she had not been able to concentrate on books, but she had had the foresight to take a few along with her to Victoria, which she knew was not overly endowed with good libraries. 'We were spoiled at Ottawa with the Parliamentary Library & its fine selection of volumes',[46] she wrote the Professor. Of the new books she read at that time, she found that Warburton Pike's *Northern Canada* was 'delightful' and Randolph Churchill's *South Africa* pleased her very much. Of interest, too, was a book about a far-off land, *Two Happy Years in Ceylon,* which reminded her of other travel books she had read in her early years in Ottawa. It was 'Beautifully written & full of information'. Frances Monck's *My Canadian Leaves,* Agnes dismissed as being 'simply horrid', without giving her reasons. Agnes also began to miss the newspapers that she had been used to reading in eastern Canada. In Victoria, 'we see only a stupid little Grit paper called I think the *Colonist',*[47] she told Pope, who dutifully sent the *Empire* and passed on an order for magazines to help bridge the cultural gap for both Agnes and Mary.

Naturally, Agnes' thoughts often turned to her brother and his health. There had been some slight improvement, but Hewitt's doctors would still not allow him to travel all the way to Victoria. He had made up his mind, under the circumstances, to stay on at the Windsor Hotel in Montreal for the winter, and this seemed to Agnes to be a sensible plan from every point of view. He would be comfortable, centrally located and near friends who could keep Agnes informed of his condition.

Her own plans for the future, as far as she could formulate any, were to go to Banff in the spring and spend a month at the cottage before going on to Ottawa. She might, she thought, even go back to live in Earnscliffe. 'Then', she wrote the Professor, 'you can come and stay ever so long with me & be so warmly and affectionately welcome as indeed you always are.'[48]

Alas for Agnes' hopes that 'By and bye I shall be stronger and able to take up the threads of life again.'[49] Instead she was dealt another blow in February when Hewitt died. This was no more unexpected than John A.'s death had been, but it brought about a further change in Agnes' life. Now, except for Mary, she *was* alone and the idea of trying to pick up the threads of life in Canada became unthinkable. By late May, she was writing the Professor, not asking him to visit her in Earnscliffe, but telling him that she and Mary would be leaving for England in a few days, taking their paid companion, Kay Peacock, with them. 'Dear friend, ever kind & true to me', she wrote, 'one who when *he* was gone did not fail me as did others, I hope we shall meet again.'[50] Then, she and her daughter were off to Montreal to board the S.S. *Vancouver*, which would take them to England whence she had gone as a young girl so many years ago, and where there were still a few cousins left to whom she could turn in her sorrow.

From that time on, as far as Canada was concerned, she was 'an exile indeed'.

11

'T'is a beautiful land! — but the joy somehow has gone out of my life',[1] wrote Agnes soon after she and Mary arrived in London in June, 1893. During those first weeks there, how many memories must have crowded in on her. She could not have helped remembering her first visit to England with Theodora, more than forty years before. At that time, she had been young, possessed of youth's excitement at the thought of seeing a new land, meeting new people. Then, after beginning another new life in Canada, with Hewitt and Richard, there had been a return to London with her mother in 1865, quite possibly following a decision not to go to Ottawa as John A.'s wife. Only a short two years later she *had* gone to Ottawa as the wife of the Prime Minister, and there had been several visits to England in that role. At other times during those twenty-five years of marriage she had had to content herself with news about the country brought home by John A. after one of his periodic visits for reasons of health or politics. Now she was back, but those closest to her were gone: Theodora, Hewitt, Richard and John A., too. She was alone, alone as she had never before been in her entire life, yet with a totally dependent daughter to care for. It was slight wonder that she found the joy *had* gone out of her life to be replaced by indecision as she faced an unknown future.

Not unnaturally, Agnes headed first for Batt's Hotel, where she had always stayed with John A. This was not only a sentimental decision. As she wrote to Pope, 'I like old Batt's and will not go into any out of the way place.'[2] She had returned to England with the idea of renewing her acquaintance with family and friends there, so she thought it wise to go to a place that was centrally located; when it became known that she was in town, everyone would know exactly where to find her. So many strands had to be picked up and woven into the fabric of the new life she hoped to create for herself and for Mary.

Gratifyingly enough, she found from the first, that she was welcome. 'I have been most kindly received by many. . . . In fact, I have so many invitations in one way or another that I need never be at home.'[3] Her relatives, too, welcomed her. Shortly after her arrival, she wrote of having 'seen so many of my cousins — We had a family gathering the other evening and I saw some I had not seen for twenty years.'[4]

Not only was she welcomed by her family, friends and acquaintances. She also received the invitations that were bound to come her way as a Peeress of the realm. In Canada, Agnes had found the title to be mostly an annoyance. She had been expected to pay more for services than were untitled persons, and she had received attention from those who thought her position might help them further their climb in society. In England, the title was much more meaningful. For a few years, at least, she very much enjoyed its prerogatives, including several Royal invitations.

In the summer of 1893, there were two important events centered on the House of Windsor. Early in July the marriage of Princess May of Teck to the Duke of York (later King George V) took place in the tiny Chapel Royal in St. James's Palace. It was so small that Agnes wrote:

very few besides the bridal procession and suites of the various Royalties assembled could get into it. My seat was just outside where with about two hundred other guests I had the most excellent view. It was a magnificent sight and so was that of the various processions as in carriages they drove through the streets. . . . London was wild that day with joy and excitement. . . . In the evening I went out with Miss Peacock to see the immense crowds and illuminations and decorations and *on top of an omnibus* (for the first time in my life) we had a capital view.[5]

The other great event that summer was a garden party at Marlborough House and, there, wrote Agnes, 'I was kindly sent for by the Queen who spoke to me very kindly in her sweet gentle gracious way — so did the Prince and Princess of Wales and our own Princess Louise — so kindly and nicely. They are all so gracious and kind.'[6]

Agnes appreciated this social life, for, as she wrote the Professor, '. . . it was a very great compliment and distinction to be asked to those very distinguished affairs'.[7]

Agnes' title gave her another right that was to prove of even more lasting interest than its social opportunities. As Barnoness Macdonald of Earnscliffe, she was entitled to a seat in the House of Lords. Having an opportunity to be so close to decision-making in the highest council in the land made up somewhat for being so far away from the old Gallery seat in Ottawa. Many times over the next few years, Agnes would be found in the House of Lords, following debates with her usual attention.

While Agnes was becoming immersed in a new political and social life, Mary, too, was finding London stimulating. She had stood the voyage from Canada far better than Agnes had dared hope would be the case, suffering only a slight chill after she had persuaded her mother to let her stay on deck one afternoon longer than Agnes thought wise. Now, in London for the first time, in London which both Agnes and John A. had told her so much about and from which her mother had brought her such pretty clothes over the years, Mary soon felt at home. It was a feeling that would never leave her; no matter where she and her mother wandered in later years, it was always for London and the English seashore that Mary pined.

During her first summer there, Mary began to get to know the area around central London, with the help of a man to push her chair and with the companionship of her mother or Kay Peacock. She discovered the near-by delights of the Aquarium and South Kensington Museum. Hyde Park, too, was a great attraction and she went there 'constantly to watch the gay throngs of carriages, horsemen and pedestrians which crowd that very fascinating *rendez-vous* from 4 to 7.30 daily.'[8]

Even before leaving for England, Agnes had planned to follow the established pattern of British society — staying in town for six weeks or so to take part in the Season, and then taking a furnished house in the country for a few months. The house had to be chosen carefully; it had to be close enough to London for her to meet a few remaining social obligations, and, it had to suit Mary's needs. Agnes found such a place in the familiar surroundings of Sydenham. The train connection with London was good and the Crystal Palace was nearby. Mary would, as her mother said, 'find endless interests and amusements down [there]. I shall get a season family ticket and we shall enjoy the lovely grounds.'[9]

Once they were more or less domesticated again, Agnes could repay some of the hospitality she had received in London. She was anxious to make firm the ties she had re-established with her cousins, Louisa Scott and Annie Broome, and with Annie's husband, Sir Frederick. There were Canadian friends, too, some visiting England for the summer, whom Agnes invited down to Sydenham.

She was particularly eager that Joseph Pope, who was in Paris as Secretary to the Canadian Commission which had been convened to hear the results of the Bering Sea Tribunal, visit her. When he arrived, some time after the middle of August, there was great rejoicing as he and Agnes discussed the findings of the Commission,[10] which they both knew would have pleased John A.

While Agnes enjoyed talking about Canadian politics once more with Pope, making it seem rather like the old days, it was another matter she wanted to discuss more urgently — what progress Pope was making in writing John A.'s biography.[11] The subject of who should write the book had come up some years before the Prime Minister's death, and 'Sir

John', Agnes revealed, when she asked Pope to take on the task, in 1892, 'declined to let me try it (with his usual wisdom) and said you were to do it'.[12] Agnes had given the former Private Secretary sole permission to use her husband's correspondence and papers. John A. had left no limitations on the work, relying on Pope's judgment as did Agnes, so her only stipulation had been, 'I want a faithful and agreeable biography.... I have nothing more to say, nor do I intend by word or — — to tie your hands.'[13]

She had, however, departed from this assurance a few months later, when replying to a remark of Pope's, who had said he was going ahead as if some of the still-active politicians with whom John A. had dealt were all dead.

> I fear we must be careful! Tupper's position is a delicate one — Galt's life hangs on a thread — Tilley's devotion to Sir John is touching — It will look badly if these facts are ignored in the *Memoirs*. I *hate* to embarrass you, even by a word of caution — and I know that by too much of it the very *pith* of the book, the very point of the story will be left out. Still we must be careful — at least I fear I think this ought to be! — I know Tilley's part will be all right in history or elsewhere — but Galt's methods and Tupper's even to a looker on were frequently peculiar and when you come to Lord Dufferin's reign I fancy your difficulties will exceed those in the case of Lord Monck....
>
> But why should I say all this — Of course you have thought of it all round and a biographer must be faithful.... I think my nature is rash to extreme — but long experience has taught me caution as it has taught me nothing else — and I cannot quite get rid of apprehension on this point.[14]

Pope seems to have been guided by Agnes' words of caution concerning writing about John A.'s contemporaries. When the *Memoirs of Sir John A. Macdonald* appeared in 1894, he expressed his own thoughts on the 'difficulty of selection [which] has been heightened by the shortness of the interval that has elapsed since [Sir John's] death'.[15]

While Agnes enjoyed Pope's visit and her many other activities in England during her first few months back, it was not long before she gave way to restlessness once more. By December, 1893, she was complaining to the Professor that the English winter weather was '. . . so gloomy and damp and dismal that [she and Mary] could not face it any longer',[16] and, by Christmas Eve, she was writing to him from the Grand Hotel des Anglais in San Remo, Italy. From their sea-front windows, she wrote, the view across the flowery terraces and the palm trees down to the 'blue glorious sunny sea' was 'all quite delicious!'[17] The whole coast was beautiful but Agnes had chosen San Remo, she said, because it was less popular, less crowded and, thus, more suitable for Mary, who was able to spend many hours outdoors. In her chair, she enjoyed 'walks' along the paths overlooking the sea or through the streets of the old town, where flowers of all kinds blossomed during the entire winter. There was also, Agnes wrote, a little English church 'just below this hotel — half hidden in olive trees. We went there this morning and liked the service very much. A church makes one feel quite at home.'[18]

But they were not at home. They were wanderers and would continue to be such for the rest of Agnes' life. The winter months Agnes would spend on the Riviera, with or without Mary. Their summers would be broken up into periods in London, short visits to friends at the close of the Season and, for Agnes, usually a month or more each autumn in Scotland. Mary would spend many days and weeks in Ramsgate or the other coastal towns of southern England. It could not have been a particularly satisfying way of life, but it was Agnes' answer to the inner aimlessness she felt now that she did not have John A. and his dedication to purpose to guide her days. At times, she excused her frequent travels by saying they were necessary for her or Mary's health, and there is abundant evidence that she did find English winter weather depressing, but it appears that she travelled for the change as much as for anything else, often making quite sudden decisions to move on.

For the winter of 1894-95, she returned to San Remo but took a house there, hoping such an arrangement would help her feel more settled. That was not the answer. Late in the next autumn she was as undecided as she had been in 1893. She wrote Pope in October, 1895, 'So far I hardly know what to do. We can't very well face an English winter and yet this moving has a thousand disadvantages.'[19] In the end, she decided to try staying in England at the Norwood hotel where she and Mary had spent part of the summer, an establishment 'so exclusive and so private that it is like ones own home. Unfortunately, it is expensive but as I cannot *decide* on remaining all winter and may at any moment have to go away I felt it prudent not to take a house.'[20] The weather, she said, was the big drawback for it was 'very depressing. . . . *Literally* we live and move and have our being in semi darkness which like that of Egypt of old, can sometimes almost be *felt*, so heavy is the mixture of fog, blacks and smoke.'[21] Still, trying to look on the bright side, 'it is *London,* the centre of the known world. Every hour full of interest and a thousand things to see — to hear — to think on.'[22]

Yet, even 'the centre of the known world' was not enough to hold Agnes, and in subsequent years she continued her migrations. When she was abroad, she claimed that she liked continental society, much preferring it to the society she would have to be a part of if she lived in England. Yet, she felt like an exile, she insisted, and always returned to England and its temptations as soon as possible after a winter abroad. Often, in England, she chose to live in a place outside of but accessible to the London society which she could neither live with nor without. That way, to some extent, at least, she could pick and choose from the invitations that came her way. And such a location could always be justified by the fact that it was good for Mary.

One continual attraction the Italian Riviera held for her in the winter was the number of acquaintances she could count on meeting there. A number were Canadians who could afford to seek refuge from their own climate. During her first winter in San Remo, Agnes paid occasional visits to the Sir David Macphersons, who had a large villa just above her hotel. The following winter, they were back, and so were Sir William Van Horne and his C.P.R. colleague, Richard Angus, and others from Montreal whom Agnes knew, as well as her New Brunswick friends, the Lords, with whom she often took tea. It made a happy diversion for her to be able to get together with these old friends in the pleasant gardens of their villas and talk over Canadian news, which she was always eager to hear. There were also British acquaintances with whom to pass the time, and, from time to time, she visited with Lady Derby, formerly Lady Stanley. The Morrows, new friends from Warwickshire, were also there and with them, one day, Agnes visited Monte Carlo. Possibly fearing that Pope might be critical of this excursion, she quickly reassured him:

Please don't imagine that *I play*. Everyone does more or less but me. I am never tempted but think Monte Carlo is a horrid place and the Casino a great bore. It does not interest me in the very least and I can't — for the life of me — see where the fascination comes in. In the end everybody loses. . . . I think the beauty of Monte Carlo greatly exaggerated and the cruel pigeon shooting makes me *ill*.[23]

What a pity Agnes so often felt that she had to justify herself in this way. Life for her now was unsatisfactory enough. In addition to her restlessness and constant need to explain her actions, she had again begun to worry (rather needlessly) about her finances and to discover that the coronet had been a costly acquisition. Living in London was generally expensive, and the social demands on a Peeress difficult to meet within her income. She was sometimes filled with the horror that she might overspend, and this mood pushed her to go too far in the opposite direction. She wrote Pope in the spring of 1895:

I shall not go out at all this season. The interest in it — if I ever had any has departed and the late hours bore me horribly. I am very well and want to keep so and not waste money. I was asked to go to Kew this afternoon with friends but declined. One is constantly being asked to things small and great.[24]

In cutting out society that summer, Agnes did not alienate herself from the Canadian community in London, expatriates like herself as well as summer visitors, of whom there seem to have been a large number in 1895. For three weeks Agnes was entrusted with the chaperonage of two young daughters of Toronto friends; Julia Jarvis, another Torontonian, was there, and so was Alec Ferguson, Agnes' solicitor. George Sparks, an old friend from Ottawa, was in town, as well as Millie White, a friend of Mary's, and members of Thomas Reynolds' family, some of whom lived in England permanently.

The following summer, Agnes was drawn back to Canada, the only time she was to return there. Mary did not go with her as her plans called for a great deal of travelling about the country to see friends and relatives, a schedule the young invalid could not have kept up with. Upon her arrival, Agnes went almost directly to Barrie, her first home in Canada. There, she wrote Pope:

> Tynehead, Barrie, (really Allandale),
> Lake Simcoe

My dear Joe:
 . . . I am enjoying every hour of my stay in this my niece's [Dora Pepler] charming little country home — a cottage about 50 yards from the bay. . . .
 Frank Pepler is a delightful fellow. They have four dear little boys all under 10. We drive and boat a good deal — last night we were out on the bay until 11.30 down to Strathallan for butter and homemade bread.[25]

It was all very pleasant and it was gratifying, too, to find that she had not been forgotten: 'All my old Barrie friends have welcomed me with *more* than friendship — of course they are very old chums — most of them dating from my early girlhood.'[26]

But Agnes had to press on. She told Pope:

Please send next [letter] to care Major Harper, Banff — I hope to be there on Friday or Saturday next — stay there three or four days and then spend two at Winnipeg. . . . I want to go to Rothsay, N.B., to see the Tilleys before returning to Ottawa and from Ottawa go direct to New York. I will be retracing my steps but on the whole that will be the best way for me.[27]

It is no wonder that when Pope was asked where Agnes might be found, he replied that she had been running all over the country. It was as if she knew this was to be her last time in Canada and she felt she had to see as many people and as much of the country as possible.

One stop-over Agnes did not make was at her old summer home in Rivière du Loup. The cottage and Les Rochers property, which she had enlarged over the years through purchases from *habitants,* had been sold the previous August to Sir Thomas Shaughnessey of the C.P.R. Pope had looked after the sale for Agnes, who had agreed to hand over the property intact since the only item of historic importance left in the house was, possibly, the 'old table Sir John always wrote at. Many an important matter concerning the C.P.R. was decided at that table. Knights and Governors, Senators and Chief Justices were made at it, and Riel hanged therefrom.'[28] This, she felt, should remain as a memento of John A.

It grieved Agnes to think of '. . . the sale of the dear old place — Sir John A.'s favourite place and where he took such infinite rest and pleasure',[29] and it was a blow to realize that she could never use it again. Yet, it was comforting to know that the place would not fall into disrepair. If only someone would buy Earnscliffe, she wished.

After returning to London in 1896, Agnes could not get Earnscliffe out of her mind. Earlier she had thought of going back there to live but had come to the regretful conclusion that this was not practical: 'Were I even 10 years younger and strong as I used to be I would go out and live there and take all risks but I am old and gouty and of no use.'[30] The obvious solution was to sell it, especially since she had seen while visiting Ottawa, how her dear old home was suffering from continued leasing.

It was not until 1900, however, that Earnscliffe found a new owner, Agnes' old friend, Ella Beatty, the wife of Charles Harriss, a well-known musician. Agnes hoped most sincerely that her friend might be 'as truly happy as I was and that her life there may be as full of content and as bright with blessing'.[31] Yet, she confessed, 'when the moment for signing came — there was no sadder woman than I in all England. There is hardly a sadder woman tonight as I sit alone and dream of the dear old days.'[32]

Agnes' trip to Canada in 1896 gave her an opportunity to see at first hand that subject she had never lost interest in — Canadian politics. Earlier in the year Pope had been named Under Secretary of State, partially because of Agnes' urging. She had written Tupper, she told Pope, 'in the strongest English I could get off the tip of my best pen. There have not been wanting those, in the past, who said I could write pretty pungently — and I used my very best effort in writing for you.'[33]

Nothing could replace first-hand observations, but Pope's new position gave her the chance to hear news close to the source, especially in 1899 when he visited London with Laurier for discussions on the Alaska Boundary Dispute. As soon as he had finished his official duties, Pope took the train out to Bushey where 'Lady Macdonald met me at the station. They live in The Hall, about half way between Bushey and Watford — a select hotel, large airey, comfortable, lovely grounds, etc.'[34] (At one time, The Hall had been a hydropathic establishment; Agnes may have been attracted to it for its therapeutic qualities in case they should help

Mary, as well as for its accessibility to London.)

Pope stayed in The Hall for the weekend. He and Agnes 'took a long tramp across country',[35] talking of Canadian affairs. Much had taken place in the Dominion since Agnes had left it in the summer of 1893. Before she sailed, Abbott had been succeeded as Prime Minister by Sir John Thompson, in spite of misgivings about the latter's Catholicism, but he had died on December 12, 1894, after only two years in office. Following his death, his wife, like Agnes after John A.'s death, had written the Governor-General to suggest a successor to her husband. Lady Aberdeen had noted in her diary, 'She was quite clear that Mr. Haggart[36] was the man that would be best able to keep the party together.'[37]

This advice, like that of Agnes in 1891, had not been taken and it had been left to Mackenzie Bowell to form an Administration. Agnes had not approved of the choice, and she had not been surprised when he later had trouble holding his Government together. She had no qualms about admitting, 'I never liked him and he never liked me. We were gently antagonistic by nature',[38] and she had seen men come and go in high office often enough to be a rather good judge of their capabilities vis-a-vis the political expediency of the moment. By the beginning of May, 1896, he had disappeared from the scene and Tupper had re-emerged to lead the Conservative party into an election.

Thus Agnes had seen her 1891 choice for the highest office of the land having his chance, at last. Forgetting her private comments to Pope about Tupper's 'frequently peculiar methods', she had praised this move by an old man, who had, for the most part, lived in London as Canadian High Commissioner since 1884. Perhaps out of loyalty to her husband and to the days when he and Tupper had worked together to create the Dominion, she had written, excitedly:

> . . . if only a strong wise active Govt. can be got together and hold on. But, I greatly fear for Tupper's health canvassing in such weather after [being] in England. But he is quite indomitable. . . and if any man can be made of any immediate use, he is the one with his promptness, vigour and courage. I don't suppose any living man ever made a greater sacrifice than Tupper when he left his charming London home, so snug and secure to fight elections during a Canadian winter. I hope Canada will appreciate this from a man over seventy and not at all strong. Nothing but a true and lofty sense of duty could possibly have activated him and he ought to be most strongly and loyally supported.[39]

In the general election that took place on June 23, 1896, (and not in the winter as Agnes seems to have expected), the country had *not* rallied around Tupper. The Conservatives had been decisively beaten and the Liberal era in Canadian politics had begun, with Laurier forming the new Government.

While this was not the result Agnes had hoped for, she had been neither very surprised nor very disappointed. 'In Canada a change was clearly and evidently wanting and wanted — and by all odds it was a Liberal's turn.'[40] All that she wanted, she had written Pope, was the good of the country, and she thought Laurier and his Cabinet should do very well. In the same letter, she had made a rather surprising admission:

You know with all my intense belief in Sir John's splendid politics, I was never an extremely strong party spirit. Never one of those truly admirable women who believe one side could never be right — and the other never wrong. Nor could I hate the Opposition with a correct and proper amount of Christian detestation.[41]

No doubt, if any Liberal other than Laurier had been at the helm of Canadian affairs, Agnes would never have admitted to such feelings, but Laurier was high in her books. She found that he resembled Sir John in so many ways and this was even more evident after he had been in office for a year: 'I hear the Govt. is going on smilingly. New brooms are pro-verbial but, to my mind, Laurier has taken in the strangest way, not only the policy but also the personality of Sir John.'[42]

In October, 1899, as Agnes and Pope walked across the countryside near Bushey, all the actions of Laurier and his Government came under scrutiny. Agnes felt much more in the picture and even more reassured about the future of the country she had seen created.

Pope and Agnes also discussed the latter's personal affairs, especially those relating to Mary's future. Mary was then thirty years old and at the peak of her mental development. Agnes knew that there was no hope of physical improvement and the question of what would become of her crippled daughter was one of great concern to her. What would happen when Mary was left alone? What plans could she make now? The two thought of various possibilities, and after Pope went back to Ottawa, Agnes discussed them with Mary. It was Mary's choice, Agnes then wrote, to return to Canada after her mother's death. She would live in Ottawa in her own house with an elderly, experienced lady in charge of the household, and no relative, under any pretext, should live there. One strong reason given by Mary for wishing to return to Canada, wrote Agnes, was so that she could be ' "near her brother" Hugh in whom she has great faith and for whom she has a warm affection'.[43]

That faith was misplaced, and during the following year, Hugh began to give Agnes almost as much concern as did Mary. A Federal election was scheduled for November, 1900, and Hugh resigned as Premier of Manitoba to enter the race. It was worrying to Agnes to see that Hugh was still so 'absolutely bound to Sir C's [Tupper's] chariot wheel', but she knew that old loyalties died hard with the Old Chief's son and, in spite of Tupper's great unpopularity in Canada at that period, Agnes hoped that Hugh would be successful in his fight for a seat.

> I *should* like to see Hugo [sic] Prime Minister of Canada — I have always told him that tho' I consider politics a most anxious, money losing, thankless, weary task, I also considered politics his *duty*, crisp and clear and advised him to stick to it as a duty. Be very sure he only does so from the very highest motives of patriotism.[44]

There were very few men, Agnes thought, with Hugh's mind: 'He is a remarkable character and always was. Few know him better than I do, none admire him more tho' I am his stepmother and by rights we ought to quarrel like cat and dog.'[45]

Unfortunately, Hugh did not have the political stamina of his father, but he had inherited the tendency to turn to drink under stress. He gave way to this weakness during the campaign and failed in his attempt to re-enter the House as Laurier's Liberals swept the field. Bad news travels fast and it was not long before Agnes knew that

> ...my dear Hugh was unable to keep in check his unfortunate tendency during the Elections. I cannot tell you how it has saddened and distressed me.... If it is true that he has again succumbed to liquor I know it will be many months before he recovers.... His system is very delicate.... The regular quiet life he loves and always tries to lead is *the only one* for him. I do trust that all his friends and mine will do all they *possibly* can to induce Hugo [sic] to remain in private life.[46]

Hugh had entered the fight out of patriotism and in loyalty to his father's memory. He had been encouraged by his wife, who liked nothing better than to think of him as a Dominion politician, and by Agnes, who had mistakenly seen him as the image of his father.

Part of Agnes' misjudgement may be excused by the fact that she had seen so little of her Canadian relatives since moving to the other side of the Atlantic. Except during her flying trip across Canada, in 1896, she had spent time only with Hugh's daughter, Daisy. In 1894, Hugh had finally given in to Agnes' urging and sent Daisy over to study in 'a first rate Brighton establishment. I have visited the school several times', Agnes wrote to the Professor, 'and know the ladies who keep it... all very satisfactory... just what I wish Daisy had enjoyed since 1891 when I wished her to be sent to an English school but Hugh thought her too young.'[47]

Daisy's education had always been of interest to Agnes, possibly giving her some measure of compensation for the fact that Mary could never go to school. When Daisy was only ten, she had spent a winter in Ottawa, attending Miss Harmon's boarding school but passing her weekends at Earnscliffe. Mary had then written Aunt Louisa:

Some of us go for her every Friday and she goes back Sunday afternoon as she is too young to get up Monday morning to be at school at nine o'clock. She takes great pains with her lessons. Mother received a letter from Miss Harmon the other day in which she praised Daisy for her good qualities and industry at her lessons.[48]

The following year, Daisy was sent to the Convent of the Sacred Heart at Sault-au-Recollet, near Montreal, since it had been agreed that she should be brought up in her mother's faith and there were very few suitable schools in Winnipeg. Holidays had still been spent at Earnscliffe and she had become a great favourite in her grandfather's family. With Agnes she had developed a special relationship that was, happily, renewed in 1894. Agnes had promised Hugh that Daisy would get to see something of Europe and of the British Isles. She joined Agnes and Mary for a holiday in San Remo over the Christmas break of 1894-95 and spent the following Easter holiday with Agnes on a tour of the Lake District. Then, in summer, Agnes took the eighteen-year-old 'Dee' to visit John A.'s part of Scotland. At one time Agnes had not found Daisy's mind very perceptive, but, gradually, she changed her opinion and now wrote, 'Daisy is I think learning to enjoy and appreciate some of what she sees. I take great pains with her.'[49] Encouraged by this growing appreciation on the part of her granddaughter, Agnes arranged to take Daisy to Switzerland in the summer and later wrote of it as being one of the most beautiful things she had ever done.

It was on her return from the trip to Scotland with Daisy that Agnes had the sad news of the Professor's death. In writing to thank Pope for representing her at the funeral, she shared some memories of long ago:

The Professor is one of the first memories of my early married life and from the day on which Sir John introduced me saying, 'Professor, this is my dear young wife' to that in which with a sisterly kiss I left the dear old man our friendship and esteem knew no check nor diminuation. [sic][50]

While the Professor had been in indifferent health for quite some time, the news was still a shock for Agnes, 'the loss of another old friend — the snapping of another link in the chain that binds me now (and always will) to the past I mourn so much.'[51]

It was not long before Agnes' family circle, already small, was still further diminished. Sir Frederick Broome, the husband of her cousin Annie, died in 1897. And the following spring saw the death of Dalton

157

McCarthy, the husband of her brother Richard's widow and the man John A. had once hoped would succeed him. Agnes had not seen McCarthy since John A. lay dying, but she still remembered 'his emotion and his kinds words'[52] at that time. She excused the fact that he had been in London several times without seeing her: 'I am sure he had some good reason, and never imagine for an instant, that he wished to show neglect, or had in any way forgotten, or ceased to be as fond of me as, truly, I was and am of him.'[53] In mourning McCarthy's death, Agnes felt not only the loss of a close family connection but a loss to the country:

His career ought to have been very different with his fine talents, charming manners, strong personality and excellent heart — he was the man to lead our party and to victory but with all his great powers, he was easily influenced and in bad hands. I always hoped the day would come when, the past forgotten and forgiven, he would take his proper place as Head of the Party. It is all over now.[54]

Whether her relatives and friends were directly involved or not, Agnes never stopped watching and commenting on both Canadian and British politics. This was, of course, a particularly tumultuous time throughout the British Empire. As early as 1896, she had written:

It is a long time since England has been so beset by enemies and troubles.
The rage against the German Emperor for his insolent and cruel telegram to Kruger[55] of the South African Republic is very great indeed.... Public opinion veers to all points of the compass... the only points that so far *stick* is that the Emperor's conduct is shameful.[56]

By 1899, war seemed inevitable in South Africa, and Laurier was caught between English-Canadian and French-Canadian feelings regarding his country's involvement, particularly since he had, for some time, resisted the philosophy that there should be strong colonial participation in all imperial defence. Patriotic sentiments ran high as the Boer War broke out, and the Prime Minister took refuge in the fact that nothing could be done, officially, without a grant from Parliament. As a precedent for this stand, Laurier used the example of none other than John A. who, in 1885, had refused to send troops to the Sudan. In the end, however, the Liberal leader had to resort to a compromise, whereby Canadian volunteers could enlist for service in South Africa, but their contingents were under the exclusive control of the British War Office.

Keeping watch in England, Agnes could not but feel proud that her husband's policies were still being honoured, while, at the same time, Laurier had found a way for Canadians to contribute to the immense outpouring of British patriotism she saw around her. 'We [i.e. Laurier and Agnes] are both Imperialists and he as much a Liberal Conservative as ever Sir John and I were. I wish with all my heart he was in our camp — soul and body as he ought to be — He is millions too good for the other and I always said so.'[57]

Within a few months Canada sent two contingents of 1,000 volunteers each. Then Lord Strathcona, the former Donald Smith of C.P.R. fame and John A.'s old enemy, spoke up. He had succeeded Tupper as Canadian High Commissioner in London in 1897, and, perhaps moved by the evidence of British feeling which he saw around him, perhaps embarrassed that Canada was not doing more to help, he 'With a gesture worthy of a feudal seigneur or a railway magnate, bore the cost of raising the six hundred rifles known as Strathcona's Horse.'[58]

The Canadian volunteers, though few in absolute numbers, certainly contributed to the eventual winning of the war, and, as Agnes noted, '. . . our brave Canadian boys — so splendid at Paardberg and elsewhere have immensely raised their country in estimation over here.'[59]

Although the war dragged on until 1902, by December, 1900, many of the Canadian volunteers, whose enlistments had been mainly for six-month terms, were on their way home. Passing through London, they were given heroes' welcomes — an inspection by Queen Victoria at Windsor Castle, and 'an apparently endless round of parades, visits, receptions and entertainments'.[60] Agnes was in London at the time and went to 'the inspection by the Prince of Wales which was very good but I only went as a spectator among the upper ten crowd'.[61] She also attended a 'handsome' farewell party, given by Lord Strathcona, for what she described as a 'large and distinguished company' in 'the large rooms in the Imperial Institute, decorated and light as day', marked by 'speeches, etc.'.[62]

During those days in London and later that spring in Cannes, Agnes was frequently called upon to defend her country's stand. As the war dwindled to a halt, Laurier continued to come under criticism from the Conservatives, who felt he should have done more, and the Quebec nationalists, who believed no troops should have been sent at all. She eagerly followed the fierce debate on the subject in the Canadian House. 'I do so often wish I could find myself just for an evening in my old gallery seat! The seat I was so rarely absent from.'[63] The next best thing was to read exactly what had been said in the debate, and Pope was asked to send the Hansards, 'like a good boy'.[64] She especially wished to read Laurier's reply to the Quebec leaders in its entirety, and she also wished her friends in Cannes to have the whole story.

Agnes, like the London *Times* and many of her English friends, had been full of praise for Laurier. When the Hansards arrived, however, she altered her opinion somewhat for she found that

Laurier tho' graceful tactful and charming (as his speeches always are) was, I think, just a little weak — No doubt (alas) he was on brittle ice and could not avoid showing that he felt so. . . .

I am sorry it has all happened as we are all so proud over here of the loyalty of the French Canadians.[65]

She did not air this partial criticism of Laurier to her acquaintances in Cannes. Rather, she presented a picture of full support for Canada's position, taking the line that 'Canada as part of the Empire naturally gave help in what the Imperial Govt. considered it was wise and necessary to do without thinking it her duty to decide on the main question.'[66] Only to Pope would she specify her own criticisms of both Canadian and English leaders:

. . . the war has been sadly mismanaged and really forced on England by the selfish millionaires here who told the Govt. that it would be a 'walk over'. Rhodes and his lot didn't care a fig for consequences — a reckless, speculating, dare-devil set who came over, their pockets full of money and dazzled English eyes to whom the sight of gold is entrancing *no matter how acquired or by whom.*[67]

And, having fired that broadside, Agnes turned her thoughts back to the immediacy of her own summer plans, which called for a visit to Switzerland before returning, once more, to England for some months, there to try to still any further criticisms of Canada and its policies, should the need arise.

12

In December, 1900, as the Canadian troops who had fought in the Boer War left England for home, Agnes expressed her regret that she 'could not have gone to more of the Canadian demonstrations but could not as I had to take turns with Mary and [besides] as a Peeress one has to "go and be and dress accordin".[1]

More and more during these years, Agnes was finding that her title imposed a financial burden, which frightened her. Her attempts to avoid its social obligations were generally impossible to achieve and, as in the case of the celebrations for the Canadian volunteers, there were functions she wanted to attend, although she would have preferred the freedom to do so without the terrifying expense involved. As early as 1896, she had written Pope:

> If only I were rid of the coronet. . . but as it is in some unfortunate way, I have got into a set in England in which it is impossible I should live easily!. . . Alas! the taking of the title was a bad day for me — but I shall get rid of it — and be Mrs. John Alex Macdonald. . . . I cannot tell you how the very word *Baroness* annoys me![2]

(There is, however, no record of her ever having made any moves towards relinquishing her title, nor could she have done so under the laws of the day.[3])

So Agnes continued to move in artistocratic circles. There were even certain occasions, especially Royal occasions, which she did enjoy to some extent, although she did not express the same excitement about them that she had shown in the months immediately after her return to England.

Among these, of course, were the festivities of the Diamond Jubilee. At the time of the Golden Jubilee, Agnes had escaped most of the Ottawa observances by leaving for her fishing trip to northern New Brunswick. On that occasion her only concern had been that her clothes be practical, and, as she recalled, she had worn 'a loose grey dress. . . and an old straw hat with a mosquito veil tightly fastened by elastic to keep out sandflies and mosquitoes'.[4] In 1897, there was no such escape. She was in London and, as a Peeress, in the thick of the celebrations, even though she had to 'go and be and dress accordin''.

By January 23, 1901, the lonely little Queen who had reigned so many years was dead, and, although the coronation of Albert Edward was not scheduled to take place for over a year, his subjects began to think of the ceremony which had not been held in such a long time. Even Agnes was thinking of the occasion. 'It will be an immense temptation. Fancy — I should have a Peeress' seat!',[5] she wrote from Cannes, where she and Mary were spending the winter. On her return to England in the spring of 1901, she found that London was almost too full of talk about the great event. 'I am tired already', she said, 'of hearing Coronation talk from morning till night. The fuss made about it is extraordinary.'[6] She went to the extent of telling Strathcona, the High Commissioner, '[I] had given up the idea of going to the Coronation but [he] understood clearly I think that I could not think it right to spend so much money on an hour's show — even tho' I should like to do so.'[7]

It was a stand that she could not maintain, possibly had no intention of maintaining, and when she returned in the spring of 1902, after wintering abroad, she confessed a little excitement: '. . . so many, in fact all my friends seemed to think I ought to go to [it]. The 1st 'Canadian Peeress' they rang the changes on it so (DV) I am going — if I am summoned, which no doubt I shall be. Summons for Peers and Peeresses come last of all — being signed by the *King's own hand.* '[8]

The summons duly arrived and, by late May, Agnes' costume was 'in hand'. She was to wear 'crimson velvet, boddice [sic] and train, petticoat of frilled chiffon and Irish lace — train and robe trimmed with miniver fur — all *most* costly — alas! I fitted on a coronet Friday.'[9] Just writing of all this luxury made her reflect:

How the wheel goes round! A small Creole child without a shilling brought to this mightly island — quite unknown — and unnoticed, and here I am among the first at the Coronation of Kings!

  It seems so strange and so undeserved a revolution. . . . But of course, every phase of life is ordered and willed. . . and I owe all from an earthly point of view, to the great man who made me his wife.[10]

The date for the Coronation was set for early July and London was already filled with visitors, both official and unofficial, when the great day had to be postponed. The King, suffering from what was described as a sudden and acute attack of appendicitis, was rushed to Guy's

Hospital, where he was operated on immediately. Both English hosts and their guests were full of consternation, but Agnes was able to report, 'The people all over England have behaved quite beautifully. My livery stable keeper's wife voiced them when she said with tears, as I consoled, "Nothing matters. We can bear any loss if only our King gets well."'[11] All the same, she wrote, the 'loss and disappointment is great in many directions. . . . *Immense* preparations of every sort had been made and no end of "stuff" of every sort and kind is on the caterers' hands.'[12]

The delay in the Coronation date imposed a financial hardship on Agnes as well as on London's caterers. 'Society has found out poor old me and I am simply deluged with invites, cards and all sorts of things. . . . I don't go to half my invites, indeed only for those which are for Colonials. . . . [They] are up in the market I can tell you! It is all the fashions to come from Fiji!!!!'[13] Many of those Colonials were, naturally, Canadians, and Lord Strathcona 'gave a magnificent reception. . . nearly 2000 present. Water Colour Institute — half a dozen fine halls crammed.'[14]

These descriptions Agnes wrote hurriedly to Pope, apologizing for her haste and explaining that she was 'up to eyes in work of sorts — amongst it helping (as one of the stall-holders) Lady Strathcona's Canadian Stall at the RB Garden on 10-11-12 July.'[15] This event, which was to benefit the Hospital for Sick Children, Great Ormond Street, had been planned for some time, and, when it was seen that the King was making a good recovery, the Queen, as Patron of the hospital, agreed to open it as scheduled. Agnes wrote, with pride,

Our Canadian stall. . . will I think be a handsome one. Mrs. Howard[16] and I are at the head of it with Lady Strathcona as ostensible chief. I need not say that all the old Lord is allowed to pay and *does* like a prince but the committee (of which I am president) agreed with me that all must not, should not be left with him and for him to do.[17]

It had been many years since Agnes had done any work of this kind and, like the 'old Lord', she was not any younger. She was fretting, too, about her 'gorgeous robes [which were] stowed away in brave hopes of being disinterred by and by. Report says in Oct. I hope not earlier — that would make still further trouble and spoil the holidays of rich and poor.'[18]

The decision as to the delayed Coronation date, however, was reached without regard for the 'rich and poor' or for Agnes' travel plans. When the date was set for Saturday, August 9, however, Londoners and their guests were able to make definite plans. Some of the foreign visitors could not wait around any longer, but many settled down to enjoy themselves for a month. Lord Strathcona had his hands full with so many Canadians in town and, besides offering his usual First of July Party, he also gave a dinner for the Colonial Premiers, to which Agnes was invited. It was, she said:

a splendid dinner.... 64 guests — 8 at each table and 8 tables. House decorated with flowers and palms. Electric light in ceiling — Each table covered with rich silver and delicate glass and a large silver basket of red roses, ferns and leaves on each. Princess Louise and the Duke of Aberdeen, etc., etc...a *first rate* dinner all beautifully done. Sir William Mulock[19] sat next to me at dinner.[20]

All these festivities were enjoyable, but hard on the purse and on the constitution, Agnes commented, noting that, as one of the popular breed of Colonials, 'I have been asked — pressed to go everywhere & have truly been 'going it' night & day!'[21] Undoubtedly she expressed the thoughts of many when she wrote, 'We crowned the King at last on Saturday.'[22] Yet, she found the ceremony

a magnificent and solemn sight.... I was with the Peeresses and had a fine view. The theatre was immediately below us — I think everything went off to perfection — The King in his Crown and robe of cloth of gold was magnificent — so was the Queen in 18 feet of royal purple velvet — embroidered with gold crowns and her underdress a standing mass of richest embroidery, jewels, costly lace, etc. The Princesses' procession was a sight to behold. Pr. of Wales grand looking in *her* velvet train and ermine and wonderful diamonds — all the Princesses were in purple.[23]

It was not until the summer of 1905 that Agnes, once more, had to look to a suitable wardrobe for Royal occasions. Early in June, she accepted an invitation to an evening Court at Buckingham Palace, an event which was, she wrote Pope, 'a fine ceremony, more interesting than a drawing room, no crowd, and people, after passing King and Queen, standing or sitting in the huge Throne Room at upper end of which the Sovereigns side by side sit in big gilded chairs.'[24] In describing what she wore that night, Agnes went into some detail 'For Minette's [Mrs. Pope's] edification'. Her costume was, she reported,

very handsome — all white (as I am always in mourning[25] and Royalties don't like black at Court) — satin dress, very fine and immense train of brocade — turned over on one side and caught back with white satin flowers and lined exquisitely with puffings of tulle and illusion — High white feathers and lappets — really a *veil* of tulle.[26]

164

In the same month Agnes also attended an afternoon party at Windsor given for the Swedish guests who had come over to attend the wedding of Margaret of Connaught and Gustav Adolph, eldest son of the Crown Prince of Sweden. 'The day was *quite* perfect', she wrote, 'and the scene one to be ever remembered. Between 5 and 6000 gorgeous company on these marvellous lawns and gardens at Windsor — all the Royalties so kind and interested and doing all sorts of nice attentions to welcome their guests.'[27] The day was especially marked for Agnes when the Duchess of Connaught 'remembered and spoke *most* graciously to me who she had not seen for 16 years!. . . it was all most satisfactory as you may imagine.'[28]

While Agnes' gowns for these and other Royal occasions were extraordinary by present-day standards, she was quite simply dressed in comparison with many other distinguished ladies who attended the Court. Her complaints about the expense of dressing for these affairs were, in many ways, justified. Nor was it simply a question of an occasional Royal invitation. Women of her station were expected to dress in the extravagent mode of the day for most social affairs, even for such a commonplace event as attending the theatre.[29]

And Agnes did go the theatre from time to time, although she was offended by many of the plays offered London audiences at the beginning of the twentieth century: 'Truth to say plays now-a-days are all so unpleasant in tone it is difficult in any way to find one commonly decent all through. Wyndham's is the best. . . and Cyril Maude won't give bad pieces. . . . Everything is beautiful at the plays — but the *morals!*'[30]

Mary, who spent her life as an observer of others, was less critical. What she wanted mostly was entertainment and, for this reason, Agnes tried to arrange a matinee attendance for her daughter now and then. Such excursions had to be well planned; as Agnes wrote, early in December 1901: 'I have been walking about Piccadilly and Long Acre this morning making arrangements for [Mary] going to the Drury Lane matinee tomorrow at 1.45. . . . I have to see entrance stairs, seats, etc. and engage lifters to convey her about when she is taken out of a Victoria at the door.'[31]

The play was *The Great Millionaire* and Mary found it to be a brilliant spectacle. A few weeks later, Agnes took her to see *Iolanthe*, which was 'quite beautifully done and pretty music. [Mary] was charmed but it is a costly outing I assure you and I am obliged to turn a deaf ear to her gentle hints about just such another.'[32]

Yet, there were continued outings of this type for Mary; late in 1904, Agnes wrote:

Mary, radiant, is just off to the Apollo Theatre to see *Veronique*, a musical play.... Bill for afternoon spree as follows

3 Theatre tickets — Balcony — £1.0.6
Lifters 4/ Chairman 3/
Page carrying chair 1/
Books, coffee and opera glass 2/
Mrs. Biden's[33] journey to and fro Sydenham 4/
Lunch-dinner and tea here for her 7/
In all £2.7.0[34]

'Meantime', Agnes continued in frank admission, 'I have a whole after-noon *all* to myself — an accident which does not often happen.'[35]

Despite the expense and the difficulties of arrangements, these were ef-forts Agnes felt obliged to make. The responsibility of meeting the needs of her daughter was enormous. Mary, she wrote, 'knows her weaknesses and said to me only this evening as I sat reading to her for hours, "I shall never grow any older, Mother, I shall always be more or less a child but so long as you doat [sic] on me that will not matter!!"'[36] It was hard on Agnes to realize that Mary was aware of her condition to this extent but 'I do all I can, day after day, year after year, so long as I shall be spared to lighten her burden and brighten her sweet gentle life.'[37]

This, of course, was what John A. and Agnes had always tried to do for their daughter, but, during these years in England, Agnes' responsibility grew greater, not only because she had no one with whom to share it, but because she saw that Mary's mind was gradually but continually im-proving. (This was a surprising change as Agnes had earlier felt Mary had reached the peak of her mental capabilities.) Her daughter was becoming 'quite companionable — very gentle but with very fixed ways and wishes',[38] and this awakened intelligence 'requires far more com-panionship than I ever dared hope she would need'.[39] It was the periods when mother and daughter were apart for any reason that Agnes worried about most. A nurse could look after Mary's physical needs but if her 'awakened intelligence' were not to suffer a set-back, it was obvious that Mary needed the companionship of an educated person, preferably her mother.

Providing such companionship and stimulation gave Agnes con-siderable problems, as well as expense. For one thing, mother and daughter were very different in character and desires. True, Mary had inherited, from her maternal grandmother, a sweet, patient nature that made her 'the most unselfish soul you could imagine...She is so courteous and dignified and high minded as a friend said the other day "a perfect lady in thought and action."'[40] On the other hand, she was also her father's daughter and had a good share of his conviviality. That

was sometimes difficult for Agnes to satisfy. For Mary, England —
preferably London or its outskirts — was where she liked to be. There, her
friends could drop in to see her, staying for tea. She had her 'story books,
her tri-weekly outings, her music and an occasional play.'[41]

Yet Agnes could not content herself with London for long periods at a
time, nor could she stand the cold, damp English winters. She was driven
to travel, alone or with friends, in search of new horizons which would
make her life a little more acceptable. Sometimes she took Mary with
her, despite the difficulties of making arrangements for an invalid, but
that rarely satisfied Mary's taste. Even the busy, gay resorts of Cannes appealed to her only briefly, as Agnes noted ruefully in March, 1901:
'[Mary] is only half reconciled to being away from England and amuses
me by her sturdy indifference to the charm of foreign life.'[42]

At other times, Agnes made complicated and expensive arrangements
for Mary to remain in England, close to her friends, while she herself
pursued her restless travels. In 1902 and, again, in 1905, Agnes travelled
during the winter to Italy with a paid *dame de companion*. She stopped
off to visit some friends on the Riviera before going on to Rome, with
Sicily being the final destination. The dry, piercing winter of Rome did
not suit Agnes' disposition any better than did the London climate, and
in 1902 two or three weeks was all she could stand before moving further
south. On the later trip, even the weather beyond Rome disappointed
her at first. They had snow on the way to Naples and a very rough crossing to Palermo — '14 hours of misery', as she said.

> We landed here at Palermo with joy without parallel.... There was the usual
> fuss about landing in Italy anywhere (never however as bad as it is in Naples)
> but it was a fine sweet morning and we drove at once to this truly beautiful
> spot — out of the town — close down to the sea — a marble and stone palace
> standing in the most charming garden — what we should call *grounds* with
> quite lovely views on every side.
>
> Terraces, balustrades, flights of steps, temples — all marble... quite a sort
> of Paradise, going down to the deepest of blue seas.[43]

After four weeks of long walks in this beautiful and historic setting,
Agnes and her companion, Mrs. Thayer, moved on to Taormina,
arriving

> in a *snow storm* as thick and as dark as any Quebec storm I can remember
> [but] in two days every vestige of snow was gone... Taormina is romantically
> lovely — a large Sicilian village high on hills — which rise beyond, above and on
> every side — in fact we are on one of the Etna range and the volcano — high
> uplifted and snowy crested rises 20 miles to the west — a glorious object
> indeed.[44]

Although the surroundings were idyllic, Agnes continued to worry about Mary, who had been left behind in England. She heard from and about her daughter frequently, but she did not think she would like to leave her for another winter. Sooner or later this chaotic life had to come to an end; she must have a more settled existence. Moreover, she had to give Mary more companionship, even if it did mean uprooting her from her beloved England. Mary would have to be able to spend winters with her mother and accept living in a foreign country for part of the year. And in that country, with Agnes to supervise, it would be possible — it would *have* to be made possible — for Mary to receive the mental stimulation she needed. When the English maid who had been with Mary for some years stoutly refused to set foot out of England again, Agnes made up her mind that she must act now. On her way home in the spring of 1905, she stopped over in Alassio, 'a sweet spot — and chiefly frequented by English people'.[45] It appealed to her so much that she decided to rent a house there for the following winter and signed a lease without further delay. The cost of running her winter home would not be too high; there would be enough money to spare so that she and Mary could go back to England each summer and keep in touch with their friends there — an all-important point for both of them.

The villa in Alassio, Casa Amena, became their winter home in late 1905. For the first time in years, Agnes faced the challenge of keeping house — and doing so in a language she knew just enough of to be able to make her way through the hassles of Italian Customs. To her credit, this did not faze her and, when they were settled, she took lessons twice a week for '. . . only one of my domestics knows a syllable of any other tongue. She has a little French *patois*.'[46]

The experiment in settling down, at least part of the year, proved a success. Agnes reported to Pope:

We spend our time very pleasantly. Every week I have two people to dinner as I am out so much every afternoon and in this way I see folk. . . . Sometimes, lonely enough, I wonder in my vague old way if I have done rightly and yet — as I sit writing today — Dec. 5, in a house where, with *warm* sunshine streaming into my large airy beautiful villa rooms and see Mary on the loggia reading. . . I feel that at my age and in her condition we are really better at Alassio.[47]

Agnes had as much social life as she wished. 'Alassio is very well-provided with a nice class of English and they call and invite and pay me every attention.'[48] She said, however, that she refused most invitations except those of the classical Greek scholar, Lewis Campbell, and his family, who were "literary and above the crowd".[49] It was pleasant,

Agnes found, to sit and listen as he read aloud from Shakespeare or from his own translations of Greek tragedies. Not surprisingly, Agnes preferred this sort of entertainment to the usual ladies' get-togethers of little teas and 'At Homes'. From her earliest days in Ottawa, she had always been an unwilling guest — or hostess — at such affairs and avoided them whenever society would allow her to do so.

By the following winter, Agnes could report:

> We are quite Alassians by this time, deep among the small English colony and social and other duties, added to housekeeping and management, superintendence, purchasing and ordering all in a foreign tongue, cut short the hours of the short winter days.[50]

Sometimes they had tea 'al fresco' in the garden of the late Sir Alfred Jones'[51] daughter, and sometimes Agnes took Mary for her favourite drive to Diano Marina:

> (all along the beautiful calm sea the drive was). There we stop in front of an hotel and tea is brought out to the carriage side and put on little tables — tea and toast and cakes and butter and honey. I am sure they thought we were Royal family to be so magnificently served outside, until they discovered that Mary could not walk! Since then they have had not been able to do enough for us and speak to her most tenderly.[52]

Mary could not walk and, according to her mother at this time, still could not speak very intelligibly. Yet, Agnes continued, 'she has all her father's charm of kindly grace and everyone loves her. It is quite remarkable how easy she makes her sad helpless life for herself as for me by her gentle civil unselfish ways.'[53]

It must have seemed to Agnes that taking Mary to Italy with her had proved the right thing to do, but the experiment did require continual planning. Mary's days had to be kept happy with teas, picnics, the companionship of new friends and her typewriter, by which she communicated with old friends. She was given, as well, a new treat in the form of 'musical afternoons [which] are her delight. I pay two and a half francs an hour, 2/1 in English money. In London the lowest "tender" was 5/6'[54]

Agnes and Mary spent almost every winter in this pleasant manner until the outbreak of the First World War. When they left Alassio for the summer, England was always their destination, although sometimes, if the heat became unbearable, they would move their departure forward to May and spend a few weeks in Switzerland on the way 'home'. Once in England, Mary would usually head for 'hateful Ramsgate',[55] as Agnes described it, or some other coastal resort, while Agnes spent some time in

London, visiting friends and replenishing her wardrobe.

In the early summer of 1907, Agnes hastily changed her plans for a month's stop in Paris on the way back from Alassio and hurried to return to England, hoping to see some of the Canadians who were there with Laurier for a Colonial Conference. She always tried to be in London during these meetings since they gave her a feeling of being close to decision-making as she had once been. Laurier, who had become Sir Wilfrid in 1902, was as popular as ever in England: 'Public opinion is struck by his fairness, moderation and good sense — all made more effective by his pleasant gentlemanly manner and quiet dignity.'[56]

Laurier had need of his good manners at this particular time. The Conference had been, on the whole, non-productive, and this had occasioned a sharp attack by Winston Churchill, then Under-Secretary for the Colonies, who had taunted the colonial delegates with receiving hospitality and giving in very little in return. He had gone so far, Agnes wrote, 'as to disgust many Radicals even. . . . I trust Sir Wilfred will do, as the Cdn. papers say he is going to do i.e. come over to Conferences on his own hook and not allow the Radicals over here to *taunt* Colonists with receiving hospitality.'[57]

Laurier continued to stand high in Agnes' estimation. 'Strong partizan [sic] as I am naturally, I can yet see both sides of a question and endorse!',[58] she assured Pope, lest he think she had swung too far in her appreciation of a Liberal. To emphasize the point, she told him about the annual Primrose League Meeting which she had attended a short time before.

The League had been founded in 1883, partly to maintain the Imperial ascendency, but more practically to provide a forum in which Conservatives of all classes could talk over the issues then current in England and, thus, strengthen the party. Agnes had attended its meetings occasionally; the first mentioned in her letters had been in 1902 in Albert Hall. Lord Salisbury, on the verge of retiring from British politics had been the speaker. His words had been, she had written, 'so wise — dignified — earnest — no flummery or nonsense — nor boast — no whine either — in its simple common sense expressed in plain easy language, it made me think of my husband!'[59] Lord Salisbury had died in the following year, but, at the 1907 meeting, at Hatfield, his widow, 'who I did not know by sight even, found me out *at once*', Agnes wrote, 'made us join her party — bade me to tea in her summer drawing room with her private friends and took me on the platform to hear the speeches — She was most civil and kind. . . . Whenever people who knew Sir John find me out they are most kind and demonstrative.'[60]

Despite such social and sentimental pleasures, it is not likely that Agnes really took much part in the Primrose League. During the days following John A.'s death, one writer of condolences had proposed that the Conservatives form such a club in Canada as a memorial to Sir John and his policies: '. . . I would suggest. . . a Woman's Society something similar to the Primrose League over the length and breadth of the land. . . to enlist in this form our mothers—aye, and daughters, too, under the grand old Conservative banner.'[61]

Agnes' answer had been tactful: 'while I strongly advocate any cooperative society for women in politics I am not able to assist in the formation of anything like a Primrose or other League as such formation will require a great deal of time and thought neither of which I could now devote to it.'[62] In truth, considering Agnes' aversion to women's meetings of any kind, it is doubtful if she would ever have become actively involved in such a club, on either side of the Atlantic, whether in memory of John A. or not. Despite her avowal of being a 'strong partizan', she probably went to the Hatfield meeting as much for the drive as anything else!

For Agnes had fallen in love with the motor car, and that summer, she was spending two months at Delrow, not very from Hatfield, as a paying guest in the home of a friend, Mrs. Brierly. To her great joy she had discovered that

Mrs. Brierly has a beautiful new motor. We have *delightful* times in it. I pay so much a mile when using it with her and more when using it alone. Petrol and wear and tear is costly and I could not, in a 2 month stay, allow Mrs. B. to convey me about *free*.

The motor with extras, insurance, etc., etc., has cost her about £1000 sterling![63]

Nor had this been her first love affair with motoring. In the summer of 1905, she had been on a holiday in Scotland, staying at Beaufort Castle, 'with the Phipps—long time Andrew Carnegie's partner—a lordly spot—deer and grouse and fishing. . . . The Phipps live of course in the greatest luxury—but what I *loved* was tearing about—thro' the most beautiful glens in the very best Mercedes motor!'[64] In the summer of 1907, when she had another opportunity of motoring, life became just a little different, a little more exciting for the seventy-one-year-old Baroness.

Indeed, during these years Agnes took to new forms of transportation with as much pleasure as she had found in tobaggoning, the C.P.R. in its infancy or fishing scows in New Brunswick. In 1900, on a visit to friends at Charlcote Park, near Warwick, she had encountered another new form: 'in the green lovely wooded park. . . I love to *tricycle*. I have learned and am very expert for the time of practice and hope—when I own a good trycycle [sic] to be very happy with it.'[65] How delighted she had been later that summer to have the use of a similar vehicle while visiting Glencoe, the Scottish home of the Donald Smiths, where she stayed often during these years.

It was in Scotland that Agnes felt most alive. Her first trip there had been at the end of the London 'Season', the year she had come back to England to live, and she had gone almost certainly because it was the thing to do. She had fallen in love with the country and returned almost every summer. In 1894 she went with friends on a driving tour through the Isle of Skye and down to Perth, and the following year she took Daisy to see her grandfather's country. The next two years Agnes brought Mary with her, thinking to share the country she loved with her daughter while giving her a bit of change from the heat of London. She rented a house in Argyllshire, where they lived very comfortably, she said, with days out on the loch and teas on the moors to which Mary was wheeled in her chair. 'This delights Mary',[66] Agnes contended, but, in truth, Mary was bored by the peace and quiet and, except for one more visit, did not return to Scotland, choosing to go the South Coast of England whenever her mother headed north. This was a welcome solution for both of them. As long as she was sure that her daughter was happy in what she was doing, Agnes could make her own plans with much more flexibility than when she had Mary's comfort and entertainment to look to, and she could organize visits to her many friends who had houses in Scotland, which allowed her to see them and save money at the same time. If Mary did need her, the South Coast was just an overnight trip away.

After the Coronation celebrations of 1902, it was with a great sense of relief that Agnes returned to Scotland, spending 'my two lovely months [there]', to recover from the 'month or six weeks of constant excitement, late hours and general society'.[67] She came back to London, feeling quite a new person, in time to welcome Hugh, Gertie and Jack on a long-delayed visit. But it was a visit with sad overtones. Jack was now a delicate eighteen-year-old and his parents had brought him to London primarily to seek medical advice, following the pattern set up by his grandfather so many years ago.

Agnes wrote Pope, 'I fear the boy is never going to be a really strong healthy man.'[68] In her opinion, Jack had 'been given too much of his own way — as to food and exercise and exposure — and political excitement when he should have been at school and games, etc. [but] Gertrude says he has never been *strong* enough to go to school.'[69]

Agnes also thought him a fine, intelligent lad, and during the visit, she tried, as she had done earlier with Daisy, to show him as much of the sights as possible. While Gertie shopped, Agnes took Hugh and Jack to many historic places, 'and we were all together as much as possible and it did me much good—and was sweet and cheering indeed but I cannot say I feel satisfied with Jack's condition.'[70]

The parting was a sad one, and Agnes' fears were borne out when Jack died less than three years later. She wrote Pope, whose telegram had broken the news, 'It has been a sad blow to us all—this tragic and early death—the boy in many ways resembled his grandfather and had he been at any time in good health would, I am sure, have been a great success.'[71]

Agnes never saw Hugh—or Gertie—again, although she tried. During the family visit to London, she had found Hugh quieter than ever, but still 'the same old boy'.[72] The year after Jack died, however, she received very disturbing news about her stepson. In his sorrow over his only son's death, he was drinking heavily again. Agnes did her best to persuade him to visit her, even offering to pay his way if he would come. 'The change and variety and ease of mind may be of the very greatest use to him', she wrote Pope, 'and we shall go at once to Scotland which I know H wants to see.... I am such a rash, bold spirited old woman that I can, in a strength not my own, face the anxiety which his visit may mean to me.'[73] Hugh, however, would not consent to make the trip.

The following years were full of concern. Occasionally Hugh's letters to his step-mother, which were type-written by a secretary, yet always affectionate and kind, encouraged her about his condition, but his 'lapses', as Agnes referred to his drinking, continued. At one time she became so worried about him that she told Pope:

I would go out [to Hugh in Canada], but I could not live in Winnipeg & I would not sacrifice poor Mary's ease by leaving her—anyway.[74]

She had to content herself with confiding her worries to Pope. It was not until 1912 that Agnes could say, 'I am filled with gratitude and joy by the news of Hugh Macdonald's blessed improvement.'[75] Hugh had written to tell her of his appointment as Police Magistrate of Winnipeg and, while it was less than many people wished for the old Chief's son, it was a mark of public respect that did much for Hugh. In the following year his self-confidence was further bolstered when he received the K.C.M.G. All of this helped heal the wound caused by the fact that he could never hope for a son to succeed him. He was the last of the line to bear the Macdonald name.[76]

The good news about Hugh was comforting in itself and, coming as it did, not very long after Annie Broome's death, also helped Agnes take her mind off this most recent sorrow. Louisa Scott had died ten years earlier, so, of the three cousins who had been born in Jamaica, Agnes was now the only one left. She must have missed Annie in particular, since after Annie had been widowed in 1897, she and Agnes had seen a great deal of each other. They had holidayed together, spent many pleasant, quiet hours as companions in London and, as titled ladies, had gone into society in each other's company. Now Agnes was left without this good friend and with the terrible feeling of being the last of a generation. For family contacts, she had to be satisfied with the occasional company of younger family members.

One such contact was with her brother Richard's eldest daughter, Dora Pepler. Although she had no opportunity to see her niece after her flying trip to Canada in 1896, she was able to entertain Dora's sons. Before Agnes left for Italy in the winter of 1907-08, Dora asked if she could 'receive and look after her eldest (living) son, Roger, for some time'.[77] Roger, who was on leave from the Calgary bank in which he worked, spent some six weeks at Alassio. It was not so long since he had been a little boy, Agnes mused, playing with his brothers in front of the cottage on Lake Simcoe, but now, he was 'a very fine good looking manly young fellow of near 22 . . . very companionable, pleasant, steady and domestic and easily pleased. . . But for a strong American accent he would be perfect, but even that we are accustomed to now.'[78]

Agnes had intended to take Roger on a trip to Sicily while he was her guest, but she succumbed to a severe attack of influenza for the first time in years and was unable to do so. This did not interfere with Roger's visit too much, since Alassio, itself, offered many diversions — masked balls, picnics, excursions and 'luncheons ad lib'. 'Such junketings which by some inexplicable combination of reasonings', Agnes lamented, 'have come — in Italy, to be gravely considered as ushering in discreetly a Religious Fast!'[79] At the end of his visit, some of Agnes' friends offered to take Roger on a motor tour of Spain, and then Agnes helped him, financially, to make an extended visit to England on his way back to Canada.

A few years later, she tried equally hard to see that his brother Eric's first European holiday was a success. This second son of Dora's was also highly approved of by Agnes and in writing of his visit to her in Switzerland, where she and Mary were spending part of the summer of 1913, Agnes said, 'I took care to make his visit profitable and pleasant [and to] show him as much as was possible.'[80]

Another such contact was with Dora's sister, May Fitzgibbon, a widow since the early 1890s. In 1895, May had visited London, bringing her daughter, Frances, with her. Agnes, remembering what a pleasant companion Richard's daughter had been on the trip to Lac St. Jean in 1892, had looked forward to May's visit eagerly and found it marred only by its brevity. In 1902, May was back in London, this time as a working woman. She had decided to make a career out of journalism and was covering the Coronation, socially, for the *Globe*. This was not, however, the year for aunt and niece to see much of each other. Agnes was busy and so was May, as Pope was informed, rather plaintively: 'I see little of her as she is in a rush of society and business — Working hard she tells me and much interested in her work. I am delighted she is helping herself especially as she thoroughly enjoys her work and has great fun into the bargain. She looks very well and is *beautifully* dressed.'[81]

May's work for the *Globe*, however, brought her back to London in several subsequent years and while she, herself, was often too busy to spend much time with her aunt, Agnes and Mary saw a good deal of Frances. In 1903, May's mother, Agnes McCarthy, was also in London. With May at work all day and seventeen-year-old Frances at school, Mrs. McCarthy 'looks pretty forlorn. She evidently does not like the climate',[82] Agnes wrote of her sister-in-law. Occasionally Agnes arranged a luncheon and sometimes they went on drives together, but there is no indication that their relationship, which had never been good, changed during this period. It was a joy, however, to get to know Frances, and during the holidays she often spent time with Agnes and Mary, in a pattern pleasantly reminiscent of the days when Daisy used to visit them from her school in Brighton.

Agnes' interest and pride in her niece's career was great and she took pleasure in being able to report that May was 'much admired...Her speaking is excellent I hear and her writing too and above all she is making herself useful to her country.'[83] By contrast, Agnes saw around her in England 'Too many women about — too many organizations and talk and so on and not enough practical work and understanding as might be desired.'[84] The country was wracked by unemployment, by questions of education and religion and by the Home Rule issue,[85] but Agnes felt that 'Women in England rule the roost and I have heard men say — do a good deal of mischief and this was, I hear, notably the case during the last elections [1906]. Some of the candidates' female supporters seem to have made things absolutely ridiculous and to have done more harm than good!!'[86]

Over the years, Agnes had not altered her thinking on women's role in society, especially in politics. She found her earlier opinion, that they either made mischief or became bores, still valid, and she was particularly impatient with the suffragettes and their willingness to achieve their aims by any means, even by destroying public property. In Agnes' view, 'They are disgusting everybody — but indeed their existence and proceedings are the outcome of the extraordinary prominence encouraged in women of all classes in England of late years.'[87] Canadian suffragettes annoyed her equally, even though their actions were not so extreme. In 1903, when there were angry demonstrations in Canada over the Alaska Boundary dispute, one group of activists joined the outbursts in Toronto. Agnes commented, 'Those silly women . . . do more harm than good — as women generally do when they put their dainty fingers into the political pie.'[88]

Both the Canadian and the British women were seeking the franchise and, while Agnes had no liking for the suffragettes' methods, she would have respected their right to their strong opinions. She, herself, had held her opinion, unchanged, over the years: a supportive role, yes, but an activist, no. She had been as closely connected with politics as she thought any woman should be and she was too old now to change her mind on the topic.

Another subject on which Agnes never changed her mind was the importance of religion to society and to herself, personally. Her religious affiliations did, however, come in for some self-scrutiny, as they had done when she had been a young bride and trying so hard to do right in all things. At that time she had compared, in her diary, the 'earnest, life pervading religion' she found exemplified in the *Life of the Last Duchess of Gordon* with

these fashionable days of outward worship. . . . I think we are all so formal and so untrue in our devotions, not intentionally but because a sort of false, formal creed is rising among us. I feel somehow in Church as if our Prayer Books were too small and too new! Mine is the dandiest thing I possess — except my new bonnet. It is so red and tiny.[89]

In the same entry, she had added 'I am afraid my turn of mind is getting Methodistical', and then had noted that she had read an article about the amendment of the Anglican rubric and 'found it much to my way of thinking. Dr. Jones would not call it orthodox but I am not orthodox, I fear.'[90] Nearly forty years later, she could become just as annoyed with the church: 'Certainly the Church of England is in a parlous state with fears and fightings and the terrible right of 'private judgment'!'[91] And a couple of years later:

Church questions and church lines in Gt. Britain are things nobody seems clearly to understand. I gave up trying long ago and have subsided into resignation only ever and always refusing to be bored by listening to arguments and controversies — Unchristian, unholy and unjust. They say I am 'Broad Church'. In my humble way I do mostly my best.[92]

Sometimes, as far as observances were concerned, Agnes' 'best' meant taking a good look at churches other than the Anglican one, to which she had always belonged. John A. had not been tied to any one church in particular, caring little, as Pope had said in his *Memoirs*, for external forms of worship. Agnes had certainly heard many discussions on the subject. At Rivière du Loup, when John A. and the Rector had walked and talked over different religious beliefs and observances, some of this was probably repeated to Agnes in the quiet evening hours. Ideas would have been exchanged with Pope, who was a Catholic. Long before, when disturbed by church squabbles in the St. Alban's congregation, John A. had passed on his opinion of matters in that church, agreeing with Agnes who found High Churchism 'too formal and too worldly. John says they (the High Anglicans) will, in 20 yrs., perhaps, go to the R.C. church.'[93]

In 1904, while preparing to leave for a visit to Rome, Agnes seemed to be thinking of doing what John A. had predicted for the High Church Anglicans. She went so far as to write Pope: 'I will... tell you how the Eternal City gets on — spite of its sad disfigurements and vulgar crowds, I think it is charming and inspiring and if I could only make up my mind to be received into your Church (as I tell the Archdeacon of London I am going to do) I should find "Roma" still more entrancing.'[94]

In her next letter — from Rome — there was no indication that she was thinking of doing anything as drastic as leaving her own church, but a report that 'We have done no end of things and seen and heard — Splendid places at the Beatification of a saint — twice — near the kneeling Pope [Pius X] — before the High Altar.'[95] She had also had 'a private interview with the Pope!!! It was all most flattering and he received us in his Cabinet de "travail".'. . . . His Holiness was most kind and delightful — the most gracious fatherly manner in his gorgeous appts. Even seeing those Vatican salons was a wonder.'[96]

In short, it sometimes seems that in religion, as in many other matters, Agnes' attention was caught more by external forms than by actual substance. Nonetheless, in her religion, as she said herself, she tried to do her humble best and, in so doing, remained faithful to the church of her childhood for the remainder of her days.

Another subject on which Agnes continued to show her own distinctive views was the line taken by political parties on both sides of the Atlantic. Here, again, she displayed some surprising departures, especially on specific issues or individuals.

One burning issue of the day was the vast numbers of unemployed and what to do about the unrest and frequent strikes the economic situation often led to. The root situation touched her heart: 'Taxation, poverty — ruin is in everybody's mouth. . . . What distresses me, day and night, is the dreadful poverty and lack of employment among the *really* poor classes. This is harrowing.'[97] She was not much impressed, however, by the actions taken to relieve the frequent unrest. In 1911, a series of rail strikes had been brought to a supposed settlement. She wrote, 'I am greatly mistaken if matters will ever fall into the old shape and if these last strikes are not the beginning of an end that will astonish us all. If you heard the common talk that I do — on the sands and beaches here — in the Parks and trains you would see what I mean.'[98] It was Lloyd George she saw as the political 'man of the situation' and predicted, quite mistakenly, that 'he may possibly, I think somehow be much changed by the outcome of his success and end up a Tory as so many of these successful fellows do!'[99]

Her own reasoning on the social discontent in England and its causes shows that she, herself, was somewhere between two political poles: 'I hate socialism of course and hope fervently we shall stop short of that — but a change of base for Gt. Britain has to be pretty soon — in my poor judgment.'[100] She felt that the strikers had much to complain about but that the Government had to be held answerable for its policies which had resulted in 'too much cheap education, too much coddling up, too much talk democratic and the masses are quick to see — to hear and learn.'[101]

She compared the attitude of the British poor with that of similarly situated Italians (whom she had a good opportunity of studying during her winters in that country) and had to admit that she found the 'idle, misguided men [of England], nurtured to constant and indiscriminate charity',[102] came out second best against the Italians who, although poor, lived on very little and did not grumble. This vision of the British poor made Agnes highly suspicious of a suggestion made in 1909 by Hugh Graham, publisher of the Montreal *Star*. While in London for a press conference, he had given a speech on the theme that 'there is no Imperial question of greater importance today than that of maintaining a commanding British sentiment in Canada',[103] and pleaded that, since British immigrants to Canada were not as numerous as were those from other countries, the unemployed of England should be sent to the Dominion. Agnes felt, however, that the 'increasing thousands [are] resolved to do nothing but what suits individual tastes and *howl* with rage when emigration is even suggested'.[104] So it was doubtful that the answer to Canada's maintenance of British sentiment lay with the immigration of the 'idle, misguided men' of England.

Agnes also noted, with a little trepidation, that the far-reaching dissatisfaction in England could have further economic results for her country: 'such a chorus of grumbling and lamentation. . . is a wonderful confirmation of the proverb about an "Ill wind, etc." that, quite seriously, I think the public mind over here is turning steadily to Canada as a place for good investment and purchase of property. I only hope they won't overdo the sentiment!'[105] Agnes was very proud that Canada remained so much to the fore in British thinking, but she was not sure she wanted to see too much investment controlled by England's hands.

Agnes could afford such a sentiment, for the economic news about

Canada had been good over the years. In 1909, she wrote, 'I hear now with a glorious pride of [Canada's] rapid development and prosperity — and my daily prayer is for both for her.'[106] Laurier was still Prime Minister, having been returned in the elections of 1904 and, again, in 1908, although this time with a reduced majority. His stand on defence matters had remained the same over the years, but, in 1910, faced with the growing menace to the Empire of Germany's increased sea power, he tried to bring in a Bill to set up a Canadian naval service. The result was an election call in 1911, and during the campaign he faced opposition from both French Canadians and the Conservatives on the issue. His appeal on the grounds of sound Canadianism was in vain and, when the votes were counted, the Conservatives, under Robert Borden, had a strong grip on the reins of power.

The news of the election result reached Agnes at Glencoe, where she had been spending some time with the Strathconas, and it did not take her long to reverse her stand on Laurier or to revert to her innate loyalty to the Conservative Party, from which only Laurier had been able to distract her.

> So the cat has jumped with a vengence [sic] and upset Sir Wilfred's [sic] applecart with amazing promptitude.
> Of course, knowing how strong a party woman I necessarily am, you will forgive my exultation and that, hearing such Imperial rejoicing over the result.... I feel strongly how gratified my dear husband would have been at this very decided 'parting of the ways'.[107]

The other plank in Laurier's election platform that had led to his downfall had been his proposal of a new tariff arrangement with the United States, one in which British politicians and press saw dangers to their country.[108] Agnes was well aware of this British concern, and, after the election, she asked Pope to pass on some advice to the new Canadian Prime Minister:

> Tell our new Premier this — !and assure him that one so ignorant and poor in judgment as I am, could not have believed in such interest and approbation over any expression Colonial, if I had not been here in England to observe it for myself —
> But with all possible speed the question of Tariff Reform ought — as it seems to me — to be re-opened.
> I have not an idea as to how[,] when or where, only, by some means let some prompt and active steps be taken from our side before enthusiasm on this side begins to cool.
> I trust Borden's Cabinet will be equal to the magnificent opportunity and *strike the iron while it is hot!*[109]

Excusing herself for this proffered advice, which she termed 'cheeky', Agnes emphasized that she gave it only because the election results had had such a profound effect in England. (Pope passed on her advice to Borden.[110] What weight it carried is open to question, although the Taft agreement proposed by Laurier was not implemented.)

Borden's attention was primarily focussed on a Naval Bill of his own, which called for urgent action and asked for a large grant of money to build three powerful battleships to be incorporated in the Imperial navy. It passed the House in April, 1913, but was defeated when it reached the largely Liberal Senate, a move that surprised Agnes, who had been informed by Hugh that 'the Senate will hardly show their teeth as the Bill is popular in Canada!.[111] As a staunch Canadian who was often exposed to British criticism of Canada's conduct, especially in matters of Imperial defence, Agnes told Pope that she was glad to see Borden sticking to his point. She had hard words to say about Laurier's role[112] in the defeat of the Bill: '*If* there is any serious consequence to Laurier's action, I shall indeed regret it — Canada's loyalty has always been a strong point and we shall be dubbed weak, traitorous, false, etc.'[113] Her parting shot at Laurier was, 'I must say, I never would have thought Sir Wilfrid's love of office (and his actions mean nothing more) would have led him into so deplorable a condition – for such it seems to me.'[114]

Whatever can be said for or against Agnes, it is obvious that she had not lost — on paper at least — any of her old zest. Sharing her thoughts with Pope, as she did consistently up to this point, she showed herself an acute observer of politics and all the life around her. As she approached her last few years, she was crusty sometimes, caustic sometimes, but, despite her little side excursions into theories and philosophies, little changed from the girl and young wife of many years earlier.

13

Politics and politicians were not the only subjects that received sharp comment from Agnes' pen during the last decades of her life. She was worried by many things—from the accommodation of her own needs and Mary's, to the travails of her few remaining relatives, to social issues of the day—but nothing caused her so much distress as her finances. Throughout the long years of her widowhood, the problem of handling money occupied much of her time and attention, and eventually her anxiety about it led her to a complete break with Pope, the person on whom she had depended for advice of all sorts for so many years.

That this should have happened and that Agnes should have expended so much energy worrying about money was sad, yet probably inevitable. Like her mother, like many Victorian women, Agnes felt totally insecure and incompetent while dealing with financial matters, yet her conscience, her independence and, quite possibly, her youthful experience with economic instability seemed to drive her into constant tinkering with them. She had no faith in her ability to manage, but she could not sit back and let someone else do all the managing for her.

The situation was exacerbated by several factors besides Agnes' personality: the high standards of dress and entertainment expected of a Peeress of the realm; Agnes' own inclinations, which John A. had long ago labelled as an expensive manner; the ever-growing expense of Mary's needs, especially as Agnes grew older, and of making separate arrangements for the invalid when her mother did not feel their schedules could be made to match. On top of all this was the fact that John A., in making his arrangements for Agnes and Mary to receive the income from his estate, had unknowingly created a problem by naming four trustees who lived in different parts of Canada. The four men he had chosen—his own son, Hugh, Edgar Dewdney, Fred White and Pope—had seemed the best individuals for the job, and it had probably appeared to John A., in 1889, when the will was drafted, that Canada was already becoming a closely knit country, bound together as it was by the C.P.R. One can argue as to whether the speed of communications advanced enough during Agnes' lifetime to have ever made this arrangement practical. What cannot be argued is that her decision to live on the other side of the Atlantic complicated the situation immensely.

For the first years of Agnes' widowhood, neither the arrangement for the trustees nor any of her other financial woes constituted grave problems. True, she was always a bit uneasy about her monthly cheques and whether the amount she received would cover her costs, but it was not until 1900 that she found real cause for alarm. In that year, two things happened to change her outlook: Alec Ferguson, solicitor for the estate, died, and Agnes got the idea that a trust company might serve her better than did her trustees.

Ferguson's death was a real blow. Agnes received the news while she was at Glencoe with the Strathconas, and she felt, 'Not only have I lost one of my very, very best, truest, kindest friends, but one whose assistance was invaluable to me — one on whom I entirely relied — whose opinion I entirely valued and whose help cannot be replaced.'[1]

Her words proved all too true and, as time went on, she began to feel more and more alone. Of the trustees, Dewdney was so far away; Hugh, she felt, should not be worried too much about her affairs lest it turn him to drinking; Fred White was soon to become too old and too ill to be of much help. That left Pope, the junior trustee, but the one on whom she was already depending heavily. There was also Lord Strathcona, who had no legal position regarding Agnes' affairs, but whose advice as a friend she was coming to prize more and more highly. This was to be especially true after she began to disagree with Pope.

The disagreement came about over the possible use of a trust company. While Agnes was in Glencoe, at the time of Ferguson's death, James Ross, another Scot connected with the building of the C.P.R., asked her if she had ever considered using such a company to look after her investments. She immediately wrote Pope, 'Have you any experience of trust companies? Do you believe in them — the Bank of Montreal Trust Company for instance? Let me know.'[2] In further discussions before leaving Glencoe, the idea of using the facilities of the Royal Trust Company of Montreal became firmly implanted in Agnes' mind, an idea likely supported by Strathcona, who was closely connected with this company.

Pope, however, turned out to be opposed to having any alterations made in the estate management. If any change were made, he told her, the trustees who had been appointed by John A. would have to resign.[3] Furthermore, he warned her, there was a possibility that her income might suffer: she might only receive four per cent from her investments and even that could not be guaranteed.[4]

Agnes insisted — and Pope dragged his feet, perhaps prompted by loyalty to the expressed wishes of his late Chief, perhaps because he really believed he was acting in Agnes' best interests. Whatever his reasons, it was nearly fourteen years before he found it possible to arrange for the estate to be transferred to a trust company, fourteen years before he found it possible to release the trustees of their responsibilities while retaining some surety that Agnes would not suffer financially from the change in management of the estate, fourteen years in which the disagreement between Pope and Agnes gradually became a rift that could never be breached.

During those fourteen years, Agnes tried, in her own way, to cut her expenses, but it was difficult. Mary's needs increased while Agnes, now that she was growing old, found she herself could not manage without extra help. Her position as a Peeress imposed a great burden and she often wished she were rid of the coronet. 'Truly for *that* whistle, Joe — Mary and I have paid dearly indeed',[5] she wrote in 1910, and, in the following year, she stayed abroad so as to avoid attending the coronation of George V, thinking back to the heavy costs she had incurred for the coronation of Edward VII. Her rueful comment on the title at that time was:

Still I would not have refused [the peerage] as the offer reflected a new lustre in my husband's great name.

The expense and added importance of such a distinction in all places and in all societies never entered my poor brain, however, so little did I, in 1891, realize life in the world I knew so little of![6]

As the transfer of the estate progressed (or did not progress, as it seemed to Agnes), she leaned more and more on Lord Strathcona. Her correspondence with Pope on the subject often mentioned how helpful John A.'s former opponent was to her: 'No brother could be kinder than is the old Lord, no near relative be more warmly interested, more truly useful, or more ready, at any moment to see me and hear me and do all he can.'[7] Yet, she felt she should be 'always very reticent. . . & careful in troubling or speaking to him – as you may imagine one would be with so rich and generous a man – !'[8] As it was, thinking back to the old political battles, she found 'his kindness, consideration and interest is beyond belief when one thinks how little I or mine deserve from him.'[9]

Lord Strathcona did actually work closely on the transfer with both Agnes and Pope. Because of his position with the Royal Trust Company, he was able to pass on the reassurance that

the security of the Estate would be undoubted [as] this Company is in as good a position as any Private Trustee to obtain a satisfactory revenue.[10]

He also hoped that his intervention would result in speeding up the process of the transfer, but the delays continued. One of the worst was occasioned by the discovery that the solicitor who had replaced Ferguson had converted some of the interest from Agnes' investments to his own use and had also kept the accounts in so chaotic a fashion that Pope felt forced to excuse himself on the grounds that 'I am neither a lawyer nor an accountant.... I had to trust somebody. That somebody turned out to be untrustworthy. In all the circumstances I think it extremely fortunate that the capital of these estates is intact. Nothing has been lost through Sinclair.[11]

This was not written until 1913 and, by then, Agnes' patience was exhausted. She had been waiting so long and found it difficult to understand why the transfer was still not complete. Her ever-present fears of handling money, of being caught between conflicting advice, of not being sure who to trust and, above all, of not having enough money to meet her own and Mary's needs, piled up on her. In May, she admitted, 'The strain of anxiety is great as I am now an old woman and I fear, losing that pluck which has carried me over many a sharp moment and hour of trial.'[12]

The next few months saw no relief from that strain. June was always a bad time for her as 'those last awful hours [of John A.'s final illness] come back to me with a vividness quite inexplicable';[13] this year it proved a time of fears and doubts that did not let up later in the summer. She remained in Alassio longer than usual to avoid the costs of London and travel in England, but, when the heat of Italy became unbearable, she went to Switzerland. There, she tried to be a good hostess to Eric Pepler and to look after Mary's needs, while waiting every day, every hour, for the news that took so long to come. At last, she could stand it no longer and returned to England, where she could be contacted more easily than on the continent. That proved no help. Indeed, in early autumn, it seemed to her that Pope's letters were concentrating more and more on the depositing of John A.'s papers in the Public Archives of Canada than on the transfer of his estate.

Her patience snapped. In a bitter letter to Pope, whom she now addressed as 'Dear Sir Joseph Pope' and not 'Dear Joe', she wrote that she hoped the papers were now in the possession of Prime Minister Borden, who would take care of them as was fitting.[14] She fully expected, too, she wrote, that the transfer of the estate would take place without further delay:

I have said my last word about the Letters and, as I have done for 13 years in the past, await with anxious concern some satisfactory conclusion in the future.

184

I also hope and expect that no more correspondence between you and me will be continued by or desired by you.[15]

Such a pungent letter might have been expected to be the end of a long and loyal relationship between John A.'s widow and Pope, and it did break any closeness between them. Yet Pope, despite the increasing responsibilities of his own work and his growing family demands, remained faithful to the memory of John A. and continued to work on the transfer. In December he was able to write to Agnes that the accounts had been passed and by February, 1914, the transfer was completed. For the first time since John A.'s death, Pope was released from responsibility for the finances of his Chief's widow, something which Agnes had long wished for him.

Considering the long years of closeness between Pope and Agnes and the care he expended on her in so many matters, it was very sad that their final contacts should have been so bitter. Had the other trustees been active in their management of the estate or had Agnes had the services of a good solicitor in those late years, things would almost certainly have worked out in a different fashion. At the age of seventy-eight, Agnes should never have had to find herself so alone. On the other hand, much of the blame, as Pope once pointed out, really rested on the manner in which John A. had named four trustees.[16] This, Agnes, ever-loyal to her husband's memory in all details, would not admit. 'I see the point', she wrote, 'about "Executors scattered over a continent" but Sir John could not look into the events of more than 20 years — If I believe in what is called "luck" — which I do not — I might say Mr. Ferguson's sudden death & Mr. Sinclair's reign were unlucky for me.'[17]

No further letters were ever exchanged between Agnes and Pope but he did not drop completely out of the lives of his old Chief's widow and daughter. As long as Agnes lived, he was to follow her movements and travails through contacts with other family members in Canada, often offering them quite sage advice on how to treat the indomitable old woman. After her death, he began a spasmodic correspondence with Mary, saying in a letter of condolence: 'I received news of your dear Mother's death with great regret. Though of late years an estrangement unfortunately grew between us, I do not forget our long friendship, nor her many kindnesses to me.'[18]

In one of several letters to Pope during this period, Mary was to comment, 'I think my Mother hoped to return to Canada as she used to talk (sometimes) of the old friends (there).'[19] In truth, however, by the latter years of her life, Agnes had long since given up any such move as impractical for both Mary and herself. It was only necessity that kept her even in England during the winter any more — necessity real or imagined — and one such time was late 1913 when she was waiting for the estate transfer. By the middle of February, 1914, when her affairs were firmly in the hands of the Royal Trust Company, she left once more for Italy.

She was taking a familiar route that would carry her back to her house in Alassio, yet she left in sorrow. The break with Pope, which she regarded as complete, was matched by another great personal loss: Lord and Lady Strathcona had recently died within a few months of each other. This had been a considerable blow to the elderly Agnes. Of Lady Strathcona's death, Agnes had written Pope (with whom she was then still in correspondence), '[It] was a shock to many. I have lost a truly kind friend and her kindness to and sympathy for Mary I cannot explain but the suddenness of her death added to the loss of a companion of more than 60 years!'[20]

Lady Strathcona's death had been in November, 1913, and had been followed by speculation that old Lord Strathcona would finally retire as Canadian High Commissioner. It was not the first time there had been such a rumour. In 1908, a similar report had circulated and Agnes, who held him in such high regard, politically and personally, had welcomed the possibility, '. . . great as the blow is for Canadian progress and interests. We all felt that at 88 it was time he should rest and his deafness *he* felt to be very much increased.'[21] That rumour had continued through the summer of 1909, when there was talk that Hugh Graham of the Montreal *Star* was to be the new High Commissioner. Agnes had continued to hope that her old friend would then take his leisure, especially as she approved of Graham as a successor:

> I don't *think a better choice could be made*. He is a man of affairs, keen and competent, industrious and successful — she gentle and nice without 'side' or vulgarity or pretentions and would go down well. What is wanted is a man accustomed to real work and with a thorough knowledge of Canada's requirements, a man whose life hitherto has been busy and modest — with a sensible practical wife. Your 'high flyers' will be laughed at and — with turned heads — do important mischief.[22]

She knew, too, in 1909, whom she did *not* want to fill the post of High Commissioner, adding 'For goodness sake, don't send us Montague Allan!! or the Cloustons'.[23]

All of her advice had been in vain, for Lord Strathcona did not leave office until his death at ninety-three in late January, 1914. Agnes' preference for a successor then, if she had one, is not known, but it is certain that she left for Italy knowing there could be no future support from either Pope or Strathcona — the men who had been her staunchest friends over the years of her widowhood. Another chapter in her life was finished.

Worse, in 1914, a new and ugly chapter in world affairs was about to begin and Agnes was uncomfortably aware of it. Although Westminster had been ignoring, to an astonishing degree, all signs of the approaching conflict, Agnes had commented as early as 1910 that some people 'think Germany intends to attack us for want of something better to do apparently!'.[24]

When the First World War did break out in the summer of 1914, Agnes and Mary had gone, once more, to Switzerland, and the declaration of war put them in an awkward position. Their plans called for them to remain in the Swiss mountains until late October and then to return to Italy. Now, what should they do? Europe was fast approaching chaotic conditions and Agnes, who was now seventy-eight years old, had to make plans not only for herself, but also for her invalid daughter and two maids, all of whom were totally dependent on her. Should they stay in Switzerland? The country, although neutral, was close to the area where the fighting would probably take place. Should they go back to England, despite the disadvantages of its climate? Would it be safe even to try? Should they return to Italy? That country was not yet in the war, but it was likely to become involved. She chose to go, nonetheless, to their usual winter home in Alassio and to go as soon as she could make arrangements. Apparently she felt her place was there, and she worked out the complicated travel arrangements in a way that showed the elderly Baroness still had some of the pluck she had feared was gone forever. Hugh wrote Pope a description of how his step-mother managed to get back to Italy by September:

> I have received two long letters from her since she left Switzerland. . . . She appears to have had a rather hard time of it getting out. . . . as English money would not be accepted and it was impossible to obtain Swiss currency. She, however, managed to engage a courier who was well off and owns a house in Milan and who fortunately had several hundred francs of Swiss money and paid the expenses of the whole party to Italy where he accepted her cheque in repayment. She writes in very good spirits and states that both she and Mary are well.[25]

The news that Agnes was in Italy was passed on to May Fitzgibbon, who was now living in Vancouver with her mother and daughter. May was almost hysterically concerned for her aunt's safety and suggested trying to persuade Agnes to leave Europe for

> the southern States with dear Mary so that we could get to her if there was any trouble. I am SO SO hoping she will do this. The USA is likely to remain neutral and be the safest place for them both, as no one can tell what Euro-

pean country may next be involved. . . . Is there anyone in London who would try to get them a safe passage across the Atlantic?[26]

May was writing to Pope (possibly not knowing of the break in his communications with Agnes), but she had also heard from Hugh, whom she was surprised to report was 'evidently not worrying about Aunt Agnes and Mary!'[27] In his reasoned reply to May, Pope assured her that, yes, there *were* people in London who would be able to help her aunt, including George Perley, who succeeded Lord Strathcona as High Commissioner, and his wife, Milly White, was an old friend of Mary's. He pointed out, however, that it should be ascertained whether or not Agnes *wished* to leave Italy.[28] Agnes was, at the moment, in Baveno on Lake Maggiore, where she had spent some time years ago, but she was making her way, slowly, back to Alassio.

Meanwhile, in Vancouver, May fretted and worried. An Atlantic crossing would be a very complicated trip for her aunt. If, on the other hand, Agnes chose to remain in Italy, what about her finances? Would she be able to receive any money? Even if she could, May wrote to Pope,

> I fear that provisions will be terribly dear and that the moment will come
> when dear Aunt A cannot get out of Italy even if she wishes to do so. . . .
> Expenses in Europe — even should the war cease — will be terribly high
> for years to come. Aunt A is no longer young and she ought to be where
> some one of her relatives could go to her if she were ill, or if anything should
> happen to her, Mary is to be thought of. . . . If she could only be induced to
> spend part of her time in the Southern States and part in Canada, I am sure it
> would be best.[29]

Agnes' reaction to May's cries of alarm was, apparently, to ignore them since she remained in the familiar Casa Amena throughout that winter while May's hysterical letters went out to poor Pope, who always seemed to be the one the family turned to in time of crisis.

> I am helpless, [May wrote] helpless because she has come to that time in
> life when she actually believes that what she is doing is sure to be best. She,
> poor soul, imagines that she is guided by Divine Inspiration, and her letter is
> full of this sort of thing, as a matter of fact, I fear she is acting simply with
> a view to the immediate future, and her fear of anything like a long journey
> with poor Mary. . . . I don't think my aunt can have any idea of what is before
> them if Italy is embroiled in the war. The taxes will be enormous and the
> Italian soldiers are as given to drunkness [sic] as the Germans. . . . I feel it is
> an impossible situation for those four lonely women in a villa where they
> will have no English neighbours this winter.[30]

Pope obviously knew Agnes' character better than did May, and he advised her that it would be wrong to let her aunt know she was the object of too great concern. He also tried to comfort May by telling her that he felt Agnes would be quite safe in Italy because, even if that country did become involved in the war, it was sure to enter on the side of the Allies. In this case, British subjects would not be in any danger and he advised May that she should best cheer up a bit.[31]

By April, 1915, Italy did enter the war on the side of the Allies, although May more than likely continued to worry as she had during the past year: 'because she [Agnes] has been so strong-minded in the past, I feel that old age may find her stranded and left to rely on a strength that is no longer there!'[32]

May should have had more confidence in her aunt's ability to cope — no matter what the circumstances. Agnes seems to have managed the war years very well indeed. She was in Italy, where she felt at home and whose people she liked; she knew, too, what she was capable of doing. One thing she would not attempt, under war-time conditions, was to make her usual summer trips to England. Despite the heat, despite Mary's undoubted desire to see her friends, she remained firmly in Italy. During the summer of 1915, she simply stayed on at Casa Amena, but the war had disrupted British travel to Italy so drastically that the owner was soon forced to sell the villa where Agnes had spent so many pleasant winters and where she felt secure. She had to move away from Alassio and decided to return to San Remo, her first place of refuge on the Italian Riviera.

The only extant correspondence from Agnes after that date is to the manager of the Royal Trust Company in Ottawa, who seemed likely to inherit Pope's place as her Canadian correspondent. In the spring of 1916, in a hand a little shakier than before, she assured him:

We are all hoping for better or rather more peaceful outlook soon — but it has been a sad experience indeed — a time of stress and strain never to be forgotten — tho' perhaps less acutely realized in Italy than elsewhere, especially on this coast where even the sick and wounded seem helped by the sunshine.[33]

A month or so later she wrote him again, telling of her pride in hearing such good reports of Canadian soldiers.

A stranger I met by chance and who does not know me at all — said, as he discussed the war 'Those Canadian boys are splendid — so fearless and ready, disciplined as old soldiers' adding some still stronger remarks as to their powers of endurance and cheery nature. I should have liked to thank the speaker but I could not for tears.[34]

(Agnes' two great-nephews, Roger and Eric Pepler, were with the Canadian forces, and Agnes' thoughts must have gone out to them as well as to other boys from Canada — her country, always.)

As to their way of life in San Remo, Agnes went on to say:

This coast has been quite quiet and unvisited by war alarms — tho' a week or two ago a submarine was reported and we villa residents were officially desired to show no lighted windows southward. . . .

Yesterday a large bark [sic] conveying coal to Genoa was overhauled by an Austrian gunboat not very far off — the crew (31) allowed to go away in boats while 4 shots sunk the bark [sic] and her cargo!

These incidents and the frequent troop-filled railway trains passing up and down are the only signs that happily we see or hear of the dreadful strife not so far off![35]

Yet, San Remo held many reminders of the fighting, and Agnes, at the age of almost eighty, had set about doing what she could to alleviate the loneliness which is a part of war:

The hospitals in San Remo (4) have all been large hotels standing in fine gardens and we see wounded creeping about among the flowers attired in hospital garb. . . . I have visited some of the hospitals — the men seem to like seeing me and to have post cards and cigarettes administered with some kind words in a very bad Italian.[36]

While Agnes clearly was not suffering the problems May had forseen, she did suffer agonies over the war itself and asked the manager that question to which there has never seemed to be an answer: 'Does it not seem to you, as it does to me, strange that no way of settling difficulties can be found, instead of the barbarous bloody senseless murdering of human beings?'[37]

As the heat set in during the summer of 1916, Agnes and Mary set out on their annual pilgrimage in search of mountain air. On July 30, while they were at Courmayeur, in the foothills of the Mont Blanc massif, Agnes suffered a stroke. Sarah Coward, maid-companion to Agnes and Mary for over ten years, took command of the situation. She wrote, at once, to Hugh to tell him how things stood:

our English Dr. . . said that the Baroness must be got away as soon as possible [and] on Wednesday morning we started off in a motor car for Turin. (The Dr. with us of course). The Baroness was very fatigued with 6 hours motor journey. . . . I am glad to say that [she] rested better last night and seems stronger this morning mentally and bodily. . . .

Dear Miss Mary trys [sic] to be courageous but her nerves are dreadfully upset.[38]

190

In Canada, the news of Agnes' illness soon became known to Pope and to May Fitzgibbon, who wailed with her usual alarm:

It is what I so dreaded and I annoyed my poor Aunt by trying in every way I could to get her to come out.... My poor mother is very broken and aging rapidly under the stress and anxiety of these terrible days and were it not that my first duty is to her, I would raise the money in some way and get to them wherever they are. But I can't. I am tied hand and foot and it almost breaks my heart to think of poor Mary. Her cup of misery is full.[39]

This was another of May's over-reactions. Within a few days, it was clear that Agnes was making a good and fairly rapid recovery. Indeed, by the middle of September, she was able to dictate a letter to her bank manager in London. She had, by then, returned to her villa in San Remo, and touches of her old spirit appeared as she explained, 'It was quite ruinous living in Turin.... I shall remain here, as the villa is paid for until the 29th of May, 1917.'[40] Money was still a major preoccupation with her and there was no sense in wasting it. By returning to her villa, she also had the advantage of having a fine, large garden and it was there she convalesced, as Coward reported to Hugh in mid-October:

[the Baroness] is still improving, getting stronger both bodily and mentally. She passes a good deal of time sitting or lying on a small bed in the garden.[She] now takes short drives nearly every day, also walks in the garden. She still requires help from nurse and myself but the last week much less than before — Today she has begun to write a letter to you — the first letter she has tried to write since July.[41]

Whether or not Agnes was able to write to Hugh is not known, but in late November, she did manage to write the Royal Trust Company's manager in Ottawa. Although her hand was decidedly shaky, her thoughts were pefectly clear and quite typical:

I am getting better and hope, by the Blessing of God, to recover completely, but I have been very suffering since Aug 3rd. with formidable bills to pay for doctors and nurses.... I have no regular nurse now but one was with me for 12 weeks.

The doctor — a very clever Italian — pronounced my illness congestion of the head from going too high in the Alps and an attack of bronchitis which still requires the greatest care....

This place is very nice and the villa very luxurious. I rented at War price until May 29th... but after that time we shall be wanderers again.[42]

And, for the next three years, Agnes and Mary did become 'wanderers again', although they did not stray very far. Their summers were spent at

Varese, in the Italian province of Lombardy, where Agnes was able to have an uninterrupted view of the Alps as far as Monte Rosa, as if to compensate for no longer being able to take the long mountain walks she had always enjoyed. In the winter they went back to San Remo.

This pattern continued unbroken until 1920 when Agnes and Mary finally returned to England, planning to stay the summer. After a brief period in London, they moved to 47 Grand Parade, Eastbourne, where they had stayed once before. It was there, sometime during the late summer, that Agnes had a second stroke, one so bad that Coward told Hugh: 'since then she has been almost absolutely helpless, and had to be carried up and down stairs.'[43]

On September 5, 1920, it was all over. A telegram sent by the Baroness Strathcona[44] to the Royal Trust Company's Montreal office informed them that 'Baroness Macdonald died this afternoon. . . Please notify Sir Hugh J. Macdonald at Winnipeg.'[45]

Mary was later to write to Pope, 'my mother's end was quite calm as she was quite unconscious and therefore did not know anyone',[46] but the condition Coward had described had lasted some weeks. Hugh, knowing how much his step-mother must have disliked being almost totally helpless, wrote upon hearing of her death, 'I am sure she must have felt death a happy release'.[47] Many who knew her well must have agreed, and the London *Times* came close to suggesting the same sentiment in the obituary tribute it paid the late Baroness: '[Her] death will be mourned by friends in every continent. A wide reader, a writer of considerable ability, a clever conversationalist with a keen sense of humour, and, above all a woman with a very large heart, she made herself popular in whatever part of the world her active nature led her steps.'[48]

Agnes, separated from most of her family and Canadian friends during the latter part of her life, was even further isolated in death. In the telegram which Baroness Strathcona sent informing the Trust Company of Agnes' death, she said, 'am arranging burial at Eastbourne unless you have any instructions to the contrary.'[49]

Hugh's information on this was, 'the mater wrote me some time ago saying she had given Mary and Coward full instructions as to what she wished done.'[50] These instructions had already been carried out when Hugh wrote this to Pope. On September 9, Agnes had been buried in Ocklynge Cemetery, Eastbourne, an ocean away from the grave of her husband whose memory she had always treasured.

Death is rarely tidy, though Agnes' left fewer loose ends and problems than many. There was really only Mary, and ever since Agnes had come to realize that there was a strong possibility that her daughter would outlive her, she had been very careful to make plans for the invalid's future. Such arrangements had been the subject of correspondence with

Pope after his visit to Agnes in 1899. They had come up again in 1904, when Agnes was looking at other bequests she wished to make. At that time she had described her concern to Pope in vivid language: 'The horror of leaving my poor helpless dependent darling in any but the best possible circumstances is dreadful to me and tho' she is extremely delicate in many ways all the doctors who have seen her think her constitution is extraordinarily strong. . . . She may live to be an old woman.'[51]

The question of what arrangements would suit Mary's needs best had been given careful consideration by Agnes and by Mary herself. Before the turn of the century, Mary had expressed a firm wish to return to Canada when her mother died, and this had been reflected in the plans Agnes made with Pope at that time. Over the years, however, the wisdom of this course had come more and more into question and, finally, it had become clear that it would be unacceptable to Mary. In 1910, Agnes had described her new plans to Pope, saying that Mary

does not wish to return to Canada—I think she and I are both convinced that her health would suffer in a cold climate. . . . Mary wishes her home to be *near London*, within reach of friends and, in a place where, when Canadians visit England, Mary should be likely to see them. . . . Mary suggested a small flat in London and this might be better if it came within her means. . . . I do not wish any relative or friend, or any other person in that capacity to live with Mary, or make any prolonged stay with her, on *any* pretext *whatever*.[52]

On the question of who should care for Mary, there had been no doubt whatsoever in Agnes' mind—Sarah Coward, the maid-companion who had won the approval and confidence of mother and daughter. Indeed, Mary had become deeply attached to the woman she called 'my Coward'. Agnes knew this and was very grateful to Coward who, she wrote Pope, at the time of changing the plans, 'has expended much time on Mary, who she has marvelously helped and improved, and I trust her in all respects implicitly. I wish her to have charge and entire care of Mary in case of my death.'[53]

And that was how it was, except that Coward married soon after Agnes' death and her husband became a member of Mary's household.[54] It seems not to have mattered. The three settled in a flat in Hove, and there Mary lived in an apparently compatible atmosphere for the rest of her days. She kept in touch with her Canadian relatives and connections, and her thoughts, like those of her mother were often on the Canadian side of the Atlantic. In one letter to Pope, she wrote:

your letter. . .seemed a link with the old time at Earnscliffe. . . . I should like to have news of some of the people whom I knew when we were all at

Stadacona Hall and Earnscliffe.... Is Gaisford still in Ottawa and what has become of old Sarah (I mean the sister of old Ben) who was my nurse when I was a little girl (in Canada).[55]

Despite the close ties with Canada, Mary was quite content to live, winter and summer, in her beloved England until her death in 1933.

She was buried in Hove Cemetery, not far from her mother's resting place. One likes to think that there remains this one physical family link for Agnes, who travelled so far, who met and won so many of the challenges life sent her, who ended with so many years of loneliness.

It was, perhaps, inevitable that Agnes, a woman of so many accomplishments and talents, would be known, from the day of her marriage until her death, as 'Sir John A.'s wife'. That was almost certainly how she saw herself. It was also part of the truth — and a very important part for Agnes, for John A. and for Canada. John A., like Disraeli, to whom contemporary commentators were fond of comparing him, acknowledged how much he owed to Agnes.[56] It was also the opinion of Canadian writers, one of whom said, 'Baroness Macdonald of Earnscliffe had the happiest influence over the late career of her husband. . . she has always been nobly associated with [his] career.'[57] Another biographer of John A. was more specific in his comparison of the roles played by the two wives, saying that Agnes '[attended] to Sir John at the late sittings of the House, as Mrs. Disraeli used to do. . . wrapping up her husband after he has made a speech and zealously guarding his health while at home and travelling.'[58]

Agnes had done that and more. The same writer proclaimed that 'In domestic life, Lady Macdonald is a model woman, lavishing tenderness upon an invalid daughter'.[59] When Pope wrote to Mary after Agnes' death, he commented on this care and devotion, saying, 'nothing can make up for a mother's tender and loving care which you have always enjoyed in unstinted measure.'[60] At the time of Agnes' death, Mary was fifty-one years old, much older than anyone had once thought it possible for her to live. During all those long and difficult years, it was true, as Pope said, Mary had had her mother's care in 'unstinted measure'. Even as Agnes approached her last years, ill and unable to take as active a part as she would have liked in Mary's life, she had supervised her as much as possible and had surely rejoiced in her planning for the years ahead and her wise choice of Coward, 'in all respects most excellent, clever, entirely trustworthy, judicious, deeply religious. . . the person Mary ought to have with her always.'[61]

As John A.'s wife, Agnes had also achieved a reputation of 'keeping a household that might be the envy of any circle'.[62] After a hesitant beginning, after much self-criticism, Agnes had finally reached the point where she no longer felt inadequate as mistress of her household. She had even adjusted to accepting her social role to the point where she was termed

the crown to [John A.'s] social success. Of the society circle [in Ottawa] she is voted preeminently the Queen where, in every project of social enterprise, she is the first and the last, and no less the favourite of the elderly and demure, than of the young folk. To go to Ottawa and mention the name Lady Macdonald to any of the young people there is, at once, to bring forth a paean in her praise.... She seems to be in the social what her husband is in the public sphere.[63]

Yet there was much more to Agnes than the Victorian ideal of devoted wife, mother and hostess. Lady Stanley, soon after coming to Canada as wife of the Governor-General, characterized her as 'a very clever stern woman'.[64] It must be hoped that the idea of Agnes being 'stern' was formed on outward appearances only and that Lady Stanley soon modified her judgment. In any event, the idea of Agnes being 'clever' would have become more and more apparent. That this was true was evidenced in the many articles she wrote, commenting on different aspects of British and Canadian politics. It was also reflected in the closeness she had to the opinions of her husband for a quarter of a century. One of her first entries in her diary had been: 'My lord never talks politics out of season, so only passing allusions were made to the subject all evening.'[65]

Yet, by the following day, he had already begun to share his views with Agnes and this had continued. It was noticed that not only was she a constant visitor in the House but 'Sir John. . . it is whispered, is in the habit of consulting her when he is about to take some important political step.'[66]

Whether or not John A. really did consult her, Agnes got a very good grasp of political affairs, good enough for her to follow them closely and comment on them shrewdly throughout the rest of her life, good enough for her writings on them to be considered worthy of inclusion in a publication with the standing of *Murray's Magazine*.

Indeed, it is often only from her writings, both public and private, that we can see Agnes as an individual. In her pieces for *Ladies' Home Journal*, her sense of humour, as well as her political acumen, shows up. That she did not write more is a pity. She had planned to do so but, as with her diary-keeping, it did not get done. In 1888, the editor of *Murray's* wrote her: 'A pink tea sounds delicious, do send me something about it. Please don't think anything too frivolous for *Murray's*.... How amusing is your account of the world.'[67] Not too long after this, however, John A. became ill and life ceased to be 'amusing' for Agnes. She could not write what she did not feel.

She never took up her pen for publication again, although she sometimes thought about it. When asked by E.M. Chadwick for information of a biographical nature for inclusion in his *Ontarian Families*, she begged Pope to 'tell him that I will never supply material for biographies. Some day I'll write all about it myself with other things in a book.'[68] Shortly after John A.'s death, she had mentioned to Pope that she would write the story of her married life.[69] Sadly, this was not done either. As she remarked in 1893, when she went to live in self-imposed exile in England, 'the joy somehow has gone out of my life'.[70]

She never regained that joy throughout the long years of her widowhood. Without John A., she could manage to keep going, manage to look after Mary as she had done for so many years, even manage to remain *au courant* with politics, but her thoughts remained in the past. As she wrote Pope in 1897, 'I am in truth only a very sad old woman — with a past, alas! wholly unforgotten & unforgettable!'[71]

The occasion for this sad statement was the rebuttal of some gossip that had reached her ears that summer, gossip to the effect that she was engaged to marry again. Toronto newspapers, long the bane of her husband's life, now annoyed Agnes to the point where she instructed Pope to 'assure all that nothing is further from my thoughts or intentions'.[72] In a rather defensive manner, Agnes went on, 'Even if I wished such an arrangement, Mary's health & condition would most effectively prevent it & in no case should I feel inclined to begin my life over again.'[73] She admitted (and Pope, who previously seems to have thought her imprudent, would likely have agreed), 'I fear I am a bit careless of what I say & do, sometimes, but, as you know, I have always had a fair share of my own way & like to please myself as to *who* I see much of & when but apart from that there is really *no shadow* of reason for such a silly unkind rumour of which I trust I shall hear no more.'[74]

It was as Agnes wished. No more such rumours circulated and Agnes continued living as 'such an idle, useless wanderer'.[75] There was little sunshine in her late years of widowhood and the spunky old Agnes showed up only when she wrote of topics close to her heart, letters of comment on Canadian, British and world politics. What was closer to her heart, however, her days of married happiness with John A., never did get the attention of her pen.

It is a pity she did not write more, as there is so much only she could have told us — about the first twenty-four years of Confederation and about herself. From the sources available — her diary, her letters to Pope and the few other papers — we get glimpses of an Agnes who merits our attention in her own right. What seems to emerge most strongly from this evidence is the picture of an Agnes who had promised, when a child, that 'for the future, I'll be good' and who, apparently, was guided as an adult by the motto Eleanor Roosevelt adopted years later: 'You cannot live at all if you do not adapt yourself to your life as it happens to be'.[76]

We are left with this tantalizing picture and, perhaps, a symbol. Agnes' grave in Eastbourne is still well kept, with funds provided at her death. It is marked by a tombstone which bears the words:

> In Loving Memory of
> Susan Agnes
> Baroness Macdonald
> of Earnscliffe
> Widow of Sir John Macdonald
> Late Prime Minister of Canada
> Died at Eastbourne, 5th Sept. 1920
> Age 84
> 'Jesu, Lover of My Soul
> Let Me to Thy Bosom Fly'

The epitaph is flat and conventional, but the grave is surrounded by flowers. They are different flowers than those which Agnes planted in her little garden beside the steps in Jamaica so long ago — different, too, than those she tended with much satisfaction in her several Canadian homes. Nor are they the Italian flowers and shrubs that enhanced the grounds of her villa in Alassio and, later, made her life brighter in San Remo when she was, at last, largely confined to a small bed in the garden. The flowers in her grave are English flowers and that, too, would have pleased Agnes for she had gone to England so many times, seeking the comfort and companionship of her relatives and friends there.

Surely these bright but tidy flowers suggest something of the way in which Agnes' spirit flamed within the mold of Victorian sensibility, something of the love and humour and intelligence she expressed often but always within the confines of contemporary convention, something of the way she did adapt herself to life 'as it happened to be'.

Notes
&
Bibliography

Notes

CHAPTER 1 NOTES

1. PAC, Macdonald Papers, MG26A, Vol. 559A, Lady Macdonald's diary,
   July 5, 1867.
2. *Ibid.*
3. PAC, Pope Papens, MG30EI, Vol. 107, Baroness Macdonald to Sir Joseph
   Pope, Nov. 25, 1911.
4. Dirty Pit, renamed Bernard Lodge, would have been of wooden construction,
   as were most houses of that period. Time and the Jamaican climate dealt with
   these buildings in their own way: those that fell into disuse after the
   Emancipation of the slaves were easy prey for the hurricanes that often hit the
   island or tumbled during the severe earthquakes that frequently shook the
   land. In the wakes of these destructive forces, nature assumed full control as
   the luxuriant tropical vegetation covered the ruins. What nature failed to
   accomplish, man did. The Bernard Lodge property is now part of the vast
   complex, including what were neighbouring farms, that makes up the Bernard
   Lodge Sugar Estate.
5. *Lady Nugent's Jamaica Journal*, ed. Philip Wright, Institute of Jamaica, 1966,
   p. 15. The journal was written during 1801 to 1805.
6. *Ibid.*, p. 25
7. *Ibid.*, p. 26
8. Pope Papers, *op. cit.*, Baroness Macdonald to Sir Joseph Pope, April 22, 1906.
9. The Huguenots had undergone centuries of persecution, occasionally
   alleviated by partial reprieves, for their religious beliefs. During the reign of
   Louis XIV some of these French Protestants were 'convinced', by means of
   legal persecutions and tortures, to adopt the Catholic faith. The time came
   when the King could assert, rightly or wrongly, that the best of his French
   subjects had seen the light and that the Edict of Nantes, by which they had
   enjoyed some degree of religious freedom, was no longer needed. With the
   Revocation of the Edict, over 250,000 Huguenots left the country, some going
   to Germany and others to England. In this latter group were members of the
   Bernard family.
10. See Burke's *Landed Gentry*, 1952, entry for Bernard of High Hall, Eng.
11. J.H. Parry and P.M. Sherlock, *A Short History of the West Indies,* 2nd ed.
    Macmillan, London, 1968.
12. In 1695, by an Act of the Scottish Parliament, a company was set up which had
    extensive trading rights in Africa and the Indies. This company decided to
    establish a colony in the Darien Isthmus and, at the same time, they thought,
    they would be securing a free trade route to the Pacific.
13. *Jamaica Almanack*, 1832, WIRL.

14. *Jamaica Almanacks*, for the years listed, WIRL.
15. PAC, Macdonald Papers, MG26A, Vol. 557, Nos. 269220-22.
16. Poem in private possession, property of the estate of the late Mrs. D.F. Pepler.
17. *Ibid.*
18. Pope Papers, *op. cit.*, Vol. 108. Baroness Macdonald to Pope, Feb. 10, 1910.
19. *Falmouth Post and Jamaica General Advertiser*, Jan. 1, 1850, WIRL. This was also Lady Nugent's view in 1801-05.
20. Letter in private possession, property of the estate of the late Mrs. D.F. Pepler.
21. Letter in private possession, property of the estate of the late Mrs. D.F. Pepler.
22. When Thomas Bernard's father, David, died in the early 1800's, his widow, Judith, had taken the other children to England, where they settled in Cheltenham, Glosc. On the Hewitt side, both of Theodora's parents were dead and she had only one sister, Susan.
23. Letter in private possession, property of the estate of the late Mrs. D.F. Pepler.
24. Agnes also saw her Uncle Walter later when he visited England to put his son, Hopton, in school there.
25. Diary in private possession, property of the estate of the late Mrs. D.F. Pepler.
26. Mary Mayne was a half-sister of Theodora's, their father having remarried after the death of the first Mrs. Hewitt.
27. Hawkstone, some miles from Shrewsbury, Shropshire, was the residence of Sir Rowland and Lady Hill. Sir Rowland, 4th Baronet of Hawkstone, was a cousin of Theodora's.
28. Sir Andrew — not identified. Possibly another cousin.
29. The Taylors — not identified, nor is Charles Hill.
30. Tixhall Lodge — another address for the Maynes in Staffordshire.
31. Mrs. Bernard's diary. In private possession, property of the estate of the late Mrs. D.F. Pepler.
32. *Ibid.*
33. Letter in private possession, property of the estate of the late Mrs. D.F. Pepler.
34. Lady Macdonald's diary, *op. cit.*, Feb. 22, 1868.
35. Mrs. Bernard's diary, *op cit.*
36. Lady Macdonald's diary, *op. cit.*, Jan. 2, 1871. Nathaniel Hawthorne lived in England in the 1850's as American Consul in Liverpool.
37. Macdonald Papers, *op. cit.*, Vol. 567, No. 271904.
38. *Ibid.*, No. 271992.
39. *Barrie Northern Advance*, June 21, 1854, p. 1, NL.
40. *Ibid.*, April 12, 1854, from an article written by a Capt. Grubb, once an official of the East India Company, but, by 1854, a resident of Barrie.
41. Agnes Macdonald, 'On A Canadian Salmon Stream', *Murray's Magazine*, London, July-Dec., 1887, p. 447.
42. Agnes Macdonald, 'On A Toboggan', *Murray's Magazine*, London, Jan.-June, 1887, p. 79.
43. Information contained on a map of Barrie, laid out by William Gibbard, January, 1854. The map is in the Simcoe County Archives.
44. Macdonald Papers, *op. cit.*, No. 271887.

Chapter 2 notes

1. PAC, Macdonald Papers, MG26A, Vol. 547, No. 258366.
2. E.B. Bigger, *An Anecdotal Life of Sir John Macdonald*, John Lovell and Sons, Montreal, 1891, p. 82.
3. James Pennington Macpherson, *Life of the Rt. Hon. Sir John A. Macdonald*, Vol. 1, Earle Publishing House, St. John, N.B., 1891, p. 81.
4. PAC, Macdonald Papers, MG26A, Vol. 559A, Lady Macdonald's diary, Mar. 22, 1868.

5. James Pennington Macpherson was the son of John Alexander Macpherson and Maria Clark, a sister of Isabella, John A.'s first wife.

6. Macpherson, *op. cit.*, p. 81.

7. Biggar, *op. cit.*, pp. 82-83.

8. The Liberal-Conservative Party was composed of the last of the members of the Family Compact — the High Tories — under Sir Allan McNab, and the moderate Conservatives under John A., with the support of the Baldwin Reform Party and some French and English in Lower Canada. The groups in Opposition, the Clear Grits and the Parti Rouge, were the forerunners of today's Liberal Party.

9. Sir George Etienne Cartier, joint premier of Canada from 1857 to 1862. Born in Canada in 1814, he died in England in 1873. He was a Member from Montreal from 1861 until his death.

10. Letter in private possession, property of the estate of the late Mrs. D.F. Pepler.

11. *Ibid.*

12. Mrs. Gowan's husband, Judge Robert James Gowan, was later knighted. From 1885 to 1907 he sat in the Senate. Mrs. Gowan was an Ardagh.

13. Letter in private possession, property of the estate of the late Mrs. D.F. Pepler.

14. *Ibid.*

15. Letter in private possession, property of the estate of the late Mrs. D.F. Pepler.

16. Sir Joseph Pope, *Memoirs of the Right Honourable Sir John Alexander Macdonald G.C.B.*, 2nd ed., The Musson Book Company, Toronto, 1930 [1st ed., 1894], p. 334.

17. Macdonald of Earnscliffe, 'A Builder of the Empire', *Pall Mall Magazine*, Sept.-Dec., 1897, p. 350.

18. PAC, Pope Papers, Macdonald Estate, MG30E1, Vol. 106, Nov. 19, 1892.

19. Letter in private possession, property of the estate of the late Mrs. D.F. Pepler.

20. Richard A. Preston, 'The British Influence of RMC' in *To Preserve and Defend: Essays on Kingston in the nineteenth century*, ed. Gerald Tulchinsky, McGill-Queens University Press, Montreal and London, 1976, p. 120.

21. Agnes Macdonald, 'On A Toboggan', *Murray's Magazine*, Jan.-June, 1888, Vol. 3, p. 80.

22. *Ibid.*, p. 81.

23. *Ibid.*, p. 82.

24. Macpherson, *op. cit.*, p. 393.

25. *Ibid.*

26. Pope, *Memoirs. . . op. cit.*, p. 334.

27. *Ibid.*

28. Biggar, *op. cit.*, p. 99.

29. *Ibid.*, p. 99.

30. See, for example, Pope, *Memoirs. . . op. cit.*, p. 334.

31. Letter, from Susan Stewart to Theodora Bernard, in private possession, property of the estate of the late Mrs. D.F. Pepler.

CHAPTER 3 NOTES

1. In November, 1861, a British steamer, the *Trent* was boarded and two Southern Confederates were removed from it by officials of an American ship. Britain protested this breach of international law, and, for a few weeks, it seemed as if war between Britain and the United States might occur.

2. These watercolours are in private possession, property of the estate of the late Mrs. D.F. Pepler.

3. Sir Joseph Pope, *Memoirs of the Right Honourable Sir John Alexander Macdonald, G.C.B.*, 2nd ed., The Musson Book Company, Toronto, 1930

[1st ed., 1894], p. 282. The letter is dated August 15, 1864.

4. Frances Monck, *My Canadian Leaves: An Account of a Visit, 1864-5*, Bentley and Son, London, 1891, pp. 152, 154.

5. *Ibid.*, p. 113.

6. Alexander Galt, Member for Sherbrooke, Lower Canada. He became Minister of Finance in the Cartier-Macdonald Administration in 1858 on condition that a federation of British North America be discussed seriously.

7. Pope, *Memoirs. . . op. cit.*, p. 300.

8. The Crystal Palace had been moved to Sydenham, on the outskirts of London.

9. PAC, Macdonald Papers, MG26A, Vol. 559A, Lady Macdonald's diary, Feb. 5, 1868.

10. Annie and Louisa were the daughters of Theodora's sister, Susan Stewart.

11. Letters in private possession, property of the estate of the late Mrs. D.F. Pepler.

12. Lady Macdonald's diary, *op. cit.*, July 6, 1867.

13. PAC, Pope Papers, Macdonald Estate, MG30E1, letter to Pope, Oct. 10, 1900.

14. John A. expressed disappointment, again, that the surrounding area was not as large as he had wished. He wanted the land through to Sparks Street as part of the Hill and also thought that a new residence for the Governor-General should be built behind the Parliament Buildings, towards Nepean Point. 'Some of my colleagues', he lamented, 'would not hear of it, and said that what had already been appropriated would suffice for the requirements of the next century.' (Pope, *Memoirs. . . op. cit.*, p. 282). By 1865, when all the Government offices moved to Ottawa, space was already at a premium.

15. The Rev. Thomas Bedford-Jones informs us that the house on Daly Street got its name in the following way: 'It was just after the Franco-Prussian War and the cession to Italy of the four famous Fortress Cities which composed the Austrian Quadrilateral lease of defense (Peschiera, Mantua, Verona and Legnano). Some wag gave their epithet to the house in St. Alban's Terrace where the four magnates had their quarters. . . .' ('How St. Alban's Church, Ottawa, Had Its Beginning', [n.d.], reprinted in *The Journal of the Canadian Church Historical Society*, Vol. III, No. 3, Toronto, May, 1957, p. 19.)

16. *Ibid.*, p. 5.

17. *Ibid.*, p. 19.

18. Irish veterans who left the army at the end of the American Civil War in 1865 were joining the Fenians. This revolutionary group, which had had a cell in the United States since 1858, felt frustrated being so far from the main cause — Ireland — which they wished to liberate from the English and began to look for a British target closer at hand.

19. PAC, Macdonald Papers, MG26A, Vol. 512, letter to Oliver Mowat, former Upper Canada delegate to Confederation Conferences, Aug. 13, 1866. John A.'s use of the word 'home' in his quote is interesting and seems to express the same philosophy as was earlier stated by colonials in Jamaica. Britain was 'home' to both.

20. E.B. Biggar, *An Anecdotal Life of Sir John Macdonald*, John Lovell and Sons, Montreal, 1891, p. 99.

21. Lady Macdonald's diary, *op. cit.*, July 6, 1867.

22. PAC, Macdonald Papers, *op. cit.*, Vol. 554, No. 262909.

23. Three of these bridesmaids were daughters of delegates — Charles Tupper, William Macdougall and Adams Archibald. Georgia Mayne was obviously a relative of the Dawson Maynes, possibly the one whom Hewitt was rumoured to be going to marry at this time but did not.

24. Ottawa *Daily Citizen*, Mar. 18, 1867.

25. *Ibid.*

26. The impressive list included: 'Lord, Lady and the Honble. Misses Monck;

Lieut-Col. the Hon. R. and Mrs. Monck; the Hon. Auberon Herbert; Sir Henry and Lady Harnage; Sir Charles and Lady Cuyler; Sir Richard and Lady Mayne; Sir Joshua and Lady Rowe; the Lord Bishop of Montreal and Metropolitan; His Excellency Governor Hincks, C.B.; the Honbles. G.E. Cartier, W. Macdougall, T. D'Arcy McGee, Mr. and Mrs. Howland and H.L. Langevin; the Honbles. Mr. and Miss Tupper, Mr. and Miss Archibald, Mr. and Mrs. Ritchie, McCully Johnson, Henry, Wilmot, Fisher, Tilley and Mitchell from Nova Scotia and New Brunswick; Montague Bernard, Esq., D.C.L.; Messrs. E.R. Bernard, Fearon, Chapman, Lieut. Col. Mayne, Captain Mayne and Mrs. Mayne, J.H. Daley. . . the groomsman was D. Bruce Gardyne.' (Ottawa *Times*, Mar. 8, 1867.)

27. Ottawa *Daily Citizen*, Mar. 8, 1867.
28. *Ibid.*
29. PAC, Macdonald Papers, *op. cit.*, Vol. 569, Nos. 276149-52.
30. Pope, *Memoirs. . . op. cit.*, pp. 336-7.
31. PAC, Macdonald Papers, *op. cit.*, Vol. 569, No. 276149.
32. Ottawa *Times*, March 16, 1867, p. 2.
33. PAC, Macdonald Papers, *op. cit.*, Vol. 569, No. 276152.
34. Pope, *Memoirs. . . op. cit.*, p. 339, letter from Monck dated May 14, 1867.

CHAPTER 4 NOTES

1. PAC, Macdonald Papers, MG26A, Vol. 559A, Lady Macdonald's diary, July 5, 1867.
2. Ottawa *Citizen*, July 5, 1867.
3. Ottawa *Times*, July 3, 1867.
4. Surprise and little concern. See Joseph Pope, *Memoirs of the Right Honourable Sir John Alexander Macdonald*, 2nd ed., The Musson Book Company, Toronto, 1930 [1st ed., 1894], p. 351. 'On that day Lord Monck informed me that I had been made a K.C.B.' The concern was over the fact that some of his colleagues from Lower Canada resented being given only the C.B.
5. The Rev. Thomas Bedford-Jones, 'How St. Alban's Church, Ottawa Had Its Beginning', [n.d.], reprinted in *The Journal of the Canadian Church Historical Society*, Vol. III, No. 3, Toronto, May, 1957, p. 13.
6. Ottawa *Citizen*, July 5, 1867.
7. 'The Parliament Buildings were brilliantly illuminated. . . . Among the principal illuminations by private individuals [was] a large illuminated transparency bearing the words Success to the new Dominion of Canada, over the door of Mrs. Scott, Confectioner. . . . Mrs. Trotter, at the Toronto House also illuminated, and Mrs. McKenna very properly did the same.' (Ottawa *Times*, July 3, 1867.)
8. *Ibid.*
9. Lady Macdonald's diary, *op. cit.*, July 5, 1867.
10. PAC, Macdonald Papers, MG26A, Vol. 569, No. 276156, March 6, 1868.
11. Lady Macdonald's diary, *op. cit.*, July 6, 1867.
12. *Ibid.*
13. *Ibid.*, July 5 , 1867.
14. *Ibid.*, July 7, 1867.
15. *Ibid.*, Nov. 17, 1868.
16. *Ibid.*, Dec. 3, 1867.
17. *Ibid.*, July 8, 1867.
18. *Ibid.*, July 10, 1867.
19. *Ibid.*
20. *Ibid.*, July 7, 1867.

21. *Ibid.*
22. *Ibid.*, July 13, 1867.
23. *Ibid.*, July 14, 1867.
24. *Ibid.*, Sept. 28, 1867.
25. *Ibid.*, Nov. 17, 1867.
26. *Ibid.*
27. Bedford-Jones, *op. cit.*, p. 7.
28. Lady Macdonald's diary, *op. cit.*, July 7, 1867.
29. Pope, *Memoirs. . . op cit.*, p. 666.
30. Lady Macdonald's diary, *op. cit.*, Nov. 17, 1867.
31. *Ibid.*, March 19, 1868.
32. *Ibid.*, April 19, 1868.
33. *Ibid.*, Nov. 17, 1868.
34. *Ibid.*, Feb. 5, 1868.
35. *Ibid.*, Jan. 12, 1868.
36. *Ibid.*, Nov. 21, 1867.
37. *Ibid.*, Jan. 3, 1868.
38. 'Kettledrum' was the fashionable term used in the late 18th century and during the 19th to denote an afternoon tea-party, sometimes followed by a larger assembly. It was a smaller affair than a 'drum'.
39. Lady Macdonald's diary, *op. cit.*, Jan. 2, 1868.
40. *Ibid.*, Jan. 11, 1868.
41. *Ibid.*, Jan. 7-8, 1868.
42. *Ibid.*, March 19, 1868.
43. *Ibid.*, March 31, 1868.
44. *Ibid.*, Jan. 1, 1868.
45. *Ibid.*, Feb. 22, 1868.
46. *Ibid.*, Jan. 11, 1868.
47. *Ibid.*, Feb. 7, 8, 1868.
48. *Ibid.*, Jan. 12, 1868.
49. *Ibid.*, Feb. 7, 8, 1868.
50. *Ibid.*, March 25, 1868.
51. *Ibid.*, March 24, 1868.
52. *Ibid.*, April 12, 1868.
53. *Ibid.*, April 15, 1868.
54. *Ibid.*, April 12, 1868.
55. *Ibid.*, April 19, 1868.
56. *Ibid.*, April 25, 1868.
57. *Ibid.*, May 1, 1868.
58. The Imperial Government had guaranteed the £4 million that the Canadian Government had to borrow to build this railway. In July, 1868, the Cabinet decided the line should follow the Bay of Chaleurs route since that was the best from a military and strategic point of view. This met with approval by the Imperial Government as the route was farthest from the U.S. —Canada border and thus regarded as the safest.
59. Lady Macdonald's diary, *op. cit.*, Aug. 28, 1868.
60. *Ibid.*, Sept. 30, 1868.
61. *Ibid.*, Jan. 27, 1869.
62. *Ibid.*, June 21, 1868.
63. *Ibid.*, Sept. 24, 1868.
64. *Ibid.*
65. *Ibid.*, Jan. 1, 1869.
66. *Ibid.*
67. *Ibid.*, Feb. 2, 1869.
68. *Ibid.*
69. *Ibid.*

70. *Ibid.*, Feb. 7, 1869.
71. *Ibid.*, April 1, 1869.
72. *Ibid.*,
73. *Ibid.*, April 25, 1869.

CHAPTER 5 NOTES

1. PAC, Macdonald Papers, MG26A, Vol. 559A Lady Macdonald's diary, May 1, 1869.
2. *Ibid.*, Nov. 7, 1869.
3. *Ibid.*
4. *Ibid.*, Jan. 27, 1869.
5. The area purchased as Rupert's Land included nearly all of what would become the provinces of Manitoba, Saskatchewan and Alberta, as well as portions of present-day Ontario, Quebec and the Northwest Territories. Originally the term had referred to those territories whose rivers flowed into Hudson Bay; as the fur trade expanded, it gradually came to include other lands to the south, west and north. Even at the time of purchase, the boundaries were poorly defined.
6. Sir Joseph Pope, *Memoirs of the Right Honourable Sir John Alexander Macdonald*, 2nd ed., The Musson Book Company, Toronto, 1930 [1st ed., 1894], p. 408.
7. Lady Macdonald's diary, *op cit.* Jan. 7, 1870.
8. *Ibid.*
9. E.B. Biggar, *An Anecdotal Life of Sir John Macdonald*, John Lovell and Son, Montreal, 1891, p. 106.
10. Pope, *Memoirs. . .*, *op. cit.*, p. 435, letter of July 3, 1870.
11. Lady Macdonald's diary, *op. cit.*, Jan. 1, 1871.
12. *Ibid.*
13. *Ibid.*
14. *Ibid.*
15. *Ibid.*, Jan. 2, 1871.
16. *Ibid.*
17. *Ibid.*, Jan. 4, 1871.
18. *Ibid.*, Jan. 3, 1871.
19. The Moncks' summers had been spent in the typical farmhouse of M. Moreau, the local blacksmith, which still stands today, though now known as the McCarthy house. Others from Quebec City who spent their summers in Rivière du Loup included the William Merideths, the Abraham Josephs and members of the Lemoine, Chouinard and Pope families.
20. The Reverend Thomas Bedford-Jones, 'How St. Alban's Church, Ottawa, Had Its Beginning', reprinted in *Journal of the Canadian Church Historical Society*, Toronto, May, 1957. Vol. III, No. 3, p. 15.
21. Lady Macdonald's diary, *op. cit.*, April 19, 1868.
22. Bedford-Jones, *op. cit.*, p. 15.
23. PAC, Macdonald Papers, MG26A Vol. 547, Nos. 28550-1, Oct. 1870.
24. *Ibid.*
25. *Ibid.*
26. Baroness Macdonald of Earnscliffe, 'A Builder of the Empire', *Pall Mall Magazine*, Vol. 13, Sept.-Dec., 1897, p. 352.
27. Lady Macdonald's diary, *op. cit.*, May 10, 1868.
28. Baroness Macdonald, *op. cit.*, p. 352.
29. Their majority was small and, in spite of all efforts, Ontario was won by the Reformers. George Brown had, however, been out of politics since being

defeated in the 1867 election and had never again entered his name for the House of Commons in elections.

30. Lady Macdonald's diary, *op. cit.*, March 18, 1872.
31. Lady Macdonald, 'By Car and by Cowcatcher', *Murray's Magazine*, Vol. 1, Jan.-June, 1887, p. 222.
32. The Marchioness of Dufferin and Ava, *My Canadian Journal, 1872-8,* John Murray, 1891, April 8, 1973.
33. Cartier died 1873; John A. had been very closely associated with him since the formation of the Liberal-Conservative Party in 1857. After watching this partnership for something over a year, Agnes had written in her diary, 'Cartier . . . the fairest of men — he always seems to me, full of life and pleasant chattiness, but he is exceedingly egotistical. He must be clever and powerful but somehow I don't think he is a favourite — I mean in public life — still his honesty must be respected.' (Lady Macdonald's diary, *op cit.* Sept. 19, 1868.)
34. Pope, *Memoirs. . .*, *op. cit.*, pp. 623-4.
35. Most historians, including Donald Creighton, have accepted the suicide-attempt story, while Pope, the ever-loyal Secretary, brought in an element of doubt. Where there can be no room for doubt is that John A. must have disappeared from Rivière du Loup in an alcoholic haze for some days in order to occasion the report by the Governor-General to his superiors in London.
36. The Marchioness of Dufferin and Ava, *op. cit.*, Oct. 23, 1873.
37. *Ibid.*, Oct. 28, 1873.
38. *Ibid.*, Nov. 3, 1873.
39. *Ibid.*, Nov. 4 , 1873.
40. Lord Dufferin wrote to John A., saying that he had been kept awake until 5 a.m. by his wife as she recounted the details of John A.'s speech. 'Round the breakfast table at Rideau Hall this morning there was a continuous chorus of admiration from all my English friends.' (PAC, Macdonald Papers, *op. cit.*, Vol. 79, Nov. 4, 1873.) These friends included Lord Rosebery, a future Prime Minister of England.
41. The Marchioness of Dufferin and Ava, *op. cit.*, Nov. 5, 1873.
42. Pope, *Memoirs. . .*, *op. cit.*, p. 561.

CHAPTER 6 NOTES

1. PAC, Macdonald Papers, MG26A, Vol. 559A, Lady Macdonald's diary, Jan. 1 , 1870.
2. *Ibid.*
3. Baroness Macdonald of Earnscliffe, 'A Builder of the Empire', *Pall Mall Magazine*, Vol. 13, Sept.-Dec., 1897, p. 352.
4. E.B. Biggar, *An Anecdotal Life of Sir John Macdonald*, John Lovell and Son, Montreal, 1891, p. 104.
5. *Ibid.*
6. Lady Dufferin was also trying to learn to skate at this time.
7. The Marchioness of Dufferin and Ava, *My Canadian Journal, 1872-8,* John Murray, London, 1891, Nov. 15, 1873.
8. Biggar, *op. cit.*, p. 256.
9. Letter dated Aug. 28, 1859. In private possession, property of the estate of the late Mrs. D.F. Pepler.
10. PAC, Macdonald Papers, MG26A, Vol. 558, Nos. 269508-9.
11. *Ibid.*, Vol. 569, No. 276609, Sept. 3, 1870.
12. *Ibid.*, Vol. 554, No. 262995, Nov. 26, 1874.
13. *Ibid.*, Vol. 569, Aug. 25, 1873.
14. *Ibid.*, Oct. 12, 1877.
15. PAC, Pope Papers, MG30E1, Vol. 107, Baroness Macdonald to Pope,

Nov. 25, 1906.

16. Biggar, *op. cit.,* pp. 103-4.
17. Lady Macdonald's diary, *op. cit.,* Nov. 17, 1867.
18. *Ibid.,* March 19, 1868.
19. *Ibid.*
20. *Ibid.,* April 19, 1868.

21. The Rev. Thomas Bedford-Jones, 'How St. Alban's Church, Ottawa, Had Its Beginning', [n.d.], reprinted in *Journal of the Canadian Church Historical Society,* Toronto, May, 1957, Vol. III, No. 3, p. 20.
22. Lady Macdonald's diary, *op. cit.,* March 11, 1875.
23. Bedford-Jones, *op. cit.,* p. 21.
24. *Ibid.*
25. *Ibid.*
26. *Ibid.,* p. 20.
27. The partners in the firm were then John A., James Patton, Robert Fleming and, after the completion of his studies at Osgoode Hall, Hugh John.
28. Built in 1872, this house was owned by John A. until 1888, when he sold to Sir Oliver Mowat. It now is part of the University of Toronto and bears a plaque identifying it as the Macdonald-Mowat House.
29. Lady Macdonald's diary, *op. cit.,* Jan. 3, 1868.
30. *Ibid.,* Jan. 4, 1868.
31. *Ibid.,* Sept. 19, 1868.
32. Macdonald Papers, *op. cit.,* Vol. 569, Dec. 6, 1873.
33. This rash of bye-elections was caused by a change in electoral boundaries, a plan of Mackenzie's that he must have regretted.
34. Hamilton *Weekly Times,* Oct. 25, 1877.
35. Lady Macdonald's diary, *op. cit.,* Aug. 27, 1868.
36. Toronto *Mail,* July 12, 1872.

CHAPTER 7 NOTES

1. PAC, Macdonald Papers, MG26A, Vol. 559A, Lady Macdonald's diary, Feb. 25, 1868.
2. The Marchioness of Dufferin and Ava, *My Canadian Journal, 1872-8,* John Murray, London, 1891, June 23, 1872.
3. Simply stated, the National Policy was an attempt to show that the Conservative Party had plans for the protection of goods manufactured in Canada. This had been a strong plank in the platform of the 1872 election campaign.
4. Lady Dufferin reported that she had heard someone shout 'Three Groans for Mackenzie' and that there were signs in the streets reminding the Vice-Regal party that not even the final route had been decided upon — one such read: 'Per Vias Recta, the Fraser Valley'. There were other 'signs' of disenchantment, such as 'a live horse, with a cloth over it, on which was written "Good, but not iron" and another had "Speed the Railway" written on a board, above which a little train moved along as we passed.' (The Marchioness of Dufferin, *op. cit.,* Aug. 16, Sept. 5 and 6, 1876.)
5. PAC, Macdonald Papers, MG26A, Vol. 569, Nos. 276205-6. Sarah and Oswald were Mary's two nurses; Thomas Reynolds' daughter lived in the cottage next to the Macdonalds'.
6. Lady Macdonald's diary, *op. cit.,* March 15, 1868.
7. *Ibid.,* March 24, 1868.
8. Macdonald Papers, *op. cit.,* Vol. 569, No. 276209.
9. *Ibid.,* No. 276210.
10. *Ibid.*

11. Sir Joseph Pope, *Memoirs of The Right Honourable Sir John Alexander Macdonald*, 2nd ed., Musson Book Company, Toronto, 1930, [1st ed., 1894] pp. 569-70.

12. Macdonald Papers, *op. cit.*, Vol. 554, No. 263271.

13. P.B. Waite, *Macdonald: His Life and World*, McGraw Hill-Ryerson, Ltd., Toronto, 1975, p. 57.

14. Douglas Library, Queen's University, Williamson Papers, May 3, 1881.

15. Macdonald Papers, *op. cit.*, Vol. 554, No. 263271. A 'dress improver', for those who are interested, was simply a bustle.

16. Baroness Macdonald of Earnscliffe, 'A Builder of the Empire', *Pall Mall Magazine*, Vol. 13, Sept.-Dec. 1897, pp. 349, 351.

17. Mrs. W.R. Eakin of Montreal inherited this house from her father, the Hon. H.J. Symington. Agnes' original deed is in Mrs. Eakin's possession.

18. Irene R. Wolfe, 'St. Patrick', an unpublished account of the one-time residents. The writer is a descendent of Abraham Joseph, one of the original residents of Rivière du Loup. This manuscript is in the hands of Mrs. W.R. Eakin of Montreal.

19. Macdonald Papers, *op. cit.*, Vol. 569, Feb. 19, 1883.

20. PAC, Pope Papers, MG30E1, Vol. 107.

21. In 1878, the Lieutenant-Governor of Quebec caused a political furor by dismissing the provincial Government, accusing it of slighting his office. Neither the Governor-General, Lord Lorne, nor John A. could decide how best to handle this situation and, on John A.'s advice, the British Government was asked for a judgment. The result was the dismissal of the Lieutenant-Governor.

22. Sir Joseph Pope, ed., *The Correspondence of Sir John Macdonald, 1840-1891*, Oxford University Press, 1921, p. 260, April 8, 1879.

23. Pope, *Correspondence. . . op. cit.*, Appendix.

24. *Ibid.*

25. General Maurice Pope, ed., *The Public Servant: The Memoirs of Sir Joseph Pope*, Oxford University Press, Toronto, 1960, Appendix, p. 24.

26. Sir Joseph Pope, *The Day of Sir John Macdonald*, Glasgow, Brook and Company, Toronto, 1915, p. 117.

27. In 1912, the *Reminiscences* of Sir Richard Cartwright, a long-time political rival of John A.'s, made sure the story circulated once more.

28. Lady Macdonald's diary, *op. cit.*, Dec. 1, 1868.

29. Macdonald's Papers, *op. cit.*, Vols, 537-38, no. 253622.

30. Frederic Nicholls and A.W. Wright, compilers, *Report of the Demonstration in honour of the 40th Anniversary of Sir John Macdonald's entrance into public life*, privately printed, Toronto, 1885, pp. 14-15.

31. *Ibid.*, p. 99.

32. *Ibid.*

33. *Ibid.*, p. 100.

34. Nicholas Flood Davin was then owner of the Regina *Leader*. He later entered politics.

35. Macdonald Papers, *op. cit.*, Vol. 547, Nos. 258694-5.

CHAPTER 8 NOTES

1. Macdonald of Earnscliffe, 'A Builder of the Empire,' *Pall Mall Magazine*, Vol. 13, Sept.-Dec. 1897, p. 353.

2. Not until 1920 did women's names appear on voters' lists for Federal elections. In provincial elections, Manitoba, Saskatchewan and Alberta were the first to grant women political equality with their menfolk, followed by British Columbia and Ontario in 1917. The provinces then ran afoul of the Borden

government, which delayed the right of women to vote, federally, until the passage of the 1918 Elections Act. Other Canadian women who were then eligible to vote were those in Nova Scotia and New Brunswick in 1919 and in Prince Edward Island in 1922, but it was not until 1940 that Quebec recognized women voters. In Newfoundland, women had voted since 1925.

3. PAC, Macdonald Papers, MG26A, Vol. 559A, Lady Macdonald's diary, March 31, 1868.

4. *Ibid.,* Aug. 27, 1868.

5. PAC, Macdonald Papers, MG26A, Vol. 547, No. 258695.

6. Frederick Nicholls and A.W. Wright, compilers, *Report of the Demonstration in honour of the 40th Anniversary of Sir John Macdonald's entrance into public life,* Toronto, 1885, p. 99.

7. The Federal government was ready to provide land, for there was plenty, but it was not the land desired by the Métis. John A. invited Riel to Ottawa to discuss the matter.

8. House of Commons Debates, 1878, p. 2564.

9. PAC, Pope Papers, Macdonald Estate, MG30E1, Vol. 107, Baroness Macdonald to Pope, April 22, 1906.

10. It is also ironical that two of the first spikes in the railway had been driven by the Macdonalds' good friends, Lord and Lady Dufferin, during the former's term as Governor-General. During the Vice-Regal trip to the West in the summer of 1877, Lady Dufferin had written that they 'drove through Fort Garry [sic] and across the Red River to a place where D. [Lord Dufferin] and I each drove a spike in the Canadian Pacific Railway, the first line in this part of Canada'. (The Marchioness of Dufferin and Ava, *My Canadian Journal, 1872-8,* John Murray, 1891, Sept. 28, 1877.)

11. Macdonald Papers, *op. cit.,* Dec. 22, 1885.

12. *Ibid.,*

13. *Ibid.,* Jan. 19, 1886.

14. The Brooks were from Sherbrooke, Quebec. From 1872 to 1882, he had been an M.P. and by 1886 had moved to the Supreme Court of Quebec.

15. William Cornelius Van Horne was the General Manager of the C.P.R.

16. Macdonald Papers, *op. cit.,* Jan. 19, 1886.

17. *Ibid.*

18. C.P.R. Archives, Van Horne Collection, Montreal, July 6, 1886.

19. *Ibid.*

20. Lady Macdonald's diary, *op. cit.,* Sept. 1, 1868.

21. *Ibid.,* Jan. 4, 1871.

22. This diary was eventually published as Maurice Pope, ed., *Public Servant: The Memoirs of Sir Joseph Pope,* Toronto, Oxford Press, 1960.

23. A high official in the North West Mounted Police.

24. Maurice Pope, ed., *op. cit.,* pp. 52-53.

25. Agnes Macdonald, 'By Car and by Cowcatcher,' *Murray's Magazine,* London, Vol. 1, Jan.-June, 1887, p. 215.

26. *Ibid.*

27. *Ibid.,* p. 216.

28. *Ibid.,* p. 218.

29. *Ibid.,* p. 219.

30. The Primrose League was founded in England in 1883 in support of the Conservative Party there.

31. Agnes Macdonald, 'By Car and by Cowcatcher,' *op. cit.,* p. 219.

32. 'Brother-in-law' is the translation of the Indian name, Kis-ta-mo-ni-mon, given to John A. by Chief Crowfoot.

33. Agnes Macdonald, 'By Car and by Cowcatcher', *op. cit.,* p. 222.

34. *Ibid.,* p. 223.

35. Maurice Pope, ed., *op. cit.,* p. 53.

36. One of the provisions in the contract to build the C.P.R. was that, for twenty years from the date of the contract, no other railway could be built in the Northwest, between the C.P.R. and the U.S. border. By Clause 15 of the contract, the only exceptions allowed were some lines that ran to the southwest or to a town or settlement as long as these did not come within fifteen miles of the international border.

37. Agnes Macdonald, 'By Car and by Cowcatcher,' *op. cit.*, p. 225.

38. *Ibid.*

39. C.P.R. Archives, *op. cit.*, July 17, 1886.

40. Maurice Pope, ed., *op. cit.*, p. 54.

41. Agnes Macdonald, 'By Car and by Cowcatcher', *op. cit.*, p. 225.

42. Poundmaker had come to an inglorious end a fortnight earlier, having choked to death while eating wild berries.

43. Agnes Macdonald, 'By Car and by Cowcatcher', *op. cit.*, p. 227.

44. Maurice Pope, ed., *op. cit.*, p. 55.

45. Agnes Macdonald, 'By Car and by Cowcatcher', *op. cit.*, p. 229.

46. *Ibid.*

47. *Ibid.*, p. 230.

48. *Ibid.*, pp. 231-32.

49. *Ibid.*, p. 232.

50. *Ibid.*, p. 233.

51. *Ibid.*

52. *Ibid.*, p. 235.

53. *Ibid.*, p. 296.

54. *Ibid.*, p. 235.

55. *Ibid.*, p. 296.

56. Maurice Pope, ed., *op. cit.*, p. 56.

57. Agnes Macdonald, 'By Car and by Cowcatcher', *op. cit.*, p. 310.

58. *Ibid.*, pp. 297-98.

59. *Ibid.*, pp. 298-300.

60. *Ibid.*, p. 303.

61. *Ibid.*, p. 305.

62. *Ibid.*, p. 308.

63. Maurice Pope, ed., *op. cit.*, p. 57.

64. *Ibid.*, p. 62.

65. If Agnes was, indeed, the anonymous writer on Canadian affairs in *Murray's Magazine*, she was in good company. Among her fellow contributors in those years were Lord Byron, the Bishop of Carlyle, 'Buffalo Bill', Matthew Arnold, S. Baring Gould and Sir J. Drummond Hay.

66. [Lady Macdonald?], 'Canadian Topics', *Murray's Magazine*, Vol. 1, Jan.-June, 1887, p. 686.

67. *Ibid.*, p. 688.

68. [Lady Macdonald?], 'Men and Measures in Canada', *Murray's Magazine*, Vol. 2, July-Dec., 1887, p. 385.

69. *Ibid.*, p. 386.

70. *Ibid.*

Chapter 9 notes

1. This baby, born in February, 1887, was the mother of Mrs. David Partridge of Toronto.

2. Agnes Macdonald, 'On A Canadian Salmon River,' *Murray's Magazine*, Vol. 2, July-Dec., 1887, p. 450.

3. *Ibid.*, pp. 451-52.

4. *Ibid.*, p. 454.

5. *Ibid.*, p. 456.
6. *Ibid.*
7. *Ibid.*
8. *Ibid.*, p. 461.
9. Not identified.
10. Agnes Macdonald, 'On A Canadian Salmon River', *op. cit.*, p. 622.
11. *Ibid.*, pp. 627-28.
12. *Ibid.*, p. 629.
13. *Ibid.*, p. 634.
14. *Ibid.*, p. 631.
15. *Ibid.*, pp. 631-32.
16. C.P.R. Archives, Montreal, Van Horne Collection, No. 13629, July 17, 1886.
17. This cottage still stands today, although much altered. Its estimated date of construction is set at 1887 according to the Canadian Inventory of Historic Buildings. The propery now belongs to the C.P.R., which acquired it in October, 1929.

    The records present some uncertainty as to how much time, if any, Mary spent in this cottage. One researcher says, without giving a source, that Agnes (and, one must presume, Mary, when she was with her mother) used this cottage in the summers of 1887, 1888, and 1889. (Bart Robinson, "Banff Springs: The Story of A Hotel", *Banff: Summer Thought*, 1973.) The Macdonald Papers, however, include a bill from the Sanatorium dated September 10, 1887, which reads: 'July 1 To Board Miss Macdonald and attendants to date, 71 days $426. Livery to date $84.50.' (PAC, Macdonald Papers, *op. cit.*, Vol. 555, No. 264058.) Since we know that Mary wrote to her father from Banff Station on April 6, 1887 (Macdonald Papers, *op. cit.*, Vol. 569), that bill seems open to two interpretations: that the party started the season in the cottage, found it unsuitable, and moved to the Sanatorium on July 1; or that they never stayed in the cottage at all and that this is the second bill presented for payment, the first not having survived to go to the PAC.

    The Archives of the Canadian Rockies at Banff shed little light on the situation. They show that Villa Lots 26 and 27 were formally leased to Agnes on September 11, 1893, at $30 per annum, but the archivists say it is evident that she had possession of these lots for an unknown length of time before this.
18. [Lady Macdonald?], 'Canadian Topics', *Murray's Magazine*, Vol. 1, Jan.-June, 1887, p. 689.
19. Macdonald Papers, MG26A, Vol. 569, Nos. 276316-29, May 31, 1887.
20. *Ibid.*
21. E.B. Biggar, *An Anecdotal Life of Sir John Macdonald*, John Lovell and Son, Montreal, 1891, p. 257.
22. Macdonald Papers, *op. cit.*, Vol. 569, Jan. 14, 1878.
23. *Ibid.*, Aug. 27, 1889.
24. *Ibid.*
25. Biggar, *op. cit.*, p. 239.
26. *Ibid.*
27. *Ibid.*
28. Joseph Pope, *Memoirs of the Right Honourable John Alexander Macdonald*, 2nd ed., The Musson Book Company, Toronto, 1930 [1st ed., 1894], pp. 613-14.
29. On July 16, 1888, the Red River Railway Act, under which construction of t¹ lines to the south had been planned, was disallowed by the Federal Government, causing an uproar.
30. Emma Albani, *Forty Years of Song*, Mills and Boone, London, 1911, pp. 211-12.
31. PAC, Stephen Papers, MG29A30, No. 291, Feb. 15, 1889.
32. Agne Macdonald, 'On A Toboggan', *Murray's Magazine*, Vol. 3, Jan.-J¹

1888, p. 86.

33. The area around the Pribilof Islands off Alaska was rich in seals and it was the slaughter of these animals, with the possibility of their eventual extinction, that started the tension between Canada and the U.S. By rights, the U.S. had jurisdiction over only three miles around the islands. The sale of seal pelts being profitable, soon the Americans laid claim to all the Bering Sea waters. This was disputed by the British, and it was not until 1893 that the matter was settled by arbitration.

34. Lady Macdonald, 'An Unconventional Holiday', *Ladies' Home Journal*, Philadelphia, Vol. 8, No. 9, Aug., 1891, p. 1.

35. *Ibid.*

36. *Ibid.*

37. *Ibid.*

38. William McKinley, twenty-fifth President of the United States, introduced a bill in 1890 which imposed high and, in some cases, almost prohibitive duties. The effect of this was felt heavily in Canada, but opposition to it came from many European countries as well.

39. Lady Macdonald, 'An Unconventional Holiday', *op. cit.*, p. 1.

40. *Ibid.*

41. *Ibid.*, Vol. 8, No. 10, Sept., 1891, p. 2.

42. Maurice Pope, ed., *Public Servant: The Memoirs of Sir Joseph Pope*, Oxford University Press, Toronto, 1960, p. 78.

43. Sir Joseph Pope, *The Day of Sir John Macdonald*, Glasgow, Brook & Co., Toronto, 1915, pp. 178-79.

44. *Ibid.*, p. 178.

45. Quoted in Mercer Adam, *Canada's Patriot Statesman*, Parish & Co., Toronto, 1891, p. 497.

46. Biggar, *op. cit.*, p. 289.

47. London *Times*, June 8, 1891. As there was no paper on Sun., June 7, 'last night' refers quite correctly to June 6, 1891.

CHAPTER 10 NOTES

1. *Letters of Queen Victoria: 1891-1895*, 3rd series, Vol. 2, John Murray, London, 1931, p. 41.

2. *Ibid.*

3. E.B. Biggar, *An Anecdotal Life of Sir John Macdonald*, Lovell and Son, Montreal, 1891, p. 289.

4. Ottawa *Daily Citizen*, June 8, 1891.

5. *Ibid.*

6. London *Daily Graphic*, June 9, 1891.

7. PAC, Tupper Papers, No. 4692, July 24, 1891.

8. PAC, Macdonald Papers, MG26A, Vol. 559, No. 270774, June 12, 1891.

9. *Ibid.*, No. 270775.

10. *Ibid.*

11. Royal Archives, Windsor Castle, England.

12. Office of the Secretary of State, Ottawa, July 29, 1891.

13. Macdonald Papers, *op. cit.*, Vol. 569, Nos. 276327-8, May 21, 1887.

14. Tupper Papers, *op. cit.*, No. 4396, July 24, 1891.

15. Toronto *Globe*, July 7, 1891, p. 4.

16. Max Jesoley, 'Unknown Wives of Well-known Men: VI — Lady Agnes Macdonald', *Ladies' Home Journal*, Vol. 8, No. 7, June, 1891, p. 3.

17. *Ibid.*

18. Maurice Pope, ed., *Public Servant: The Memoirs of Sir Joseph Pope*, Oxford

University Press, Toronto, 1960, p. 79.
19. *Ibid.*
20. PAC, Thompson Papers, MG26D, Vols. 288-291, No. 00783A.
21. Tupper Papers, *op. cit.*, No. 4454, Nov. 4, 1891.
22. Ottawa *Daily Citizen*, June 11, 1891.
23. C.P.R. Archives, Montreal, Van Horne Collection, June 16, 1891.
24. Toronto *Globe*, July 17, 1891, p. 4.
25. The other trustees of the Macdonald estate were Edgar Dewdney, Fred White and Hugh John Macdonald.
26. PAC, Pope Papers, Macdonald Estate, Vol. 107, Nov. 21, 1891.
27. *Ibid.*
28. *Ibid.*
29. G. Mercer Adam, *Canada's Patriot Statesman*, Parish & Co., Toronto, 1891, pp. 545-46.
30. *Ibid.*, p. 546.
31. Pope Papers, *op. cit.*, Feb. 25, 1892.
32. *Ibid.*
33. *Ibid.*
34. Queen's University, Douglas Library, Williamson Papers, July 3, 1892.
35. On her way down to Rivière du Loup, Agnes had stopped off in Montreal to visit her friends, the Stephens.
36. Pope Papers, *op. cit.*, Sept. 12, 1892.
37. Williamson Papers, *op. cit.*, Sept. 12, 1892.
38. *Ibid.*, Nov. 3, 1892.
39. Pope Papers, *op. cit.*, Nov. 3, 1892.
40. *Ibid.*
41. *Ibid.*
42. *Ibid.*, Nov. 19, 1892.
43. *Ibid.*
44. *Ibid.*
45. *Ibid.*
46. Williamson Papers, *op. cit.*, Dec. 10, 1892.
47. Pope Papers, *op. cit.*, Nov. 19, 1892.
48. Williamson Papers, *op. cit.*, Nov. 8, 1892.
49. *Ibid.*
50. *Ibid.*, May 23, 1893.

CHAPTER 11 NOTES

1. PAC, Pope Papers, MG30E1, Vol. 107. Baroness Macdonald to Pope, June 11, 1893.
2. *Ibid.*
3. *Ibid.*
4. Douglas Library, Queen's University, Williamson Papers, July 11, 1893.
5. *Ibid.*
6. *Ibid.*
7. *Ibid.*
8. *Ibid.*
9. *Ibid.*
10. The American actions regarding this fishing ground had been condemned. The Bering Sea had been held to be part of the high seas, so the seals that were caught there by American agents were illegal catches.
11. Two books on John A. — one by his nephew, James Pennington Macpherson, the other by E.B. Biggar — had appeared in 1891 and been very badly received by Agnes and other members of the Macdonald family. Biggar's book was

anecdotal and contained stories well known to the public, but ones which Agnes, possibly, could not tolerate hearing repeated so soon after John A.'s death. The Macdonalds' dislike of Macpherson's work is harder to understand. As a member of the family, he had first-hand knowledge of John A., but this was not enough, supposedly, without the papers to which Pope alone was given access. For whatever reason, the book made for a family row that ended with that branch cutting off Agnes, summarily, much to her sorrow.

12. Pope Papers, *op. cit.*, Sept. 12, 1892.
13. *Ibid.*
14. *Ibid.*, Nov. 28, 1892.
15. Sir Joseph Pope, *Memoirs of the Right Honourable Sir John Alexander Macdonald,* 2nd ed., The Musson Book Company, Toronto, 1930, [1st ed., 1894], preface to 1st ed.
16. Williamson Papers, *op. cit.*, Dec. 24, 1893.
17. *Ibid.*
18. *Ibid.*
19. Pope Papers, *op. cit.*, Oct. 19, 1895.
20. *Ibid.*, Jan. 8, 1896.
21. *Ibid.*
22. *Ibid.*
23. *Ibid.*, March 14, 1901.
24. *Ibid.*, May 26, 1895.
25. *Ibid.*, June 16, 1896.
26. *Ibid.*
27. *Ibid.*
28. *Ibid.*, Aug. 4, 1895.
29. *Ibid.*
30. *Ibid.*, Jan. 8, 1896.
31. *Ibid.*, May 16, 1900.
32. *Ibid.*
33. *Ibid.*, Jan. 30, 1896.
34. PAC, Pope Papers, Special Journals, Visits to England re Alaska, 7 Sept. to 31 Oct., 1899. Entry for Sat., 14 Oct., 1899.
35. *Ibid.*, Entry for Sun., 15 Oct., 1899.
36. John Haggart, M.P., and member of Bowell's Cabinet.
37. *Journal of Lady Aberdeen,* Champlain Society, Oxford University Press, Toronto, 1960, Dec. 13, 1894.
38. Pope Papers, *op. cit.*, Jan. 8, 1896.
39. *Ibid.*, Jan. 30, 1896.
40. *Ibid.*, Oct. 4, 1896.
41. *Ibid.*
42. *Ibid.*, Oct. 17, 1897.
43. PAC, Macdonald Papers, MG26A, Vol. 558, No. 269299.
44. Pope Papers, *op. cit.*, Oct. 10, 1900.
45. *Ibid.*
46. *Ibid.*, Dec. 3, 1900.
47. Williamson Papers, *op. cit.*, Jan. 9, 1895.
48. Macdonald Papers, *op. cit.*, Vol. 569, Dec. 10, 1887.
49. Pope Papers, *op. cit.*, Aug. 11, 1895.
50. *Ibid.*, Oct. 19, 1895.
51. *Ibid.*
52. *Ibid.*, May 30, 1898.
53. *Ibid.*
54. *Ibid.* McCarthy had not only rejected John A.'s overtures to lead the Conservatives but, in 1889, had broken with the party and led the revolt against the Jesuit Estates Bill in Quebec. From then on, he sat on an

Independant, heading the Equal Rights Movement and strongly opposing Separate Schools in Manitoba. When Laurier became Prime Minister, McCarthy gave him partial support.

55. There had long been unsatisfactory relations between Great Britain and the Boers, the Dutch-speaking Republics of the Transvaal and the Orange Free State. In 1896, the discovery of gold on the Rand in the Transvaal brought a flood of British immigrants and gave the British Government an excuse to move the Boers back. Sir Cecil Rhodes led the ill-fated Jameson Raid into the area, and it was after the defeat of this expedition that the German Kaiser sent a telegram of congratulations to Kruger, the Boer leader. From the British view-point, the Kaiser's aim seemed to be to persuade France and Germany of their hostility to Britain and thus provoke a European war.

56. Pope Papers, *op. cit.*, Jan. 8, 1896.
57. *Ibid.*, April 2, 1900.
58. O.D. Skelton, *Life and Letters of Sir Wilfred Laurier*, Carleton Library Series, Vol. 2, McClelland and Stewart, Toronto, 1965, p. 41.
59. Pope Papers, *op. cit.*, May 16, 1900.
60. Desmond Morton, *The Canadian General, Sir William Otter*, Hakkert, Toronto, 1974, p. 234.
61. Pope Papers, *op. cit.*, Dec. 11, 1900.
62. *Ibid.*
63. *Ibid.*, March 16, 1901.
64. *Ibid.*
65. *Ibid.*, April 22, 1901.
66. *Ibid.*
67. *Ibid.*

CHAPTER 12 NOTES

1. PAC, Pope Papers, MG30E1, Vol. 107, Baroness Macdonald to Pope, Dec. 11, 1900.
2. *Ibid.*, Oct. 4, 1896.
3. Not until 1963, by the Peerage Act, was the disclaiming of peerages made possible.
4. See Chapter 9, note 10.
5. Pope Papers, *op. cit.*, April 22, 1901.
6. *Ibid.*, May 5, 1902.
7. *Ibid.*, Jan. 26, 1902.
8. *Ibid.*, May 18, 1902.
9. *Ibid.*
10. *Ibid.*
11. *Ibid.*, July 3, 1902.
12. *Ibid.*
13. *Ibid.*
14. *Ibid.*
15. *Ibid.*
16. Margaret Charlotte, the Strathconas' only child, was married to R.J.B. Howard, M.D.
17. Pope Papers, *op. cit.*, July 9, 1902.
18. *Ibid.*, July 3, 1902.
19. Sir William Mulock sat for North York in the Canadian House of Commons from 1882 to 1905.
20. Pope Papers, *op. cit.*, Aug. 12, 1902.
21. *Ibid.*
22. *Ibid.*

23. *Ibid.*
24. *Ibid.*, June 22, 1905.
25. This was mourning for Hugh's son, Jack, who had died that summer.
26. Pope Papers, *op. cit.*, June 22, 1905.
27. *Ibid.*
28. *Ibid.*
29. George Bernard Shaw, writing to the *Times*, London, July 3, 1905, had words on contemporary fashionable dress for men, which he thought reasonable in every aspect. 'Evening dress [is] cheap, simple, durable, prevents rivalry and extravagance. . . annihilates class distinctions and gives men who are poor and doubtful of their social position. . . a sense of security and satisfaction.' By comparison, he had harsh words for ladies' fashions.
30. Pope Papers, *op. cit.*, Dec. 4, 1901.
31. *Ibid.*
32. *Ibid.*, Jan. 26, 1902.
33. Mrs. Biden was a widowed friend of Mary's. The third ticket was for Cox, Mary's maid.
34. Pope Papers, *op. cit.*, Dec. 17, 1904.
35. *Ibid.*
36. *Ibid.*, Dec. 25, 1900.
37. *Ibid.*, May 17, 1901.
38. *Ibid.*, Nov. 3, 1900.
39. *Ibid.*, June 16, 1901.
40. *Ibid.*, Dec. 15, 1900.
41. *Ibid.*, Feb. 3, 1904.
42. *Ibid.*, Mar. 14, 1901.
43. *Ibid.*, Jan. 26, 1905
44. *Ibid.*, Feb. 26, 1905
45. *Ibid.*, Apr. 6, 1905.
46. *Ibid.*, Dec. 5, 1905.
47. *Ibid.*
48. *Ibid.*
49. *Ibid.*
50. *Ibid.*, Jan. 13, 1907.
51. Sir Alfred Jones (1824-1906), Liberal M.P. for Halifax in the House of Commons and, later, Lieut.-Gov. of Nova Scotia, 1900-1906.
52. Pope Papers, *op. cit.*, Nov. 25, 1906.
53. *Ibid.*
54. *Ibid.*, Apr. 22, 1906.
55. *Ibid.*
56. *Ibid.*, June 3, 1907.
57. *Ibid.*
58. *Ibid.*
59. *Ibid.*, May 18, 1902.
60. *Ibid.*, June 3, 1907.
61. PAC, Macdonald Papers, MG26A, Vol. 557, Nos. 269251-2.
62. Pope Papers, *op. cit.*, Aug. 15, 1891.
63. *Ibid.*, June 8, 1907.
64. *Ibid.*, Sept. 10, 1905.
65. *Ibid.*, June 24, 1900.
66. *Ibid.*, Sept. 3, 1896.
67. *Ibid.*, Nov. 8, 1902.
68. *Ibid.*
69. *Ibid.*, Dec. 3, 1902.
70. *Ibid.*
71. *Ibid.*, June 22, 1905.

72. *Ibid.*, Nov. 8, 1902.
73. *Ibid.*, May 21, 1906.
74. *Ibid.*, Sept. 10, 1905.
75. *Ibid.*, Feb. 19, 1912.
76. Hugh's daughter, Daisy, married Hugh Gainsford and had two sons, Hugh (who still lives in Winnipeg) and Lionel (who died a few years ago). There are two adopted children in the Gainsford family.
77. Pope Papers, *op. cit.*, Feb. 16, 1908.
78. *Ibid.*
79. *Ibid.*, Mar. 26, 1908.
80. *Ibid.*, July 14, 1913.
81. *Ibid.*, July 3, 1902.
82. *Ibid.*, Dec. 26, 1903.
83. *Ibid.*, Jan. 7, 1906.
84. *Ibid.*, Dec. 5, 1905.
85. Home Rule for Ulster (now Northern Ireland) divided loyalties and the Party.
86. Pope Papers, *op. cit.*, May 21, 1906.
87. *Ibid.*, Oct. 27, 1906.
88. *Ibid.*, Nov. 23, 1906.
89. PAC, Macdonald Papers, MG26A, Vol. 559A, Lady Macdonald's diary, Dec. 1, 1867.
90. *Ibid.*
91. Pope Papers, *op. cit.*, Dec. 17, 1904.
92. *Ibid.*, Apr. 22, 1906.
93. Lady Macdonald's diary, *op. cit.*, Apr. 19, 1868.
94. Pope Papers, *op. cit.*, Dec. 17, 1904.
95. *Ibid.*, Jan. 16, 1905.
96. *Ibid.*
97. *Ibid.*, Oct. 25, 1910.
98. *Ibid.*, Aug. 20, 1911.
99. *Ibid.*
100. *Ibid.*
101. *Ibid.*
102. *Ibid.*, Dec. 6, 1908.
103. London *Times*, June 26, 1909.
104. Pope Papers, *op. cit.*, Dec. 6, 1908.
105. *Ibid.*, Oct. 25, 1910.
106. *Ibid.*, Nov. 2, 1909.
107. *Ibid.*, Oct. 6, 1911.
108. Had the propositions of the Taft Agreement been implemented, it was feared by many that Canada would become a mere adjunct of the United States.
109. Pope Papers, *op. cit.*, Oct. 6, 1911.
110. *Ibid.*, May 17, 1913.
111. During the debate on the Bill, Laurier's Liberals opposed it as it did not provide for a Canadian navy. At the same time, they made light of the 'emergency' cries raised by the Conservatives, saying that, if there was an emergency, Britain did not know it existed.
112. Pope Papers, *op. cit.*, May 17, 1913.
113. *Ibid.*
114. *Ibid.*

CHAPTER 13 NOTES

1. PAC, Pope Papers, MG30E1, Vol. 107, Aug. 28, 1900.
2. *Ibid.*, Sept. 18, 1900.

3. Strathcona did not think this necessary, but his argument did not carry weight with Pope. The latter was suspicious of much of the advice Agnes received from her friends in England. He found justification for this attitude a few years later when Agnes sold her personal C.P.R. stock on the advice of Baron Mount Stephen. The stock continued to rise in value.

4. Pope Papers, *op. cit.*, Vol. 112, Dec. 12, 1900. At the time, Agnes was receiving an income of about five percent from John A.'s estate, Hewitt's small estate and some money she held outright. Added to the $3,000 she continued to receive from the Testimonial Fund, this gave her an income of some $9,000 a year. (April 23, 1901.)

5. *Ibid.,* July 3, 1911.

6. *Ibid.,* April 30, 1910.

7. *Ibid.,* Nov. 24, 1908.

8. *Ibid.,* April 22, 1906.

9. *Ibid.,* Oct. 12, 1909.

10. Letter from H. Robertson, Manager, Royal Trust Company, Montreal, to E.S. Clouston, Montreal, April 19, 1913.

11. Pope Papers, *op. cit.*, Dec. 31, 1913.

12. *Ibid.,* May 17, 1913.

13. *Ibid.,* June 7, 1913.

14. Agnes had written directly to Sir Robert Borden, refusing to accept any payment for herself but insisting that Pope be paid as some recompense for all the work he had done for her over the years. The sum of $5,000 was duly paid him by cheque No. 172, 1913-14 accounts, by the Office of the Auditor General.

15. Pope Papers, *op. cit.*, Sept. 13, 1913.

16. *Ibid.,* Jan. 17, 1913.

17. *Ibid.,* March 5, 1913.

18. *Ibid.,* Vol. 110, Sept. 15, 1920.

19. *Ibid.,* March 25, 1921.

20. *Ibid.,* Vol. 107, Nov. 29, 1913.

21. *Ibid.,* Dec. 13, 1908.

22. *Ibid.,* Oct. 12, 1909.

23. *Ibid.*

24. *Ibid.,* June 14, 1912.

25. *Ibid.,* Vol. 110, Sept. 25, 1914.

26. *Ibid.,* Aug. 12, 1914.

27. *Ibid.,* Oct. 12, 1914.

28. *Ibid.,* Aug. 18, 1914.

29. *Ibid.,* Sept. 28, 1914.

30. *Ibid.,* Oct. 12, 1914.

31. *Ibid.,* Oct. 19, 1914.

32. *Ibid.,* Sept. 28, 1914.

33. Royal Trust Company Archives, Ottawa, letter to C.A. Eliot, Apr. 29, 1916.

34. *Ibid.,* June 18, 1916.

35. *Ibid.*

36. *Ibid.*

37. *Ibid.*

38. Pope Papers, *op. cit.*, Vol. 2, Aug. 4, 1916.

39. *Ibid.,* Vol. 110, Sept. 14, 1916.

40. Royal Trust Company Archives, Ottawa, Sept. 14, 1916.

41. Pope Papers, *op. cit.*, Vol. 2, Oct. 15, 1916.

42. Royal Trust Company Archives, Ottawa, letter to C.A. Eliot, Nov. 23, 1913.

43. Pope Papers, *op. cit.*, Vol. 110, Sept. 10, 1920.

44. Under John A.'s will, his four trustees and Agnes had been appointed Mary's guardians. This was clearly intended to continue until Mary's death with no

consideration given to what then seemed the unlikely event of Agnes predeceasing Mary. In Agnes' will of June 12, 1914, she appointed English guardians for Mary, 'so far as I have the power to do so'. One was Donald Smith's (Lord Strathcona's) daughter, Margaret, who became a Baroness on the death of her father. The other two were Mary Evelyn Dymond of Matravers, Dorset, and Alexander Lang of the Bank of Montreal. Hugh agreed that it was more appropriate that Mary should have guardians who lived in England as she did.

45. Pope Papers, *op. cit.*, Vol. 110, Sept. 5, 1920, copy from Royal Trust Company, Montreal office.
46. *Ibid.*, Sept. 28, 1920.
47. *Ibid.*, Sept. 10, 1920.
48. London *Times*, Sept. 7, 1920.
49. Pope Papers, *op. cit.*, Sept. 5, 1920, copy from Royal Trust Company, Montreal office.
50. *Ibid.*, Sept. 10, 1920.
51. *Ibid.*, Vol. 107, May 3, 1904.
52. PAC, Macdonald Papers, MG26A, Vol. 558, Nos. 269307-8, June 2, 1910.
53. *Ibid.*
54. Sarah became Mrs. Charles Clarke and lived until Dec. 2, 1944.
55. Pope Papers, *op. cit.*, Vol. 110, March 25, 1921.
56. E.B. Biggar, *An Anecdotal Life of Sir John Macdonald*, John Lovell and Son, Montreal, 1891, p. 301. For John A's acknowledgment, see n. 32 to chapter 7 of this book.
57. Biggar, *op. cit.*, p. 301.
58. G. Mercer Adam, *Canada's Patriot Statesman*, Parish and Co., Toronto, 1891, p. 546.
59. *Ibid.*
60. Pope Papers, *op. cit.*, Vol. 110, Sept. 15,, 1920.
61. Macdonald Papers, *op. cit.*, Vol. 558, No. 269308, June 2, 1910.
62. Adam, *op. cit.*, p. 546.
63. *Ibid.*
64. *Letters of Queen Victoria, 3rd Series, 1886-1890*, John Murray, London, 1891, Sept. 30, 1888.
65. PAC, Macdonald Papers, MG26A, Vol. 559A. Lady Macdonald's diary, July 5, 1867.
66. Adam, *op. cit.*, p. 546.
67. Letter from the editor, *Murray's Magazine*, March 24, 1888.
68. Pope Papers, *op. cit.*, Vol. 110, May 26, 1895.
69. *Ibid.*, Sept. 6, 1891.
70. *Ibid.*, Vol. 107, June 11, 1893.
71. *Ibid.*, Oct. 17, 1897.
72. *Ibid.* Unfortunately, research has not yet discovered the newspaper articles which so annoyed Agnes.
73. *Ibid.*
74. *Ibid.*
75. *Ibid.*, Nov. 3, 1892.
76. Joseph P. Lash, *Eleanor and Franklin*, W.W. Norton & Co., Inc., New York, 1971, p. 722.

Bibliography

Material Read and Quoted:

BOOKS:

Adam, G. Mercer *Canada's Patriot Statesman*, Parish & Co., Toronto, 1891
Albani, Emma *Forty Years of Song*, Mills and Boone, London, 1911
Biggar, E.B. *An Anecdotal Life of Sir John Macdonald*, John Lovell and Sons, Montreal, 1891
Macpherson, James Pennington *Life of the Rt. Hon. Sir John A. Macdonald*, Earle Publishing House, Saint John, N.B. 1891
Morton, Desmond *The Canadian General: Sir William Otter*, Hakkert, Toronto, 1974
Parry, J.H., and Sherlock, P.M. *A Short History of the West Indies*, 2nd ed., Macmillan, London, 1968
Pope, Joseph *Memoirs of the Right Honourable Sir John Alexander Macdonald*, 2nd ed. The Musson Book Co., Toronto, 1930 [1st ed., 1894]
— — — *The Day of Sir John Macdonald*, Glasgow, Brook and Co., Toronto, 1915
— — — ed. *The Correspondence of Sir John Macdonald, 1840-1891*, Oxford University Press, 1921
Pope, Maurice, ed. *The Public Servant: the Memoirs of Sir Joseph Pope*, Oxford University Press, Toronto, 1960
Skelton, O.D. *Life and Letters of Sir Wilfred Laurier* (Carleton Library Series, Vol. 2), McClelland and Stewart, Toronto, 1965
Tulchinsky, Gerald, ed. 'The British Influence of RMC', by R.A. Preston, in *To Preserve and Defend: Essays on Kingston in the nineteenth century*, McGill-Queens University Press, Montreal and London, 1976
Victoria, Queen *Letters of Queen Victoria*, 3rd Series, Vols. 1 and 2, John Murray, London, 1930
Waite, P.B. *Macdonald: His Life and World*, McGraw-Hill, Ryerson Ltd., Toronto, 1975

DIARIES

Aberdeen, Lady *Journal of Lady Aberdeen*, Champlain Society, Oxford University Press, Toronto, 1960
Bernard, Theodora   Diary. In private possession, property of the estate of the late Mrs. D.F. Peplar.
Dufferin and Ava, The Marchioness of, *My Canadian Journal, 1872-8*, John Murray, London, 1891
Macdonald, Agnes   Diary, 1867-75. PAC. Macdonald Papers, MG26A, Vol. 559A.

Monck, Frances A.   *My Canadian Leaves: an Account of a Visit, 1864-5,* Bentley and
Sons, London, 1891
Wright, Philip, ed.   *Lady Nugent's Jamaican Journal,* Institute of Jamaica, 1966

ARTICLES, AND PAMPHLETS:

Bedford-Jones, The Rev. Thomas   'How St. Alban's Church, Ottawa, Had Its
Beginning', *Journal of the Canadian Church Historical Society,* Vol. III, No. 3,
Toronto, May, 1957
Jeseley, Max   'Unknown Wives of Well-known Men, VI. Lady Agnes Macdonald',
Ladies Home Journal, Vol. 8, No. 7, Philadelphia, June, 1891
Macdonald, Agnes   'By Car and by Cowcatcher', *Murray's Magazine,* Vol. 1, John
Murray, London, Jan.-June, 1887
———   'On a Toboggan', *Murray's Magazine,* Vol. 3, John Murray, London,
Jan.-June 1887
———   'On A Canadian Salmon Stream', *Murray's Magazine,* Vol. 2, John Murray,
London, July-Dec. 1887
———   'An Unconventional Holiday', *Ladies' Home Journal,* Vol. 8, Nos. 9 and 10,
Philadelphia, Sept., 1891
[———?]   'Canadian Topics', *Murray's Magazine,* Vol. 1, John Murray, London,
Jan.-June, 1887
[———?]   'Men and Measures in Canada', *Murray's Magazine,* Vol. 2, John Murray,
London, July-Dec. 1887
[———?]   'A Builder of the Empire', *Pall Mall Magazine,* Vol. 13, Sept.-Dec. 1897
Nicholls, Frederic, and Wright, A. W., comp.   *Report of the Demonstration in Honour
of the 40th Anniversary of Sir John Macdonald's entrance into public life,* privately
printed, Toronto, 1885
Wolfe, Irene   'St. Patrick', Rivière du Loup, Que. (n.d.) unpublished, in private
possession, Mrs. W.R. Eakin, Montreal

NEWSPAPERS

Jamaica: *Falmouth Post and Jamaica General Advertiser,* Jan. 1, 1850

Canada: *Barrie Northern Advance,* Barrie, Ont., Various
                The Islander, Charlottetown, P.E.I., July 8, 1870
                The Weekly Times, Hamilton, Ont., Oct. 25, 1877
                Ottawa Citizen, Ottawa, Ont., Various
                Times, Ottawa, Ont., Various
                Globe, Toronto, Ont., Various
                Mail, Toronto, Ont., July 12, 1872
England: *Times,* London, Various
                The Daily Graphic, London, June 9, 1891

ARCHIVES

Canada: PAC   Macdonald, Sir John A., Papers. MG26A
                ———   Pope, Sir Joseph, Papers, MG3E1
                ———   Pope, Sir Joseph, Special Journals — Visits to England
                        re Alaska, 7 Sept. to 31 Oct. 1899
                ———   Stephen, Baron, Papers. MG29A30

— — — Thompson, Sir John, Papers. MG26D
　　　— — — Tupper, Sir Charles, Papers
　　　C.P.R. Archives (Montreal)　Van Horne Collection
　　　Queen's University Archives (Kingston, Douglas Library)
　　　　Williamson Papers
　　　Royal Trust Company Archives
　　　Simcoe County Archives (Minesing, Ont.)

Great Britain:　　Royal Archives, Windsor Castle

Jamaica:　　Jamaica Archives (JA) and the West Indies Reference Library
　　　(WIRL), various folios dealing with land transactions, births,
　　　deaths, marriages on the Island. Also estate maps in WIRL and
　　　manuscripts of Fuertado, W.A. (WIRL) and Jamaica
　　　Almanacks for various years.

Material Consulted But Not Quoted

BOOKS:

Adam, G. Mercer　*Toronto Old and New,* Mail Printing Co. of Toronto, 1891
Augier, Gordon, Hall and Rickard　*The Making of the West Indies,* Longmans, Green,
　London, 1960
Berton, Pierre　*The National Dream,* McClelland and Stewart, Toronto, 1970
— — —　*The Last Spike,* McClelland and Stewart, Toronto, 1971
Black, C.V.　*A New History of Jamaica,* William Collins and Sangster (Jamaica) Ltd.,
　1973
Bond, Courtney C.J.　*City on the Ottawa,* Queen's Printer, Ottawa, 1961
Borden, Henry ed.　*Robert Laird Borden: His Memoirs,* Macmillan and Co.,
　London, 1938
Brennard, Frank　*The Young Churchill,* New English Library, London, 1965
Briggs, Asa　*Victorian People,* Pelican, London, 1975
Carey, Robinson　*The Fighting Maroons of Jamaica,* William Collins and Sangster
　(Jamaica) Ltd., 1968
Collins, Robert　*The Formative Years: Canada, 1812-1871,* Ryerson Press, Toronto,
　1965
Cowan, John　*Canada's Governors-General,* York Publishing Co., Toronto, 1965
Creighton, Donald　*The Young Politician,* Macmillan, Toronto, 1952
— — —　*The Old Chieftain,* Macmillan, Toronto, 1955
Dafoe, J.W.　*Laurier: A Study in Politics,* McClelland and Stewart, Toronto, 1922
Fulford, Robert　*Hanover to Windsor,* Fontana/Collins, 1960
Glazebrook, G.P. de T.　*Life in Ontario,* University of Toronto Press, 1968
Hardy, J. Russell, ed.　*Portrait of a Period: A Collection of Notman Photographs,*
　McGill University Press, Montreal, 1967
Hibbert, Christopher　*1851 and the Crystal Palace,* 1st ed., John Murray, London, 1950
Hunter, Andrew F.　*The History of Simcoe County,* sponsored by the Historical
　Committee of Simcoe County, Barrie, Ont., 1948 ed.
Johnson, J.K. ed.　*Affectionately Yours: the Letters of Sir John A. Macdonald and His
　Family,* Macmillan of Canada, Toronto, 1969
— — — ed.　*Letters of Sir John A. Macdonald,* Macmillan of Canada, Toronto, 1968
Lawrence-Archer, J.H., compl.　*Monumental Inscriptions of the British West Indies,*
　Chatto and Windus, 1875

Leggett, Robert *Rideau Waterway,* rev. ed., University of Toronto Press, Toronto, 1972

Longord, Elizabeth *Victoria RI,* Pan Books, London, 1966

Lower, A.R.M. *Colony to Nation,* Longmans, Green, Co., Toronto, 1946

Monk, Lorraine, ed. *Stones of History: Canada's Houses of Parliament, 1867,* National Film Board of Canada, 1967

Martin, Chester *Foundations of Canadian Nationhood,* University of Toronto Press, Toronto, 1955

Martin, Ralph G. *Jennie,* Vols. 1 and 2, Signet Press, London, 1970-72

Mitchell, R.J. and Lays, M.D.R. *A History of London Life,* Penguin Books, London, 1964

Morris, James 'The Imperialists' in *Horizon,* Spring, 1968

Mulvaney, C. Pelham *Toronto: Past and Present until 1882,* W.E. Caiger, Toronto, 1884

Newman, Lena *The John A. Macdonald Album,* Tundra Books, Montreal, 1974

Oliver, V.L. *Caribbiana,* Vol. 5, Mitchell, Hughes and Clark, London, 1916

Parkin, George R. *Sir John A. Macdonald,* Morand and Co., Ltd., Toronto, 1908

Plumb, J.H. 'The Victorians' in *Horizon,* Autumn, 1969

— — — 'The Edwardians' in *Horizon,* Autumn, 1971

Priestley, J.B. *The Edwardians,* Sphere Books, London, 1972

— — — *Victoria's Heyday,* Penguin Books, London, 1974

Smith, [?] 'Canada: Past, Present and Future' in *Historical Sketches of Simcoe County,* Ontario County Atlas

Swainson, Donald *John A. Macdonald, the Man and the Politician,* Oxford University Press, Toronto, 1971

Taylor, Robert Lewis *Winston Churchill,* Doubleday and Co., New York, 1952

Wade, Mason *The French Canadians, 1760-1945,* Macmillan and Co., London, 1955

Walker, Harry and Olive *Carleton Saga,* Runge Press, Ottawa, 1968

Watt, D.C. *A History of the World in the 20th Century, Part I, 1899-1918,* Pan Books Ltd., London, 1970

Whittle, Tyler *Albert's Victoria,* W. Heinemann Ltd., London, 1972

Index